THE NEW AMERICAN MILITARISM

THE NEW
AMERICAN MILITARISM

How Americans Are Seduced by War

ANDREW J. BACEVICH

OXFORD
UNIVERSITY PRESS

OXFORD
UNIVERSITY PRESS

Oxford University Press is a department of the University of Oxford.
It furthers the University's objective of excellence in research, scholarship,
and education by publishing worldwide.

Oxford New York
Auckland   Cape Town   Dar es Salaam   Hong Kong   Karachi
Kuala Lumpur   Madrid   Melbourne   Mexico City   Nairobi
New Delhi   Shanghai   Taipei   Toronto

With offices in
Argentina   Austria   Brazil   Chile   Czech Republic   France   Greece
Guatemala   Hungary   Italy   Japan   Poland   Portugal   Singapore
South Korea   Switzerland   Thailand   Turkey   Ukraine   Vietnam

Oxford is a registered trade mark of Oxford University Press
in the UK and certain other countries

Published in the United States of America by
Oxford University Press
198 Madison Avenue, New York, NY 10016

Library of Congress Cataloging-in-Publication Data
Bacevich, A. J.
 The new American militarism : how Americans are seduced by war /
by Andrew J. Bacevich.
 p. cm.
Includes bibliographical references and index.
ISBN-13: 978-0-19-993176-7
ISBN-10: 0-19-517338-4
 1. Militarism—United States—History—21st century.
 2. United States—Military policy.
 3. United States—Foreign relations—2001-.
 4. Conservatism—United States-History—21st century.
 5. United States—Politics and government—2001-.
 I. Title.
UA23.B14 2005
355.02'130—973 dc22
2004023277

ISBN-13: 978-0-19-993176-7

Book design and composition by Mark McGarry, Texas Type & Book Works
Set in Stempel Garamond

9 8 7 6 5 4 3 2

Printed in the United States of America
on acid-free paper

To the memory of

George M. Blough
1947–2003

Casualty of a misbegotten war

Contents

A Note to the Reader

WHEN IT FIRST APPEARED in 2005, this book straddled past and present. Looking toward the past, it recounted the origins of new attitudes toward military power that had emerged in the United States during the decades following the Vietnam War. It decried those attitudes as perverse and found that they had given birth to a variant of militarism. Surveying the present, the book described—and lamented—what militarism had wrought, most notably the then-ongoing war in Iraq.

Today U. S. troops have left Iraq and the American people have wasted little time in forgetting the Iraq War. With the passage of time, *The New American Militarism* has now clearly become a work of history. Yet the passage of time, along with the ongoing unfolding of events, has validated its findings and reinforced its relevance. American militarism persists.

So apart from the addition of an afterword, which updates the story, the text that follows is unchanged from the original edition.

December 2012
Notre Dame, Indiana

Preface

THIS IS A BOOK about the new American militarism—the misleading and dangerous conceptions of war, soldiers, and military institutions that have come to pervade the American consciousness and that have perverted present-day U.S. national security policy.

Implicit in the argument that follows, in the selection and interpretation of evidence, and in the conclusions drawn from that evidence is a set of presumptions or predispositions that ought to be made explicit. Although in researching and writing this account I have sought to be fair and to keep my own prejudices in check, the views expressed cannot be detached from the author's personal background and outlook. Hence this brief prefatory note, consisting of four observations.

First, I am a Vietnam veteran. As one commentator famously noted, the United States military did not fight a decade-long war to preserve South Vietnam; rather, it fought a one-year war ten times over. My own year fell in the conflict's bleak latter stages, from the summer of 1970 to the summer of 1971—after Tet, after the Cambodian incursion, and long after an odor of failure had begun to envelop the entire enterprise.

Several of my college classmates died in Vietnam. Other friends came away from the war physically or psychologically scarred, the boyhood chum and brother-in-law to whose memory this volume is dedicated not least among them.

For me, the experience was merely baffling and, indeed, has become even more so with the passage of time. Vietnam provides the frame of reference within which I interpret much else, a tendency that some readers may well judge excessive. But there is no point in trying to conceal what is probably self-evident: this book represents one manifestation of a continuing effort to sift through the wreckage left by that war and to reckon fully with its legacy.

Second, after returning from Vietnam, I stayed on in the U.S. Army and became a professional soldier. In essence, my service coincided with the latter half of the Cold War, an ostensibly simpler time that some have already made an object of nostalgia. But from a military officer's perspective these were roller-coaster years. No one who served during the interval stretching from the abruptly terminated presidency of Richard Nixon to the crowded but abbreviated era of the elder George Bush will recall this as a time of stability or easy living.

Yet inside the cocoon of military life, there existed one fixed point of absolute and reassuring clarity. Those of us whose day-to-day routine centered on furiously preparing to defend the so-called Fulda Gap, the region in western Germany presumed to be the focal point of any Warsaw Pact attack, had no need to torment ourselves with existential questions of purpose. Indeed, our purpose was self-evident: it was to defend the West against the threat posed by Communist totalitarianism.

Here was the lodestar that endowed military service after Vietnam with its peculiar savor. Even when the country seemed not to care—and during much of that period it obviously didn't—we were keeping the Soviets at bay and therefore preserving freedom. So at least we believed, with an unwavering conviction.

This—not conquest, regime change, preventive war, or imperial policing—we understood to be the American soldier's true and honorable calling. That old-fashioned understanding of soldierly purpose, now perhaps rendered obsolete, also informs much of what follows.

The third point concerns politics, to which I am a latecomer. Although the prevarications and outright lies surrounding Vietnam had left the American military professional ethic much the worse for wear, enough of it survived that most young officers still understood in that war's aftermath that when it came to politics they were to have none. To be a serving soldier in my day was by definition to be apolitical. Although many of us voted, we did so less as an expression of partisanship than from a sense of civic obligation.

Only upon leaving the army, already well into middle age, did I experience the raising of political consciousness that my fellow baby boomers had undergone back in the heady days of youth. As much in response to deeply felt religious convictions as anything else, I became a self-described conservative. During the 1990s I began to contribute with some regularity to magazines identified with the political right, including the *Weekly Standard, National Review,* and *First Things.*

As long as we shared in the common cause of denouncing the foolishness and hypocrisies of the Clinton years, my relationship with modern American conservatism remained a mutually agreeable one. But even before the disputed election of 2000 resolved itself, it became clear, to me at least, that conservatives were susceptible to their own brand of foolishness and hypocrisy. At that point, my ties to the conservative literary establishment began to fray and soon dissolved.

Today, I still situate myself culturally on the right. And I continue to view the remedies proffered by mainstream liberalism with skepticism. But my disenchantment with what passes for mainstream conservatism, embodied in the present Bush administration and its groupies, is just about absolute. Fiscal irresponsibility, a buccaneering foreign policy, a disregard for the Constitution, the barest lip service as a response to profound moral controversies: these do not qualify as authentically conservative values.

On this score my views have come to coincide with the critique long offered by the radical left: it is the mainstream itself, the professional liberals as well as the professional conservatives, who *define* the problem. Two parties monopolize and, as if by prior agreement, trivialize national politics. Each panders to the worst instincts of its core constituents. Each is seemingly obsessed with power for its own sake. The historian Walter Karp's acerbic assessment of early twentieth-century politics strikes me as equally applicable to the early twenty-first century: "Behind the hoopla of partisanship, the leaders of the two parties worked together in collusive harmony."[1] The Republican and Democratic parties may not be identical, but they produce nearly identical results. Money buys access and influence, the rich and famous get served, and those lacking wealth or celebrity status get screwed—truths not at all unrelated to the rise of militarism in America.

I have no doubt that the world of politics is not without men and women of honor. But the system itself is fundamentally corrupt and functions in ways inconsistent with the spirit of genuine democracy. This anyone with eyes to see recognizes.

So what follows bears an unmistakably conservative stamp, notably in attributing great significance—perhaps too great—to the 1960s, in the eyes of devout right-wingers the locus of all the ills afflicting contemporary America. But it is also the account of someone who understands that many of those who in occupying the public eye pass themselves off as conservatives share responsibility for those afflictions, the excessive militarization of U.S. policy not least among them.

Some will misread this as cynicism. It is instead the absence of illusion.

The final point concerns my understanding of history. Before moving into a career focused on teaching and writing about contemporary U.S. foreign policy, I was trained as a diplomatic historian. My graduate school mentors were scholars of great stature and enormous gifts, admirable in every way. They were also splendid teachers, and I left graduate school very much under their influence. My own abbreviated foray into serious historical scholarship bears the earmarks of their approach, ascribing to Great Men—generals, presidents, and cabinet secretaries—the status of historical prime movers.

I have now come to see that view as mistaken. What seemed plausible enough when studying presidents named Wilson or Roosevelt breaks down completely when a Bush or Clinton occupies the Oval Office. Not only do present-day tendencies to elevate the president to the status of a demigod whose every move is recorded, every word parsed, and every decision scrutinized for hidden meaning fly in the face of republican precepts. They also betray a fundamental misunderstanding of how the world works.

What is most striking about the most powerful man in the world is not the power that he wields. It is how constrained he and his lieutenants are by forces that lie beyond their grasp and perhaps their understanding. Rather than bending history to their will, presidents and those around them are much more likely to dance to history's tune. Only the illusions churned out by public relations apparatchiks and perpetuated by celebrity-worshipping journalists prevent us from seeing that those inhabiting the inner sanctum of the West Wing are agents more than independent actors. Although as human beings they may be interesting, very few can claim more than marginal historical significance. So while the account that follows discusses various personalities—not only politicians but also soldiers, intellectuals, and religious leaders—it uses them as vehicles to highlight the larger processes that are afoot.

Appreciating the limits of human agency becomes particularly relevant when considering remedial action. If a problem is bigger than a particular president or single administration—as I believe the problem of American militarism to be—then simply getting rid of that president will not make that problem go away. To pretend otherwise serves no purpose.

In offering this account of the new American militarism and its origins, I make no claim to having unearthed the definitive version of truth. This is not likely to be the last word on the subject. I expect that some readers may judge the findings offered here as more suggestive than conclusive. Certainly, someone for whom service in Vietnam did not figure as a formative experience or who does not share my own Catholic conservative inclinations might well interpret the same facts differently. An alternative ideological slant or view of American politics and history could yield different insights and different remedies.

With all of that in mind—and in the common cause of restoring good sense and realism to American thinking about war, armies, and soldiers—I welcome suggestions, corrections, and amendments.

Acknowledgments

In the course of writing *The New American Militarism*, I accrued many debts. Colleagues, bosses, friends old and new, and kind strangers all helped in ways too numerous to recount. Although I am responsible for any errors or shortcomings, others surely can claim a share of the credit for whatever value this book may possess.

I am mightily grateful for the wise counsel of my friend and agent John Wright, who knows more about the book business than anyone else I have ever met. I thank Bob Dallek for putting me in touch with John in the first place.

Tim Bartlett, my editor at Oxford University Press, has been superb, offering just the right mix of encouragement and you-can-do-better-than-this prodding. Also at Oxford, Joellyn Ausanka, Mary Ann Benner, India Cooper, Sara Leopold, and Peter Harper facilitated the transformation from manuscript to finished book. It was a treat for me to work with such a professional team.

The Smith Richardson Foundation, which has supported my work for several years, deserves a special commendation for sticking with me on a journey that included a severe midcourse correction. In that regard, I thank Marin Strmecki and Nadia Schadlow for their patience and understanding.

Boston University granted me a semester-long sabbatical, which enabled me to complete the manuscript on schedule. I am grateful to my dean, Jeff Henderson, and to the Department of International Relations for giving me the time off from teaching. I also thank my colleague Bob Jackson for pinch-hitting as director of the Center for International Relations during my absence.

During that semester I had the extraordinary privilege to be a fellow at the American Academy in Berlin. Led by its executive director, Dr. Gary Smith, the Academy is a jewel of an institution, offering an ideal environment for creative work. My debt to Gary and to the members of the Academy's splendid staff is beyond calculating. Best of all was the opportunity to share in the intellectual life of the small community of scholars and artists whose time at the Academy coincided with my own. My fellow fellows proved to be an endless source of stimulation and gave me a taste of the liberal education that I had previously failed to acquire. We became a merry band.

As the project approached its conclusion, Tom Rempfer, Chris Farrell, and Geoff Lyon volunteered to comment on portions of the text and offered valuable insights. I thank them all.

My old friends Christopher Gray, Paul Miles, and John Richardson, shrewd observers of the American political-military landscape, showered me with leads and suggestions and kept me on my toes.

A troika of intrepid research assistants, Margaret Hickey, Jessica Strunkin, and George Whitney, came through time and again, despite my frequently less than adequate guidance. They are terrific.

Both in Boston and while I was on the road, my assistant Jain Yu did yeoman work in relieving me of the cares and burdens of administration. I deeply appreciate all of her hard work.

When I first made the leap into academe, Richard H. Kohn was there offering encouragement, advice, and wisdom. I have relied on him ever since and he has never let me down. Although I expect Dick will not agree with all of the conclusions reached in this account, I do know that his influence pervades the book. He is a scholar of remarkable distinction, a true patriot, and a man of profound decency and rocklike integrity. It is difficult for me to express how much I have come to value his friendship.

The best comes last. My wife, Nancy, stuck with me through this as she has through so many other adventures and misadventures, as always at considerable personal sacrifice. I wish to record here my measureless appreciation for all that she has done for me and for our children. I love her dearly and always will. Like the song says: when I say always, I mean forever.

THE NEW AMERICAN MILITARISM

East were the dead
Kings and the remembered sepulchres:
West was the grass.

—Archibald MacLeish,
"America Was Promises" (1939)

INTRODUCTION

TODAY AS NEVER BEFORE in their history Americans are enthralled with military power. The global military supremacy that the United States presently enjoys—and is bent on perpetuating—has become central to our national identity. More than America's matchless material abundance or even the effusions of its pop culture, the nation's arsenal of high-tech weaponry and the soldiers who employ that arsenal have come to signify who we are and what we stand for.

When it comes to war, Americans have persuaded themselves that the United States possesses a peculiar genius. Writing in the spring of 2003, the journalist Gregg Easterbrook observed that "the extent of American military superiority has become almost impossible to overstate." During Operation Iraqi Freedom, U.S. forces had shown beyond the shadow of a doubt that they were "the strongest the world has ever known,... stronger than the Wehrmacht in 1940, stronger than the legions at the height of Roman power." Other nations trailed "so far behind they have no chance of catching up."[1] The commentator Max Boot scoffed at comparisons with the German army of World War II, hitherto "the gold standard of operational excellence." In Iraq, American military performance had been such as to make "fabled generals such as Erwin Rommel and Heinz Guderian seem positively incompetent by comparison."[2] Easterbrook and Boot concurred on the central point: on the modern battlefield Americans had located an arena of human endeavor in which their flair for organizing and deploying technology offered an apparently decisive edge. As a consequence, the

United States had (as many Americans have come to believe) become masters of all things military.

Further, American political leaders have demonstrated their intention of tapping that mastery to reshape the world in accordance with American interests and American values. That the two are so closely intertwined as to be indistinguishable is, of course, a proposition to which the vast majority of Americans subscribe. Uniquely among the great powers in all of world history, ours (we insist) is an inherently values-based approach to policy.

Furthermore, we have it on good authority that the ideals we espouse represent universal truths, valid for all times. American statesmen past and present have regularly affirmed that judgment. In doing so, they validate it and render it all but impervious to doubt. Whatever momentary setbacks the United States might encounter, whether a generation ago in Vietnam or more recently in Iraq, this certainty that American values are destined to prevail imbues U.S. policy with a distinctive grandeur. The preferred language of American statecraft is bold, ambitious, and confident.

Reflecting such convictions, policymakers in Washington nurse (and the majority of citizens tacitly endorse) ever more grandiose expectations for how armed might can facilitate the inevitable triumph of those values. In that regard, George W. Bush's vow that the United States will "rid the world of evil" both echoes and amplifies the large claims of his predecessors going at least as far back as Woodrow Wilson.[3] Coming from Bush the warrior-president, the promise to make an end to evil is a promise to destroy, to demolish, and to obliterate it.

One result of this belief that the fulfillment of America's historic mission begins with America's destruction of the old order has been to revive a phenomenon that C. Wright Mills in the early days of the Cold War described as a "military metaphysics"—a tendency to see international problems as military problems and to discount the likelihood of finding a solution except through military means.[4]

To state the matter bluntly, Americans in our own time have fallen prey to militarism, manifesting itself in a romanticized view of soldiers, a tendency to see military power as the truest measure of national greatness, and outsized expectations regarding the efficacy of force. To a degree without precedent in U.S. history, Americans have come to define the nation's strength and well-being in terms of military preparedness, military action, and the fostering of (or nostalgia for) military ideals.[5]

Already in the 1990s America's marriage of a militaristic cast of mind with utopian ends had established itself as the distinguishing element of contemporary U.S. policy. The Bush administration's response to the horrors of 9/11 served to reaffirm that marriage, as it committed the United States to waging an open-ended war on a global scale. Events since, notably the alarms, excursions, and full-fledged campaigns comprising the Global War on Terror, have fortified and perhaps even sanctified this marriage. Regrettably, those events, in particular the successive invasions of Afghanistan and Iraq, advertised as important milestones along the road to ultimate victory, have further dulled the average American's ability to grasp the significance of this union, which does not serve our interests and may yet prove our undoing.

The New American Militarism examines the origins and implications of this union and proposes its annulment.

Although by no means the first book to undertake such an examination, *The New American Militarism* does so from a distinctive perspective.

The bellicose character of U.S. policy after 9/11, culminating with the American-led invasion of Iraq in March 2003, has, in fact, evoked charges of militarism from across the political spectrum. Prominent among the accounts advancing that charge are books such as *The Sorrows of Empire: Militarism, Secrecy, and the End of the Republic,* by Chalmers Johnson; *Hegemony or Survival: America's Quest for Global Dominance,* by Noam Chomsky; *Masters of War: Militarism and Blowback in the Era of American Empire,* edited by Carl Boggs; *Rogue Nation: American Unilateralism and the Failure of Good Intentions,* by Clyde Prestowitz; and *Incoherent Empire,* by Michael Mann, with its concluding chapter called "The New Militarism."

Each of these books appeared in 2003 or 2004. Each was not only written in the aftermath of 9/11 but responded specifically to the policies of the Bush administration, above all to its determined efforts to promote and justify a war to overthrow Saddam Hussein.

As the titles alone suggest and the contents amply demonstrate, they are for the most part angry books. They indict more than explain, and whatever explanations they offer tend to be ad hominem. The authors of these books unite in heaping abuse on the head of George W. Bush, said to combine in a single individual intractable provincialism, religious zealotry, and the reckless temperament of a gunslinger. Or if not Bush himself, they finger his lieutenants, the cabal of warmongers, led by Vice President Dick Cheney and senior Defense Department officials, who whispered persuasively in the president's ear and used him to do their bidding. Thus, according to Chalmers Johnson, ever since the Persian Gulf War of 1990–1991, Cheney and other key figures from that war had "wanted to go back and finish what they started." Having lobbied unsuccessfully throughout the Clinton era "for aggression against Iraq and the remaking of the Middle East," they had returned to power on Bush's coattails. After they had "bided their time for nine months," they had seized upon the crisis of 9/11 "to put their theories and plans into action," pressing Bush to make Saddam Hussein number one on his hit list.[6] By implication, militarism becomes something of a conspiracy foisted on a malleable president and an unsuspecting people by a handful of wild-eyed ideologues.

By further implication, the remedy for American militarism is self-evident: "Throw the new militarists out of office," as Michael Mann urges, and a more balanced attitude toward military power will presumably reassert itself.[7]

As a contribution to the ongoing debate about U.S. policy, *The New American Militarism* rejects such notions as simplistic. It refuses to lay the responsibility for American militarism at the feet of a particular president or a particular set of advisers and argues that no particular presidential election holds the promise of radically changing it. Charging George W. Bush with responsibility for the militaristic tendencies of present-day U.S. foreign policy makes as much sense as holding Herbert Hoover culpable for the Great Depression: whatever its psychic satisfactions, it is an exercise in scapegoating that lets too many others off the hook and allows society at large to abdicate responsibility for what has come to pass.

The point is not to deprive George W. Bush or his advisers of whatever credit or blame they may deserve for conjuring up the several large-scale campaigns and myriad lesser military actions comprising their war on terror. They have certainly taken up the mantle of this militarism with a verve not seen in years. Rather it is to suggest that well before September 11, 2001, and before the younger Bush's ascent to the presidency a militaristic predisposition was already in place both in official circles and among Americans more generally. In this regard, 9/11 deserves to be seen as an event that gave added impetus to already existing tendencies rather than as a turning point. For his part, President Bush himself ought to be seen as a player reciting his lines rather than as a playwright drafting an entirely new script.

In short, the argument offered here asserts that present-day American militarism has deep roots in the American past. It represents a bipartisan project. As a result, it is unlikely to disappear anytime soon, a point obscured by the myopia and personal animus tainting most accounts of how we have arrived at this point.

The New American Militarism was conceived not only as a corrective to what has become the conventional critique of U.S. policies since 9/11 but as a challenge to the orthodox historical context employed to justify those policies. In this regard, although by no means comparable in scope and in richness of detail, it continues the story begun in Michael Sherry's masterful 1995 book, *In the Shadow of War*, an interpretive history of the United States in our times. In a narrative that begins with the Great Depression and spans six decades, Sherry reveals a pervasive American sense of anxiety and vulnerability. In an age during which war, actual as well as metaphorical, was a constant, either as ongoing reality or frightening prospect, national security became the axis around which the American enterprise turned. As a consequence, a relentless process of militarization "reshaped every realm of American life—politics and foreign policy, economics and technology, culture and social relations—making America a profoundly different nation."[8]

Yet Sherry concludes his account on a hopeful note. Surveying conditions midway through the post–Cold War era's first decade, he suggests in a chapter entitled "A Farewell to Militarization?" that America's preoccupation with war and military matters might at long last be waning. In the mid-1990s, a return to something resembling pre-1930s military normalcy, involving at least a partial liquidation of the national security state, appeared to be at hand.

Events since *In the Shadow of War* appear to have swept away these expectations. *The New American Militarism* tries to explain why and by extension offers a different interpretation of America's immediate past. The upshot of that interpretation is that far from bidding farewell to militarization, the United States has nestled more deeply into its embrace.

Briefly told, the story that follows goes like this. The new American militarism made its appearance in reaction to the 1960s and especially to Vietnam. It evolved over a period of decades, rather than being spontaneously induced by a particular event such as the terrorist attack of September 11, 2001. Nor, as mentioned above, is present-day American militarism the product of a conspiracy hatched by a small group of fanatics when the American people were distracted or otherwise engaged. Rather, it developed in full view and with considerable popular approval.

The new American militarism is the handiwork of several disparate groups that shared little in common apart from being intent on undoing the purportedly nefarious effects of the 1960s. Military officers intent on rehabilitating their profession; intellectuals fearing that the loss of confidence at home was paving the way for the triumph of totalitarianism abroad; religious leaders dismayed by the collapse of traditional moral standards; strategists wrestling with the implications of a humiliating defeat that had undermined their credibility; politicians on the make; purveyors of pop culture looking to make a buck: as early as 1980, each saw military power as the apparent answer to any number of problems.

The process giving rise to the new American militarism was not a neat one. Where collaboration made sense, the forces of reaction found the means to cooperate. But on many occasions—for example, on questions relating to women or to grand strategy—nominally "pro-military" groups worked at cross purposes. Confronting the thicket of unexpected developments that marked the decades after Vietnam, each tended to chart its own course.

In many respects, the forces of reaction failed to achieve the specific objectives that first roused them to act. To the extent that the 1960s upended long-standing conventions relating to race, gender, and sexuality, efforts to mount a cultural counterrevolution failed miserably. Where the forces of reaction did achieve a modicum of success, moreover, their achievements often proved empty or gave rise to unintended and unwelcome consequences. Thus, as we shall see, military professionals did regain something approximating the standing that they had enjoyed in American society prior to Vietnam. But their efforts to reassert the autonomy of that profession backfired and left the military in the present century bereft of meaningful influence on basic questions relating to the uses of U.S. military power.

Yet the reaction against the 1960s did give rise to one important by-product, namely, the militaristic tendencies that have of late come into full flower.

In short, the story that follows consists of several narrative threads. No single thread can account for our current outsized ambitions and infatuation with military power. Together, however, they created conditions permitting a peculiarly American variant of militarism to emerge. As an antidote, the story concludes by offering specific remedies aimed at restoring a sense of realism and a sense of proportion to U.S. policy. It proposes thereby to bring American purposes and American methods—especially with regard to the role of military power—into closer harmony with the nation's founding ideals.

The marriage of military metaphysics with eschatological ambition is a misbegotten one, contrary to the long-term interests of either the American people or the world beyond our borders. It invites endless war and the ever-deepening militarization of U.S. policy. As it subordinates concern for the common good to the paramount value of military effectiveness, it promises not to perfect but to distort American ideals. As it concentrates ever more authority in the hands of a few more concerned with order abroad rather than with justice at home, it will accelerate the hollowing out of American democracy. As it alienates peoples and nations around the world, it will leave the United States increasingly isolated. If history is any guide, it will end in bankruptcy, moral as well as economic, and in abject failure.

"Of all the enemies of public liberty," wrote James Madison in 1795, "war is perhaps the most to be dreaded, because it comprises and develops the germ of every other. War is the parent of armies. From these proceed debts and taxes. And armies, debts and taxes are the known instruments for bringing the many under the domination of the few. . . . No nation could preserve its freedom in the midst of continual warfare."[9] The purpose of this book is to invite Americans to consider the continued relevance of Madison's warning to our own time and circumstances.

Chapter One

WILSONIANS UNDER ARMS

THE TWENTIETH CENTURY was an age of massive conceits, devised by ideologues who entertained heady dreams of bending history to suit their will. In the end, colossal fascist and Marxist ambitions produced not utopia but Auschwitz and the Gulag. Modern man's effort to replace the one true God in whom he had lost faith with a god of his own devising produced only carnage and suffering. The consort of hubris was catastrophe. If there is one lesson that deserves to be drawn from the bloodstained decades stretching from 1914 to 1989, surely that is it.

Americans contributed mightily to the destruction of these false gods. In the course of doing so, various architects of U.S. policy, beginning with President Woodrow Wilson, nourished their own heady dreams, hardly less ambitious than those of the Marxist and fascist true believers whom they resembled in spirit.

Circumstances conspired to restrain twentieth-century American ideologues. For Wilson, there was Henry Cabot Lodge and a Senate that stubbornly refused to "take its medicine." The Senate responded to presidential demands that it ratify the Treaty of Versailles precisely as negotiated in Paris by rejecting the treaty altogether. As a result, the League of Nations that was central to Wilson's vision of world peace came into existence without the United States as a member. For Franklin D. Roosevelt, Wilson's direct heir, there was a master politician's acute sensitivity to the public's yearning for normalcy after long years of depression and then war. Far from revolutionizing world affairs, his blueprint for a new League—the United Nations—made palatable to others a new balance of power favoring

American interests. For John F. Kennedy, perhaps Wilson's equal in eloquence, restraint came in the form of a nuclear-armed adversary; as a consequence, the hallmark of JFK's brief administration became not "pay any price" idealism but sober-minded pragmatism. For Lyndon Johnson, the first Southerner since Wilson to occupy the White House, the Vietnam War made short shrift of wild-eyed schemes for a New Deal to transform life along the Mekong. For Jimmy Carter, Wilson's equal in religious fervor, the inconvenient but inevasible fact of the Soviet invasion of Afghanistan meant that worldwide nuclear disarmament would have to wait another day. Thus did reality time and again curb Wilsonian enthusiasms.

Curb, but not discredit. For despite Wilson's own manifest failures as a statesman and despite the limited success enjoyed by his successors in reshaping the world consistent with Wilson's expectations, the Wilsonian paradigm—as worldview and as a basis for charting and articulating the nation's purpose—left an indelible imprint on American statecraft. As Henry Kissinger has observed, "It is to the drumbeat of Wilsonian idealism that American foreign policy has marched since his watershed presidency, and continues to march to this day."[1]

What were the essential elements of Wilson's vision? At its core, it sought a world remade in America's image and therefore permanently at peace. This was true when Wilson first articulated that vision and remains true today.

Wilson's own aim, as he famously declared, was "to end all wars" by eliminating the conditions that produced them. Wilson hoped to scrap the Old World's reliance on rivalries among competing powers and install in their place a community of nations. Such a community, Wilson believed, was already evolving in the New World under American auspices. In that regard, the then existing Pan-American Union, a precursor to today's Organization of American States, provided a model suitable for worldwide application. But although nominally a community of equals, the Pan-American system was actually anything but that. It existed to enhance and perpetuate the hemispheric primacy of the United States.

In a speech delivered to the U.S. Senate in January 1917, but directed over the heads of foreign governments to peoples around the world, Wilson spelled out the details of his proposed New Diplomacy. Sketching out a preliminary version of what would emerge a year later as his Fourteen Points—to include self-determination, freedom of the seas, economic openness, disarmament, nonintervention, and replacement of the balance of power with a "covenant of cooperative peace"—Wilson presented terms not only for ending the ongoing European struggle but for rendering war itself forever obsolete. The adoption of this formula would result in a world of sovereign states committed to the principles of liberal democracy and free enterprise—that is to say, committed to the values distinguishing the United States itself. As Wilson assured the Congress in his peroration, "These are American principles, American policies. We could stand for no others." Indeed, he concluded, "they are the principles of mankind and must prevail."[2]

God Himself willed the universal embrace of American principles. Of this, the president was certain. This certainty—about history and about the role of the United States in bringing history to its predetermined destination—was an article of faith, central to the unfolding drama about to commence with the hitherto unimaginable: America's entry into Europe's stalemated war. Indeed, for Wilson himself, possessed of a deep-seated aversion to armaments, militarism, and killing, only the certainty that he was acting as a divine agent, that America's mission was a providential one, could justify his decision in the spring of 1917 to intervene. America's purpose was as unambiguous as it was immense: to "make the world itself at last free."[3] Only a cause of such surpassing importance could warrant sending young Americans into the abattoir of the Western Front, which had become the ultimate expression of how far the Old World had deviated from God's plan. For Wilson, reflecting a long-standing but then still vigorous American tradition, the resort to arms could for the United States never be more than an expedient, a temporary measure reluctantly employed, not a permanent expression of the nation's character.

Our own day has seen the revival of Wilsonian ambitions and Wilsonian certainty, this time, however, combined with a pronounced affinity for the sword. With the end of the Cold War, the constraints that once held American ideologues in check fell away. Meanwhile, in more than a few quarters, America's unprecedented military ascendancy, a by-product of victory in the Cold War, raised the alluring prospect that here at last was the instrument that would enable the United States to fulfill its providential mission.

In the 1980s, Ronald Reagan, Wilson's truest disciple, launched that revival, reasserting for the United States the "power to begin the world over again." In the 1990s, Bill Clinton, schooled by Reagan's success against the Soviet Union and with the American electorate, elaborated on the theme. Finding that the United States represented "the right side of history," Clinton insisted that viable alternatives to democratic capitalism and the American vision of a globalized world had ceased to exist. Although intellectuals continued their quarrel about whether or not "the end of history," and therefore the final triumph of liberal democratic capitalism, was indeed at hand, the president of the United States declared the issue moot: history had spoken, and the answer it provided was definitive. Few of the president's political adversaries, otherwise despising Clinton and all that he stood for, challenged his reading of history. Conservatives no less than liberals shared in the conviction that the triumph of democratic capitalism over all comers was self-evident and irreversible.[4]

Then, in the present decade, following the catastrophe of September 11, 2001, George W. Bush—who as a candidate had promised to restore humility to U.S. policy—revealed his true colors, becoming in the eyes of his admirers "the most Wilsonian president since Wilson himself."[5] That Bush, a man of limited historical knowledge, few intellectual pretensions, and a professed aversion to anything that smacks of "nation-building," should advert with such alacrity and apparent passion to Wilsonian precepts is but one sign of how deeply they have burrowed into the collective American psyche. For Bush as for Wilson, the connection between America's calling and God's will was self-evident. "The ideal of America is the hope of all mankind," he declared on the first anniversary of 9/11, resorting to powerful scriptural imagery to drive his point home. "That hope still lights the way," he continued. "And the light shines in the darkness. And the darkness will not overcome it."[6]

The Bush administration's *National Security Strategy of the United States of America*, issued one year after the 9/11 attacks, testified eloquently to this Wilsonian revival. In his preamble to that document, the president declared that the great ideological struggles of the twentieth century had yielded an unqualified judgment. During the course of that century, freedom had vanquished totalitarianism. A direct result of this victory was to affirm now and forever the existence of "a single sustainable model for national success: freedom, democracy, and free enterprise." In the century just begun, any nation refusing to adhere to that model—embodied by the

United States—was doomed to fail. The ultimate and irrevocable triumph of freedom—"the non-negotiable demand of human dignity; the birthright of every person"—beckoned, if only humanity would seize the opportunity. It remained, according to Bush, America's "responsibility to lead in this great mission."

Bush's national security strategy and his other sweeping post-9/11 statements (frequently laced with references to presidential insights into God's purpose) strike some observers as uniquely presumptuous. Arguably presumptuous, they are anything but unique. As Henry Kissinger observed in 1994, "whenever America has faced the task of constructing a new world order, it has returned in one way or another to Woodrow Wilson's precepts."[7] The shattering events of September 2001 challenged the Bush administration to build just such a new order, and it turned instinctively to Wilson. Indeed, the administration's response demonstrates how *little* the unprecedented attacks on the World Trade Center and the Pentagon affected the assumptions underlying U.S. foreign policy; the terrorists succeeded only in reinvigorating the conviction that destiny summons the United States, the one true universal nation, to raise up a universal civilization based on American norms. "America did not change on September 11," Robert Kagan has rightly observed. "It only became more itself." Becoming more themselves, Americans persisted in the project in which they had been engaged not only "over the past decade, but for the better part of the past six decades, and, one might even say, for the better part of the past four centuries." According to Kagan, the aim of that project from the outset was mastery: "It is an objective fact that Americans have been expanding their power and influence in ever-widening arcs since even before they founded their own independent nation."[8]

In short, when it comes to ends, little of the thinking that informs this new Wilsonian moment qualifies as genuinely new. Whether credited to Reagan, Clinton, and the younger Bush—or, alternatively and perhaps more aptly, to the collapse of communism, the spurious New Economy of the 1990s, and the rise of al Qaeda—the fin-de-siècle Wilsonian revival simply represents the full flowering of ideological claims asserted and reasserted by American statesmen throughout most of the last century.[9]

What is new and what deserves far more attention than it has received is the means by which Americans today aim to achieve those ends. The key point is this: at the end of the Cold War, Americans said yes to military power. The skepticism about arms and armies that informed the original Wilsonian vision, indeed, that pervaded the American experiment from its founding, vanished. Political leaders, liberals and conservatives alike, became enamored with military might.

The ensuing affair had and continues to have a heedless, Gatsby-like aspect, a passion pursued in utter disregard of any consequences that might ensue. Few in power have openly considered whether valuing military power for its own sake or cultivating permanent global military superiority might be at odds with American principles. Indeed, one striking aspect of America's drift toward militarism has been the absence of dissent offered by any political figure of genuine stature. Members of the political class, Democrats and Republicans alike, have either been oblivious to the possibility that something important might be afoot or else have chosen to ignore the evidence.

Contrast this with earlier turning points in U.S. military history. When the United States in 1917 plunged into the European war, Senator Robert M. La Follette, a stalwart progressive from Wisconsin, warned Americans that "under a pretext of carrying democracy to the rest of the world," Woodrow Wilson was actually doing "more to undermine and destroy democracy in the United States than it will be possible for us as a Nation to repair in a generation."[10] Two decades later, as Franklin Roosevelt maneuvered the country toward a second world war, Senator Robert A. Taft, stalwart conservative from Ohio, testified eloquently to the results likely to follow. If the United States took it upon itself to protect the smaller countries of the Old World, he said in a speech on May 17, 1941, "we will have to maintain a police force perpetually in Germany and throughout Europe." As Taft saw it, this was not America's proper role. "Frankly, the American people don't want to rule the world," he said, "and we are not equipped to do it. Such imperialism is wholly foreign to our ideals of democracy and freedom. It is not our manifest destiny or our national destiny."[11] Nor were La Follette's and Taft's the only voices raised against war and militarism.

The point here is not to argue that in their time La Follette and Taft got things exactly right. They did not—although events proved them to be more prescient than either Wilson or FDR, each of whom prophesied that out of war would come lasting peace. Rather, the point is that in those days there existed within the national political arena a lively awareness that war is inherently poisonous, giving rise to all sorts of problematic consequences, and that military power is something that democracies ought to treat gingerly. Today, in sharp contrast, such sensitivities have been all but snuffed out. When it comes to military matters, the national political stage does not accommodate contrarian voices, even from those ostensibly most critical of actually existing policy.

For example, when Senator John Kerry, Democrat of Massachusetts, ran for the presidency in 2004, he framed his differences with George W. Bush's national security policies in terms of tactics rather than first principles. Kerry did not question the wisdom of styling the U.S. response to the events of 9/11 as a generations-long "global war on terror." It was not the prospect of open-ended war that drew Kerry's ire. It was rather the fact that the war had been "extraordinarily mismanaged and ineptly prosecuted."[12] Kerry faulted Bush because, in his view, U.S. troops in Iraq lacked "the preparation and hardware they needed to fight as effectively as they could." Bush was expecting too few soldiers to do too much with too little. Declaring that "keeping our military strong and keeping our troops as safe as they can be should be our highest priority," Kerry promised if elected to fix these deficiencies. Americans could count on a President Kerry to expand the armed forces and to improve their ability to fight.[13]

Yet on this score Kerry's circumspection was entirely predictable. It was the candidate's way of signaling that he was sound on defense and had no intention of departing from the prevailing national security consensus.

Under the terms of that consensus, mainstream politicians today take as a given that American military supremacy is an unqualified good, evidence of a larger American superiority. They see this armed might as the key to creating an international order that accommodates American values. One result of that consensus over the past quarter century has been to militarize U.S. policy and to encourage tendencies suggesting that American society itself is increasingly enamored with its self-image as the military power nonpareil.

This new American militarism manifests itself in several different ways. It does so, first of all, in the scope, cost, and configuration of America's present-day military establishment.

Through the first two centuries of U.S. history, political leaders in Washington gauged the size and capabilities of America's armed services according to the security tasks immediately at hand. A grave and proximate threat to the nation's well-being might require a large and powerful military establishment. In the absence of such a threat, policymakers scaled down that establishment accordingly. With the passing of crisis, the army raised up for the crisis went immediately out of existence. This had been the case in 1865, in 1918, and in 1945. The general principle was to maintain the minimum force required and no more. Thus, for example, the million-man Union Army of 1865 shrank within a year to a mere fifty-seven thousand and within another five years was reduced to fewer than thirty thousand. Even in the aftermath of World War II, when the United States had shouldered the responsibilities of global power, this pattern pertained. On V-J Day in 1945, the U.S. Army consisted of over eight million officers and men. Within a year, 1.8 million remained on active duty, a number halved again within the following year. By 1947, the army was little more than an occupation force, its combat capabilities virtually nonexistent.[14]

Since the end of the Cold War, having come to value military power for its own sake, the United States has abandoned this principle and is committed as a matter of policy to maintaining military capabilities far in excess of those of any would-be adversary or combination of adversaries. This commitment finds both a qualitative and quantitative expression, with the U.S. military establishment dwarfing that of even America's closest ally. Thus, whereas the U.S. Navy maintains and operates a total of twelve large attack aircraft carriers, the once-vaunted Royal Navy has none—indeed, in all the battle fleets of the world there is no ship even remotely comparable to a Nimitz-class carrier, weighing in at some ninety-seven thousand tons fully loaded, longer than three football fields, cruising at a speed above thirty knots, and powered by nuclear reactors that give it an essentially infinite radius of action. Today, the U.S. Marine Corps possesses more attack aircraft than does the entire Royal Air Force—and the United States has two other even larger "air forces," one an integral part of the Navy and the other officially designated as the U.S. Air Force. Indeed, in terms of numbers of men and women in uniform, the U.S. Marine Corps is half again as large as the entire British Army—and the Pentagon has a second, even larger "army" actually called the U.S. Army—which in turn also operates its own "air force" of some five thousand aircraft.[15]

All of these massive and redundant capabilities cost money. Notably, the present-day Pentagon budget, adjusted for inflation, is 12 percent larger than the average defense budget of the Cold War era. In 2002, American defense spending exceeded by a factor of twenty-five the *combined* defense budgets of the seven "rogue states" then comprising the roster of U.S. enemies.[16] Indeed, by some calculations, the United States spends more on defense than all other nations in the world together.[17] This is a circumstance without historical precedent.

Furthermore, in all likelihood, the gap in military spending between the United States and all other nations will expand further still in the years to come.[18] Projected increases in the defense budget will boost Pentagon spending in real terms to a level higher than it was during the Reagan era. According to the Pentagon's announced long-range plans, by 2009 its budget will exceed the Cold War average by 23 percent—despite the absence of anything remotely resembling a so-called peer competitor.[19] However astonishing this fact might seem, it elicits little comment, either from political leaders or the press. It is simply taken for granted. The truth is that there no longer exists any meaningful context within which Americans might consider the question "How much is enough?"

On a day-to-day basis, what do these expensive forces exist to do? Simply put, for the Department of Defense and all of its constituent parts, defense per se figures as little more than an afterthought. The primary mission of America's far-flung military establishment is global power projection, a reality tacitly understood in all quarters of American society. To suggest that the U.S. military has become the world's police force may slightly overstate the case, but only slightly.

That well over a decade after the collapse of the Soviet Union the United States continues to maintain bases and military forces in several dozens of countries—by some counts well over a hundred in all—rouses minimal controversy, despite the fact that many of these countries are perfectly capable of providing for their own security needs.[20] That even apart from fighting wars and pursuing terrorists, U.S. forces are constantly prowling around the globe—training, exercising, planning, and posturing—elicits no more notice (and in some cases less) from the average American than the presence of a cop on a city street corner. Even before the Pentagon officially assigned itself the mission of "shaping" the international environment, members of the political elite, liberals and conservatives alike, had reached a common understanding that scattering U.S. troops around the globe to restrain, inspire, influence, persuade, or cajole paid dividends. Whether any correlation exists between this vast panoply of forward-deployed forces on the one hand and antipathy to the United States abroad on the other has remained for the most part a taboo subject.

The indisputable fact of global U.S. military preeminence also affects the collective mindset of the officer corps. For the armed services, dominance constitutes a baseline or a point of departure from which to scale the heights of ever greater military capabilities. Indeed, the services have come to view outright supremacy as merely adequate and any hesitation in efforts to increase the margin of supremacy as evidence of falling behind.

Thus, according to one typical study of the U.S. Navy's future, "sea supremacy beginning at our shore lines and extending outward to distant theaters is a necessary condition for the defense of the U.S." Of course, the U.S. Navy already possesses unquestioned global preeminence; the real point of the study is to argue for the urgency of radical enhancements to that preeminence. The officer-authors of this study express confidence that given sufficient money the Navy can achieve ever greater supremacy, enabling the Navy of the future to enjoy "overwhelming precision fire-power," "pervasive surveillance," and "dominant control of a maneuvering area, whether sea, undersea, land, air, space or cyberspace." In this study and in virtually all others, political and strategic questions implicit in the proposition that supremacy in distant theaters forms a prerequisite of "defense" are left begging—indeed, are probably unrecognized.[21] At times, this quest for military dominion takes on galactic proportions. Acknowledging that the United States enjoys "superiority in many aspects of space capability," a senior defense official nonetheless complains that "we don't have space dominance and we don't have space supremacy." Since outer space is "the ultimate high ground," which the United States must control, he urges immediate action to correct this deficiency. When it comes to military power, mere superiority will not suffice.[22]

The new American militarism also manifests itself through an increased propensity to use force, leading, in effect, to the normalization of war. There was a time in recent memory, most notably while the so-called Vietnam Syndrome infected the American body politic, when Republican and Democratic administrations alike viewed with real trepidation the prospect of sending U.S. troops into action abroad. Since the advent of the new Wilsonianism, however, self-restraint regarding the use of force has all but disappeared. During the entire Cold War era, from 1945 through 1988, large-scale U.S. military actions abroad totaled a scant six. Since the fall of the Berlin Wall, however, they have become almost annual events.[23] The brief period extending from 1989's Operation Just Cause (the overthrow of Manuel Noriega) to 2003's Operation Iraqi Freedom (the overthrow of Saddam Hussein) featured nine major military interventions.[24] And that count does not include innumerable lesser actions such as Bill Clinton's signature cruise missile attacks against obscure targets in obscure places, the almost daily bombing of Iraq throughout the late 1990s, or the quasi-combat missions that have seen GIs dispatched to Rwanda, Colombia, East Timor, and the Philippines. Altogether, the tempo of U.S. military interventionism has become nothing short of frenetic.

As this roster of incidents lengthened, Americans grew accustomed to—perhaps even comfortable with—reading in their morning newspapers the latest reports of U.S. soldiers responding to some crisis somewhere on the other side of the globe. As crisis became a seemingly permanent condition so too did war. The Bush administration has tacitly acknowledged as much in describing the global campaign against terror as a conflict likely to last decades and in promulgating—and in Iraq implementing—a doctrine of preventive war.

In former times American policymakers treated (or at least pretended to treat) the use of force as evidence that diplomacy had failed. In our own time they have concluded (in the words of Vice President Dick Cheney) that force "makes your diplomacy more effective going forward, dealing with other problems."[25] Policymakers have increasingly come to see coercion as a sort of all-purpose tool. Among American war planners, the assumption has now taken root that whenever and wherever U.S. forces next engage in hostilities, it will be the result of the United States consciously choosing to launch a war. As President Bush has remarked, the big lesson of 9/11 was that "this country must go on the offense and stay on the offense."[26] The American public's ready acceptance of the prospect of war without foreseeable end and of a policy that abandons even the pretense of the United States fighting defensively or viewing war as a last resort shows clearly how far the process of militarization has advanced.

Reinforcing this heightened predilection for arms has been the appearance in recent years of a new aesthetic of war. This is the third indication of advancing militarism.

The old twentieth-century aesthetic of armed conflict as barbarism, brutality, ugliness, and sheer waste grew out of World War I, as depicted by writers such as Ernest Hemingway, Erich Maria Remarque, and Robert Graves. World War II, Korea, and Vietnam reaffirmed that aesthetic, in the latter case with films like *Apocalypse Now, Platoon,* and *Full Metal Jacket.*

The intersection of art and war gave birth to two large truths. The first was that the modern battlefield was a slaughterhouse, and modern war an orgy of destruction that devoured guilty and innocent alike. The second, stemming from the first, was that military service was an inherently degrading experience and military institutions by their very nature repressive and inhumane. After 1914, only fascists dared to challenge these truths. Only fascists celebrated war and depicted armies as forward-looking—expressions of national unity and collective purpose that paved the way for utopia.[27] To be a genuine progressive, liberal in instinct, enlightened in sensibility, was to reject such notions as preposterous.

But by the turn of the twenty-first century, a new image of war had emerged, if not fully displacing the old one at least serving as a counterweight. To many observers, events of the 1990s suggested that war's very nature was undergoing a profound change. The era of mass armies, going back to the time of Napoleon, and of mechanized warfare, an offshoot of industrialization, was coming to an end. A new era of high-tech warfare, waged by highly skilled professionals equipped with "smart" weapons, had commenced. Describing the result inspired the creation of a new lexicon of military terms: war was becoming surgical, frictionless, postmodern, even abstract or virtual. It was "coercive diplomacy"—the object of the exercise no longer to kill but to persuade. By the end of the twentieth century, Michael Ignatieff of Harvard University concluded, war had become "a spectacle." It had transformed itself into a kind of "spectator sport," one offering "the added thrill that it is real for someone, but not, happily, for the spectator." Even for the participants, fighting no longer implied the prospect of dying for some abstract cause, since the very notion of "sacrifice in battle had become implausible or ironic."[28]

In war-as-spectacle, appearances could be more important than reality, because appearance often ended up determining reality. Force had acquired symbolic value. The aim was no longer anything so crude as laying waste to the enemy. Merely demonstrating that one possessed the ability to do so was itself expected to suffice. To use force was to strike a posture, to manipulate perceptions, or to send a message. According to General Wesley Clark, the limited bombing campaign that he designed to usher the Serbs out of Kosovo in 1999 amounted to "a low-cost, low-risk statement of intent." As commander of NATO, Clark "knew from personal experience"—or fancied that he knew—"that this was just the kind of straight threat that would carry weight with [Slobodan] Milosevic and his cronies in Belgrade."[29] A little dab of airpower stood as a hint of more to come and Clark felt sure that Milosevic would take the hint.

This image of war transformed derived from—but also meshed with and seemed to validate—the technology-hyped mood prevailing during the final decade of the twentieth century. By common consent, the defining characteristics of this age were speed, control, and choice. Information empowered the individual. It reduced the prevalence of chance and surprise and random occurrences. Everything relevant could be known and, if known, could be taken into account. In the computer age, even when something "crashed," no one got hurt and nothing was damaged. The expected result was to lessen, if not eliminate, uncertainty, risk, waste, and error and to produce quantum improvements in efficiency and effectiveness.

The potential for applying information technology to armed conflict, long viewed as an area of human endeavor especially fraught with uncertainty, risk, waste, and error, appeared particularly promising. Given access to sufficient information, man could regain control of war, arresting its former tendency to become total. Henceforth, swiftness, stealth, agility, and precision would characterize the operations of modern armies. Economy, predictability, and political relevance would constitute the hallmarks of war in the information age. Technology, wrote Admiral William Owens, "can give us the ability to see a 'battlefield' as large as Iraq or Korea—an area 200 miles on a side—with unprecedented fidelity, comprehension, and timeliness; by night or day, in any kind of weather, all the time." Unprecedented visibility brings within reach an unprecedented ability to dominate. In future wars, continued Owens, the American field commander

> will have instant access to a live, three-dimensional image of the entire battlefield displayed on a computer screen.... The commander will

know the precise location and activity of enemy units—even those attempting to cloak their movements by operating at night or in poor weather, or by hiding behind mountains or under trees. He will also have instant access to information about the U.S. military force and its movements, enabling him to direct nearly instantaneous air strikes, artillery fire, and infantry assaults, thwarting any attempt by the enemy to launch its own attack.

Combat in the information age promised to overturn all of "the hoary dictums about the fog and friction" that had traditionally made warfare such a chancy proposition. American commanders, affirmed General Tommy Franks, could expect to enjoy "the kind of Olympian perspective that Homer had given his gods."[30]

In short, by the dawn of the twenty-first century the reigning postulates of technology-as-panacea had knocked away much of the accumulated blood-rust sullying war's reputation. Thus reimagined—and amidst widespread assurances that the United States could be expected to retain a monopoly on this new way of war—armed conflict regained an aesthetic respectability, even palatability, that the literary and artistic interpreters of twentieth-century military cataclysms were thought to have demolished once and for all. In the right circumstances, for the right cause, it now turned out, war could actually offer an attractive option—cost-effective, humane, even thrilling. Indeed, as the Anglo-American race to Baghdad conclusively demonstrated in the spring of 2003, in the eyes of many, war has once again become a grand pageant, performance art, or a perhaps temporary diversion from the ennui and boring routine of everyday life. As one observer noted with approval, "public enthusiasm for the whiz-bang technology of the U.S. military" had become "almost boyish."[31]

Reinforcing this enthusiasm was the expectation that the great majority of Americans could count on being able to enjoy this new type of war from a safe distance. The old-fashioned style of warfare, emphasizing mass and the sustained application of force on a colossal scale, had been a participatory activity. From 1914 to 1918 and again from 1939 to 1945, it had consumed whole generations, with even liberal democracies conscripting willing and unwilling alike to provide the generals with the requisite steady flow of cannon fodder. But in the new style of technowar, mass became an impediment; large formations simply offered easily identifiable, slow-moving, and highly vulnerable targets. Postindustrial warfare emphasized compact formations consisting of highly skilled and highly motivated volunteers—thereby encouraging the average citizen to see war as something to be experienced vicariously.

This new aesthetic has contributed, in turn, to an appreciable boost in the status of military institutions and soldiers themselves, a fourth manifestation of the new American militarism.

Since the end of the Cold War, opinion polls surveying public attitudes toward national institutions have regularly ranked the armed services first. While confidence in the executive branch, the Congress, the media, and even organized religion is diminishing, confidence in the military continues to climb.[32] Otherwise acutely wary of having their pockets picked, Americans count on men and women in uniform to do the right thing in the right way for the right reasons. Americans fearful that the rest of society may be teetering on the brink of moral collapse console themselves with the thought that the armed services remain a repository of traditional values and old-fashioned virtue. With Americans becoming ever "more individualistic, more self-absorbed, more whiney, in a sense, more of a crybaby nation," the columnist George Will told midshipmen at the U.S. Naval Academy, it is all the more important for the military to serve as a model for the rest of society, preserving values that others might deem "anachronistic." According to Will, "it is a function of the military to be exemplars."[33]

Confidence in the military has found further expression in a tendency to elevate the soldier to the status of national icon, the apotheosis of all that is great and good about contemporary America. The men and women of the armed services, gushed *Newsweek* in the aftermath of Operation Desert Storm, "looked like a Norman Rockwell painting come to life. They were young, confident, and hardworking, and they went about their business with poise and élan."[34] A writer for *Rolling Stone* reported after a more recent and extended immersion in military life that "the Army was not the awful thing that my [anti-military] father had imagined"; it was instead "the sort of America he always pictured when he explained ... his best hopes for the country." According to the old post-Vietnam-era political correctness, the armed services had been a refuge for louts and mediocrities who probably couldn't make it in the real world. By the turn of the twenty-first century a different view had taken hold. Now the United States military was "a place where everyone tried their hardest. A place where everybody ...

looked out for each other. A place where people—intelligent, talented people—said honestly that money wasn't what drove them. A place where people spoke openly about their feelings." Soldiers, it turned out, were not
only more virtuous than the rest of us, but also more sensitive and even
happier.[35] Contemplating the GIs advancing on Baghdad in March 2003,
the classicist and military historian Victor Davis Hanson saw something
more than soldiers in battle. He ascertained "transcendence at work."
According to Hanson, the armed services had "somehow distilled from the
rest of us an elite cohort" in which virtues cherished by earlier generations
of Americans continued to flourish.[36]

Soldiers have tended to concur with this evaluation of their own moral
superiority. In a 2003 survey of military personnel, "two-thirds [of those
polled] said they think military members have higher moral standards than
the nation they serve.... Once in the military, many said, members are
wrapped in a culture that values honor and morality."[37] Such attitudes leave
even some senior officers more than a little uncomfortable. Noting with
regret that "the armed forces are no longer representative of the people they
serve," retired admiral Stanley Arthur has expressed concern that "more
and more, enlisted as well as officers are beginning to feel that they are special, better than the society they serve." Such tendencies, concluded Arthur,
are "not healthy in an armed force serving a democracy."[38]

In public life today, paying homage to those in uniform has become
obligatory and the one unforgivable sin is to be found guilty of failing to
"support the troops." In the realm of partisan politics, the political Right
has shown considerable skill in exploiting this dynamic, shamelessly pan-
dering to the military itself and by extension to those members of the public laboring under the misconception, a residue from Vietnam, that the
armed services are under siege from a rabidly anti-military Left.[39]

In fact, the Democratic mainstream—if only to save itself from extinction—has long since purged itself of any dovish inclinations. "What's the
point of having this superb military that you're always talking about,"
Madeleine Albright demanded of General Colin Powell, "if we can't use
it?"[40] As Albright's Question famously attests, when it comes to advocating
the use of force, Democrats can be positively gung ho. Moreover, in comparison to their Republican counterparts, they are at least as deferential to
military leaders and probably more reluctant to question claims of military
expertise.

Even among Left-liberal activists, the reflexive anti-militarism of the 1960s has given way to a more nuanced view. Although hard-pressed to match self-aggrandizing conservative claims of being one with the troops, progressives have come to appreciate the potential for using the armed services to advance their own agenda. Do-gooders want to harness military power to their efforts to do good. Thus, the most persistent calls for U.S. intervention abroad to relieve the plight of the abused and persecuted come from the militant Left. In the present moment, writes Michael Ignatieff, "empire has become a precondition for democracy." Ignatieff, a prominent human rights advocate, summons the United States to "use imperial power to strengthen respect for self-determination [and] to give states back to abused, oppressed people who deserve to rule them for themselves."[41]

Likewise, liberals have grown comfortable with seeing the military establishment itself not as an obstacle to social change but as a venue in which to promote it, pointing the way for the rest of society on matters such as race, gender, and sexual orientation. Advanced thinking on the Left calls not for bashing Colonel Blimp or General Halftrack as a retrograde warmonger but for enlisting his assistance (willing or not) on behalf of progressive causes.

The imperative of political leaders always and in every case offering unconditional and unequivocal support for the troops gives rise to a corollary—one that illustrates militarization's impact on the calculus governing elite political behavior on questions of war and peace.

Occasionally, albeit infrequently, the prospect of an upcoming military adventure still elicits opposition, even from a public grown accustomed to war. For example, during the run-up to the U.S. invasion of Iraq in the spring of 2003, large-scale demonstrations against President Bush's planned intervention filled the streets of many American cities. The prospect of the United States launching a preventive war without the sanction of the U.N. Security Council produced the largest outpouring of public protest that the country had seen since the Vietnam War. Yet the response of the political classes to this phenomenon was essentially to ignore it. No politician of national stature offered himself or herself as the movement's champion. No would-be statesman nursing even the slightest prospects of winning high national office was willing to risk being tagged with not supporting those whom President Bush was ordering into harm's way. When the Congress took up the matter, Democrats who denounced George W. Bush's policies in every other respect dutifully authorized him to invade Iraq. For up-and-coming politicians, opposition to war had become something of a third rail: only the very brave or the very foolhardy dared to venture anywhere near it.

Democratic supporters of the war could perhaps argue—and indeed, in the invasion's ugly aftermath some did argue—that they had been snookered. Whatever slight credence this argument deserves stems from the fact that, on military matters, members of Congress as a class have become increasingly easy marks. They can be had in part because few have made any effort to educate themselves regarding issues of national security. Exacerbating the prevailing level of strategic illiteracy is the fact that so few members have any firsthand military experience. Among current sitting members of Congress, the percentage of veterans is now lower than at any time since the end of World War II. In the typical Congress of the Cold War era, approximately three-fourths of senators and more than half of House members were veterans. Those numbers have steadily declined so that following the election of 2000, only 36 percent of senators and 29 percent of House members were veterans. And the trend lines all point south.[42]

The reason for this dearth of veterans in Congress—and in the upper ranks of other national institutions—is clear: since Vietnam, the American elite has largely excused itself from military service. Minority and working-class kids might serve; the sons and daughters of those who occupy positions of influence in the corporate, intellectual, academic, journalistic, and political worlds have better things to do. Even after 9/11, writes one acute observer, "patriotism among the affluent classes has amounted to sticking an American flag decal on the tax-deductible Hummer."[43]

To put it another way, the revival of Wilsonianism and of military metaphysics has coincided with the demise of the ancient American tradition of the citizen-soldier.

This represents a remarkable departure. Through the first two centuries of U.S. history, Americans remained leery of the threat that a large "standing army" might pose to liberty at home. As a result, placing their faith in the citizen-soldier as the guarantor of their security and ultimate guardian of their freedom, they accepted a common obligation to share in the responsibility for the country's defense. Long after the War for Independence had faded into a distant memory, the Minuteman or Ralph Waldo

Emerson's "embattled farmer"—that is, not the regular or professional soldier—remained the emblematic figure in U.S. military history. For the generations that fought the Civil War and the world wars, and even those who served in the 1950s and 1960s, citizenship and military service remained intimately connected. Indeed, those to whom this obligation to serve did not apply—including at various times the poor, people of color, and women—were thereby marked as ineligible for full citizenship.

In our own time, all of that has changed.[44] Critics of the Bush administration make much of the fact that few of today's most prominent war hawks have themselves spent even so much as a day in uniform. Neither, with a handful of exceptions, have the critics themselves.

There is a simple explanation for this fact. As with so many other aspects of life in contemporary America, military service has become strictly a matter of individual choice. On that score, beginning with the Vietnam War and continuing to the present day, members of the elite, regardless of political persuasion, have by and large opted out.

Thus, for example, Dick Cheney has explained unapologetically that as a young man in the 1960s he "had other priorities" that took precedence over military service.[45] Those unhappy with the bellicose stance attributed to Cheney as defense secretary and vice president have on this point subjected him to all manner of abuse. In their eyes, he is the embodiment of the "chicken hawk"—someone who having managed to miss the war of his youth is all too eager to send *others* to risk death or dismemberment.

In fact, Cheney's explanation for his failure to serve is an eminently defensible one. In an era that exalts individual autonomy above all other values, the state as a practical matter has long since forfeited its authority to command citizens to defend the nation. In deciding that raising a family and finishing his education was *for him* more important than military service, Cheney was simply exercising the prerogative claimed by his Vietnam-era peers, a prerogative subsequently extended to the general population when President Richard Nixon created the All-Volunteer Force (AVF) in January 1973.

The implications of this development for subsequent U.S. military policy remain insufficiently appreciated. Whereas previously Americans had recognized a link between citizenship and military service—for example, according to veterans a privileged status in American public life—Vietnam all but severed that relationship. This very much suited the interests of those who during the 1960s had contrived to evade the draft. In this regard, the views of the conservative Cheney and the liberal Bill Clinton coincided: for each, the decision to serve or to avoid service was a matter of personal choice, devoid of civic connotations; for each, any suggestion that the choice, having been made, might have larger consequences—limiting their access to positions of authority or otherwise prejudicing their future—was highly objectionable. In the emergent "limited liability model of citizenship," military service, and the risk that service might entail, was strictly a matter of personal prefer-ence.[46] In the decades since Vietnam, this view has come to prevail.

Here we confront a central paradox of present-day American mili-tarism. Even as U.S. policy in recent decades has become progressively mil-itarized, so too has the Vietnam-induced gap separating the U.S. military from American society persisted and perhaps even widened.[47] Even as American elites have become ever more fascinated with military power and the use of force—Vice President Cheney, for example, is a self-professed war buff with a passion for military history—soldiering itself is something left to the plebs.[48] "The volunteer military," the writer John Gregory Dunne has observed, "has always been most enthusiastically, even devoutly, embraced by those who would not themselves dream of volunteering—or of encouraging their children to do so."[49]

Even middle-class Americans, although professing deep regard for members of the armed services, tend to admire soldiers from a safe distance. The All-Volunteer Force—a euphemism for what is, in fact, a professional army—does not even remotely "look like" democratic America. As the *New York Times* reported at the outset of Operation Iraqi Freedom, while "the nation's wealthy and more educated youth have shunned the military," minorities and the underprivileged, along with the offspring of the officer class, have picked up the slack. In 2000, for example, minorities comprised 42 percent of the Army's enlisted force. In the growing population of female soldiers, African Americans easily outnumber whites.[50] Whereas 46 percent of the total civilian population has studied at the undergraduate level, only 6.5 percent of the eighteen- to twenty-four-year-olds filling the military's enlisted ranks have had any college education.[51]

As with their favorite professional football team, Americans cheer the troops on with verve and enthusiasm. Increasingly, however, they have about as much in common with real warriors as they do with the gridiron warriors inhabiting a typical NFL locker room.

The attitude prevailing on the civilian side of the civil-military divide can be summarized briefly: although we don't know you, rest assured that we admire you—now please go away. Thomas Friedman, foreign affairs columnist of the *New York Times,* has nicely captured this perspective. Describing his attendance at the 2004 Super Bowl, Friedman recorded his outrage that the flamboyant halftime show had not paid respect to U.S. soldiers then fighting in Iraq. The halftime entertainment "really captured what has bothered me about how this war is being conducted," he wrote.

> The whole burden is being borne by a small cadre of Americans—the soldiers, their families and reservists—and the rest of us are just sailing along, as if it has nothing to do with us. . . . The message from the White House has been: "You all just go about your business of being Americans, pursuing happiness, spending your tax cuts, enjoying the Super Bowl halftime show, buying a new Hummer, and leave this war to our volunteer Army. No sacrifices required.

Such an outlook, Friedman declared, "is morally and strategically bankrupt."

Following the game, seeking an "antidote to all the creeps in that Super Bowl show," Friedman journeyed to Tampa, Florida, and called at the headquarters of United States Central Command, responsible for the conduct of the Iraq war. What he saw there made a deep impression. To visit with American men and women in uniform is to come away with "one overriding feeling."

> We do not deserve these people. They are so much better than the country . . . they are fighting for.[52]

Having thus made plain his personal disdain for crass vulgarity and support for moral rectitude, Friedman in the course of a single paragraph drops the military and moves on to other pursuits. His many readers, meanwhile, having availed themselves of the opportunity to indulge, ever so briefly, in self-loathing, put down their newspapers and themselves move on to other things. Nothing has changed, but columnist and readers alike feel better for the cathartic effect of this oblique, reassuring encounter with an alien world.

Today, having dissolved any connection between claims to citizenship and obligation to serve, Americans entrust their security to a class of military professionals who see themselves in many respects as culturally and politically set apart from the rest of society.[53] That military is led by an officer corps that has evolved its own well-defined worldview and political agenda. Senior military leaders have sought, albeit with mixed results, to wield clout well beyond the realm falling within their nominal purview. They aim not simply to execute policy; they want a large say in its formulation.

Highly protective of their own core institutional interests, these senior officers have also demonstrated considerable skill at waging bureaucratic warfare, manipulating the media, and playing off the executive and legislative branches of government against each other to get what they want. The present-day officer corps, writes the historian Richard H. Kohn, is "more bureaucratically active, more political, more partisan, more purposeful, and more influential" than at any earlier time in American history.[54] The resulting fractious, at times even dysfunctional, relationship between the top brass and civilian political leaders is one of Washington's dirty little secrets—recognized by all of the inside players, concealed from an electorate that might ask discomfiting questions about who is actually in charge. This too is an expression of what militarism has wrought.

Rendering this civil-military relationship even more problematic is the ongoing process of militarizing the presidency itself. The framers of the Constitution designated the president as commander-in-chief as a means of asserting unambiguous civilian control. Their clear expectation and intent was that the chief executive would be in all respects a civilian. This point was not lost even on generals elected to the office: upon becoming president, for example, George Washington, Ulysses S. Grant, and Dwight D. Eisenhower each went out of his way to set aside his prior soldierly identity.

Since the day that Michael Dukakis took his ill-advised ride in an M1 Abrams tank, if not before, it has been a political truism that any would-be president must at least be able, when called upon, to strike a soldierly pose. In recent years, however, serving presidents have gone further, finding it politically expedient to blur the hitherto civilian character of their office. Astute political operatives have learned that when it comes to concealing embarrassing blemishes, outfitting a president in battle dress may be even more effective than wrapping him in the flag. In the theater of national politics, Americans have come to accept the propriety of using neatly turned-out soldiers and sailors as extras, especially useful in creating the right background for presidential photo ops.[55] Of late, they have also become accustomed to their president donning military garb—usually a fighter jock's snappy leather jacket—when visiting the troops or huddling with his advisers at Camp David.

More recently still, this has culminated in George W. Bush styling himself as the nation's first full-fledged warrior-president. The staging of Bush's victory lap shortly after the conquest of Baghdad in the spring of 2003—the dramatic landing on the carrier USS *Abraham Lincoln*, with the president decked out in the full regalia of a naval aviator emerging from the cockpit to bask in the adulation of the crew—was lifted directly from the triumphant final scenes of the movie *Top Gun*, with the boyish George Bush standing in for the boyish Tom Cruise. For this nationally televised moment, Bush was not simply mingling with the troops; he had merged his identity with their own and made himself one of them—the president as warlord. In short order, the marketplace ratified this effort; a toy manufacturer offered for $39.99 a Bush look-alike military action figure advertised as "Elite Force Aviator: George W. Bush—U.S. President and Naval Aviator."[56]

Inevitably, given the nature of American politics, the partisan advantage that President Bush derived from portraying himself as a warrior-leader induced a partisan reaction. As the 2004 presidential campaign heated up, Democrats scrutinized Bush's military bona fides and claimed to find his duty performance as a Vietnam-era reservist to be sketchy at best. The more extreme critics asserted that Bush had been AWOL—absent without leave. They contrasted this with the heroics of the Democratic candidate, Massachusetts Senator John Kerry, who had been wounded and decorated for valor for his Vietnam service. Thirty years after the fact, Kerry was still milking his membership in the "brotherhood" of warriors for all of the political benefit that it was worth and, indeed, presented himself to the nation as his party's presidential nominee with a smart salute and the announcement that he was "reporting for duty." Thus did the 2004 presidential election turn, at least in part, around questions of military service in a war three decades past.[57]

Oblivious to the implications of this creeping militarism, Americans have for the most part simply accepted it—indeed, in unexpected quarters have embraced it with an enthusiasm that is nothing short of inexplicable. How else to characterize the call of Professor Harold Bloom, Sterling Professor of Humanities at Yale and a self-described liberal Democrat, for Americans to install "a military personage as president"? With "the American Empire, like the Roman before it, seek[ing] to impose a Roman peace upon the world," the times required an explicitly imperial presidency—with the "wise and compassionate" General Wesley Clark being Bloom's preferred candidate for the job.[58]

Dissent, confined to the Far Left and the Old Right, has been sporadic, marginal, and ineffective. Given the impoverished state of national political discourse and the exceedingly narrow range of views deemed permissible, efforts to call attention to the potentially adverse consequences of becoming smitten with military power, whether offered by the venerable *Nation*, by Patrick Buchanan's freshly minted *American Conservative*, or by websites like the feisty Antiwar.com, have made little headway. The same can be said regarding efforts to propose a plausible alternative to Wilsonianism under arms.

Thus, if only by default, the nation's status as the greatest military power the world has ever seen has come to signify for the great majority of citizens a cosmic verdict of sorts, a compelling affirmation of American Exceptionalism. At least as measured by our capacity to employ violence, we are indeed Number One. The providential judgment seems indisputable: the nation charged with the responsibility for guiding history to its predetermined destination has been endowed with the raw power needed to do just that.

In fact, our present-day military supremacy represents something quite different. All of this—seeing armed force as the preeminent expression of state power and military institutions as the chief repositories of civic virtue, the expectation that revolutionary advances in military technology might offer a tidy solution to complex problems, the outsourcing of defense to a professional military elite, the erosion of civilian control—distorts if it does not altogether nullify important elements of the American birthright.

Recall that at the outset the New World was intended to be radically and profoundly *new*. The vision of freedom animating the founders of seventeenth-century Anglo-America and of the eighteenth-century American republic distinguished their purpose from that of the Old World, constantly embroiled in bloody disputes over privilege and power.

Princes, armies, and perpetual war defined Europe. The *absence* of these things was to provide a point of departure for defining America. Determined to preserve their freedom and their experiment in popular self-government, Americans knew instinctively that militarism was perhaps the foremost threat to their prospect of doing so. Military power was poison—one not without its occasional utility, but a poison all the same and never to be regarded otherwise.

In our time, oblivious to the potential consequences, we have lost sight of that truth. We have chosen to marry the means of the Old World to the ends of the New, relying on force and the threat of force to spread the American Way of Life, or, as the writer Max Boot has with unusual candor observed, "imposing the rule of law, property rights and other guarantees, at gunpoint if need be."[59]

Thus has the condition that worried C. Wright Mills in 1956 come to pass in our own day. "For the first time in the nation's history," Mills wrote, "men in authority are talking about an 'emergency' without a foreseeable end." While in earlier times Americans had viewed history as "a peaceful continuum interrupted by war," today planning, preparing, and waging war has become "the normal state and seemingly permanent condition of the United States." And "the only accepted 'plan' for peace is the loaded pistol."[60]

Chapter Two

THE MILITARY PROFESSION AT BAY

OPPONENTS OF WAR have long blamed its persistence on warmongers. But war, as the historian Charles Beard observed long ago, "is not the work of a demon. It is our very own work, for which we prepare, wittingly or not, in times of peace."[1] Much the same may be said about the creeping American militarism of our own day.

Militarism qualifies as our very own work, a by-product of our insistence on seeing ourselves as a people set apart, unconstrained by limits or by history. More specifically, in this case, militarism has grown out of the Vietnam War and the way that arguments about that war's meaning worked their way through American politics and American culture during the last quarter of the twentieth century.

For Americans who came of age in the 1960s and 1970s—that is to say, for the generation that today dominates national life—Vietnam was a defining event, the Great Contradiction that demolished existing myths about America's claim to be a uniquely benign great power and fueled suspicions that other myths might also be false. Among other things, it gave rise by war's end to a mood of pervasive and seemingly permanent anti-militarism. But Vietnam also induced a powerful reaction from Americans who refused to accept the war's apparent verdict and who viewed with alarm the changes the war gave birth to or encouraged.

Coming out of Vietnam, members of the officer corps aligned themselves with the forces of reaction. They did so at least initially not out of partisan considerations (although that came later) but out of a determination to reassert claims to professional autonomy and collective status that the war had destroyed. The comprehensive and sophisticated strategy conceived to achieve this end produced a remarkable rebirth of American military power and seemed, for a moment, to restore the profession of arms to something like the stature that it had enjoyed immediately following World War II when generals like George C. Marshall, Dwight D. Eisenhower, and Douglas MacArthur had enjoyed the status of folk heroes, towering over the scene and wielding influence that extended well beyond the military arena.

But that very success had unintended consequences, one of which was to give rise to militaristic tendencies antithetical to the well-being of the armed services and incompatible with traditional conceptions of military professionalism that had set apart war as a separate domain, subject primarily to the authority of military officers. With few exceptions, American soldiers are not warmongers. But soldiers made militarism possible, and soldiers have ended up paying much of the price.

No war is to be welcomed, least of all by those who fight them. But if the United States was destined to fight a war in the Persian Gulf, the timing of the Iraqi invasion of Kuwait in 1990 could not have been more opportune. In one of the great ironies of military history, forces made redundant by the end of the Cold War and soon to be disestablished were handed the reprieve of one final mission. The American-led response to this act of aggression culminated in an extraordinarily one-sided victory, liberating a small desert oligarchy from the clutches of a ham-handed invader possessed of a large army but no nuclear weapons.

If for the people of Kuwait Operation Desert Storm meant deliverance, for the U.S. military and its officer corps it meant something even more gratifying. Victory over Iraq vindicated a massive effort of recovery and renewal launched in the immediate aftermath of Vietnam. The performance of U.S. forces during the course of the brief campaign dazzled the American people and the world at large and overturned a historical judgment that had lingered ever since the defeat in Southeast Asia. For the generation of soldiers who had fought in Vietnam, victory in the Gulf meant redemption.

Senior American officers took pains to situate Desert Storm in this larger context. "This war didn't take 100 hours to win," Major General Barry McCaffrey explained to the Senate Armed Services Committee afterward, "it took 15 years."[2] Brigadier General Robert Scales, principal author of the U.S. Army's own history of the campaign, chose as his theme the long journey "from disillusionment and anguish in Vietnam to confidence and certain victory in Desert Storm."[3] To appreciate what had occurred in the Gulf, it was necessary to appreciate first all the ground that the armed services had traversed in getting there.

In the estimation of those who had actually made that fifteen-year-long trek—to which the American people had attended fitfully at best—the journey was one of biblical proportions. "Ten years had been lost wandering in the jungles of Vietnam," General Scales wrote, reflecting a view common among soldiers of his generation.[4] After the jungles came exile—at least so it seemed to members of an officer corps that felt itself cut off from and abandoned by American society and betrayed by the civilian elites who had sent American soldiers into battle and then lost their nerve.

But the military did not waste its years in the wilderness, which became instead a time of intense purification and rigorous preparation. The end of the Vietnam War found the U.S. military establishment in a state of advanced decay. Writing in 1971, Marine Colonel Robert D. Heinl Jr. found the U.S. armed forces "clobbered and buffeted from without and within by social turbulence, pandemic drug addiction, race war, sedition, civilian scapegoatise, draft recalcitrance and malevolence, barracks theft and common crime," unsupported by the Congress, and "distrusted, disliked, and often reviled by the public."[5]

Through Herculean exertions, the services beginning in the mid-1970s purged their ranks of the pathologies bred of defeat. Out went the dopers and the bigots, the malcontents and the untrainable.

That was just the beginning. Evincing a hitherto uncharacteristic passion for operational excellence, the U.S. military set out to reinvent itself. The result was sustained innovation on a massive scale: new doctrine, sophisticated new weapons, more rigorous approaches to training and the development of leaders, large-scale changes to organizations and tactics—all developed over the period of a decade and more and fully unveiled for the first time during the pummeling administered to Saddam Hussein's army.[6]

But viewed from inside the military itself, the reform agenda was never confined to mere tangibles like hardware or warfighting. From the outset, it included a moral component. For the officer corps, the ultimate purpose of the journey was to salvage the American profession of arms, thoroughly discredited and even dishonored in Vietnam by events such as the My Lai

Massacre and by soldiers such as Lieutenant William Calley and those who had conspired to cover up his crimes. "I will be damned," insisted an angry Vietnam-era general, "if I will permit the U.S. Army, its institutions, its doctrine and its traditions to be destroyed just to win this lousy war."[7] But the Army was all but destroyed—not only destroyed but also defeated and cast aside. No matter what the cost, the officer corps resolved to prevent this from ever happening again.

The journey of renewal culminating with Operation Desert Storm even included its own prophet, who, like Moses, pointed the way but did not live to see the Promised Land. This prophet of American military professionalism whose purpose was seemingly fulfilled in Operation Desert Storm was General Creighton Abrams.

Americans know Abrams today, to the extent that they know him at all, as the namesake of the M1 main battle tank. Commissioned in 1936 upon his graduation from West Point, Abrams served in the U.S. Army until his death in 1974. During World War II, he gained a reputation as George Patton's favorite frontline soldier, commanding a tank battalion with verve and courage during the drive across France and into the Third Reich. The years following the war brought key assignments and a steady advance through the ranks. By 1964, having progressed through a succession of senior command positions, he was a four-star general and vice chief of staff of the Army. In 1968, he became senior U.S. commander in Vietnam, succeeding his West Point classmate William C. Westmoreland. In 1972, he succeeded Westmoreland again to become Army chief of staff, a position in which he was serving when he succumbed to cancer two years later. [8]

If this qualifies as an exceptionally successful military career, it was hardly a unique one. The thing that set Abrams apart was not what he did but what he stood for. Abrams embodied a particular set of values. To an officer corps reeling from Vietnam, the *absence* of those values among the senior officers who had bought into the ill-advised war conceived by Robert McNamara and his Whiz Kids stood out as one very large, if generally unspoken, explanation for the disaster that ensued.

Although the comparison was cruelly unfair, Abrams came to be seen as the antithesis of Westmoreland and others among the top brass who either had gotten Vietnam dead wrong or in silencing their doubts had become complicit in all that followed. They were—or at least in retrospect appeared to have been—too smooth, too clever, and too detached from real soldiers and real soldiering. Abrams was—and with his passing came to personify— the blunt, unassuming warrior, crusty but compassionate, far more at ease in the field than in the polished corridors of the Pentagon. They were starched khakis and spit-shined shoes. Abrams was rumpled fatigues and muddy boots. They were trimmers. He was a truth-teller.

His efforts cut short by his untimely passing, Abrams was not by any measure the most important contributor to the post-Vietnam reconstruction of America's armed forces. That project was a collaborative one, with many key players, virtually all of them long since lost to public memory, their accomplishments largely uncredited. But Abrams, present at the creation, remained thereafter the project's preeminent symbol.

In death, "Abe" became for the American officer corps the *chevalier sans peur et sans reproche,* the subject of cultlike devotion especially in the U.S. Army. Late nineteenth-century Southerners had memorialized Robert E. Lee as a beau ideal of the Confederate soldier, the honor and virtue that they imputed to Lee sanctifying the Lost Cause itself, at least among its devotees. So too did late twentieth-century survivors of America's other lost cause consciously set out to mythologize Creighton Abrams. Throughout the 1970s and 1980s, generals making the case for reform and restoration laced their speeches with parable-like stories about Abrams, usually revolving around the importance of candor, selflessness, and empathy for young soldiers. To members of the officer corps, celebrating his soldierly virtues suggested a way of salvaging something noble from the debris of Vietnam. Long after he had passed from the scene, Abrams exerted continuing influence as inspiration, model, touchstone, and source of folk wisdom.

Victory in Operation Desert Storm served as a dramatic announcement that efforts to reconstitute American power had succeeded—indeed, had surpassed the expectations of the officer corps itself. But that victory also served to vindicate the moral enterprise in which Creighton Abrams figured so centrally. In the deserts of Kuwait and southern Iraq, the American profession of arms recovered the dignity and honor lost in Vietnam.

Expunging the facts of My Lai and the memory of Lieutenant Calley lay beyond reach; but Desert Storm showed that My Lai had been an aberration and that Calley did not represent and never had represented the officer corps as a whole. This at least is how the United States military itself wished to tell the story. And that version of the story is not without truth. But the full story is more complicated and the full truth more ambiguous—as the actual stewardship and legacy of Creighton Abrams are themselves more ambiguous.

Creighton Abrams's chief contribution to post-Vietnam military reforms was to begin the process of making it more difficult for civilian authorities to opt for war. That is, as Army chief of staff he took it upon himself to circumscribe the freedom of action permitted to his political masters. He did this by making the active army operationally dependent on the reserves, placing into the reserves functions without which the conduct of a major campaign was all but impossible. Several stateside U.S. Army divisions, for example, consisted of a mix of active and reserve units. To deploy a division's worth of combat power required first the activation of that division's "round-out brigade." In effect, no president could opt for war on any significant scale without first taking the politically sensitive and economically costly step of calling up America's "weekend warriors."

This initiative—subsequently referred to as the Total Force policy—responded directly to what was already one of the military's own canonical "lessons" of Vietnam, namely that the Johnson administration had erred fundamentally at the war's outset in disregarding the advice of the Joint Chiefs to mobilize the reserves. In other recent conflicts such as World War II, mobilizing the reserves had implied that the nation was moving to a war footing. It elevated military requirements to the top of the national agenda. But President Lyndon B. Johnson had no intention of allowing Vietnam to dictate his priorities. A big, expensive foreign war was sure to interfere with his dreams of creating a "Great Society" at home. Rejecting calls to mobilize America's citizen-soldiers reflected President Johnson's determination to keep the war small.

The result was, in effect, to send the Army off to fight while leaving the country behind. As the struggle in Vietnam intensified and dragged on, the two camps drifted ever further apart. In Vietnam, recalled General H. Norman Schwarzkopf, "we had drafted young Americans, ordered them to fight, and then blamed them for the war when they came home." General Frederick M. Franks was even more unsparing: "The leaders abandoned the warriors."[9] As Americans became indifferent or even hostile to the war, the enemy accrued a priceless advantage for which those bearing the actual burden of combat paid dearly. Schwarzkopf spoke for a generation of American officers when he observed that "we all remembered feeling abandoned by our countrymen."[10]

In Vietnam, the American army had been hung out to dry. Abrams intended to ensure that that would never happen again. "They're *never* going to take us to war again without calling up the reserves," he said.[11] The civil-military propriety of this maneuver, conceived according to one four-star general "with malice aforethought" and explicitly aimed at curbing civilian authority, was highly questionable.[12] But the importance that Abrams assigned to nurturing interdependence between active and reserve forces also provides a glimpse of the underlying aims of the post-Vietnam reform project. For Abrams and other uniformed leaders, that project had purposes that went well beyond simply reviving American military strength and restoring lost professional honor. It was also about status and prerogatives—the standing of the military, especially of the officer corps, within American society and the ability of the officer corps, especially its most senior members, to influence basic national security policy.

Successful reform, that is to say, required two things: first, restoring the bonds between American soldiers and the American people, torn asunder by Vietnam; and second, shifting the balance of civil-military authority on decisions relating to war and its conduct. Ever since the advent of nuclear weapons, that balance had been tilting in favor of civilian officials like Robert McNamara, in military eyes an execrable figure. The debacle of Vietnam showed that the tilt had gone much too far.

In this regard, opinion among American officers was virtually unanimous. In Vietnam, the civilians had routinely disregarded professional military advice. As Colonel Harry Summers caustically observed in a widely acclaimed post-mortem of that war, "our civilian leadership in the Pentagon, the White House, and in the Congress evidently believed the military professionals had no worthwhile advice to give."[13] As a consequence, Summers continued, "the military had allowed strategy to be dominated by civilian analysts." These "political scientists in academia and systems analysts in the defense bureaucracy" had persuaded senior officials in the Johnson administration to impose wholesale restrictions on the conduct of the war.[14] Thus, Johnson and McNamara had refused even to countenance an invasion of North Vietnam, placed whole categories of targets off-limits, mandated a foolish policy of gradual escalation, and signaled weakness through periodic "bombing halts" and peace initiatives. Together, these had made victory impossible. Civilians had intruded where they didn't belong and decided things they had no business deciding. The image of the president and his secretary of defense hunched over a map of North Vietnam picking targets for the Air Force to bomb etched itself in the collective consciousness of the officer corps as the ultimate expression of all that had gone wrong. "Bomb a little bit, stop it a while to give the enemy a chance to cry uncle, then bomb a bit more but never enough to really hurt," Westmoreland complained. "That was no way to win."[15]

In short, Vietnam had demonstrated that when it came to deciding when to go to war and how to fight, civilians were not to be trusted. According to Westmoreland, the events in Southeast Asia had shown definitively that war had become "too complex to be entrusted to appointed officials who lack military experience, a knowledge of military history, and an ability to persevere in the face of temporary adversity."[16] It was imperative, therefore, to redress that imbalance in ways that gave generals a greater voice, perhaps even a decisive one.

The Abrams initiative constituted only a first step toward the twin objectives of reconstructing the connecting tissue between soldiers and society and rebalancing the relationship between civilian and military elites, but it was suggestive of much that followed and casts the military's wilderness years in a different light. Institutional self-interest as much as a concern for the national interest guided the officer corps during its long, hard journey toward Desert Storm, although it is unlikely that Abrams himself and other senior military leaders drew any distinction between the two.

The importance attributed to restoring the status and prerogatives of the military profession helps to explain why the officer corps launched its post-Vietnam reform effort by slamming the door shut on the war it had just fought. When the French army in the 1950s returned home from its defeat at the hands of the Viet Minh, it devoted considerable energy to figuring out how it ought to have fought that war and how it was going to win next time. For French officers, the complex political-military struggle that they had encountered in Indochina typified "modern war."[17] They expected to confront it again and soon did in Algeria.

When American soldiers in the 1970s returned home from defeat, in contrast, they had had a bellyful of guerrillas, insurgents, people's warfare, and vainly trying to win hearts and minds. For American officers, the starting point for retrieving professional legitimacy lay in avoiding altogether future campaigns even remotely similar to Vietnam.

As a result, the officer corps that came back from Southeast Asia devoted precious little energy to dissecting the defeat it had just endured. Doing so would have advanced the cause of professional revival only minimally, if at all. Rather, soldiers threw themselves headlong into an effort to devise a definition of modern war more congenial to their own purposes. This meant first of all restoring the utility of force, making the case that battle offered the prospect of decision rather than pointing ineluctably toward stalemate and quagmire. But beyond restoring war's status as the ultima ratio of princes and presidents, professional revival also meant delineating war once again as a unique domain falling exclusively within the purview of warriors. The key, wrote Colonel Summers, was to draw a "clear distinction between war and peace."[18] In Vietnam, a murky conflict that had dragged on endlessly and aimlessly, that distinction had been lost, and with it the prerogatives and standing of military professionals. The American officer corps now set out to undo all of that.

In that regard, American officers responded to failure in ways reminiscent of German officers during the 1920s and 1930s.[19] But the task facing American soldiers after their defeat in Vietnam was even more difficult than that which German soldiers had faced after their defeat in World War I. For the Americans had to deal with the skepticism of observers persuaded by Hiroshima on the one hand and by Vietnam itself on the other that all war had become an exercise in futility and the profession of arms obsolete.

The bind to which these critics pointed was a real one. The post-Vietnam U.S. military attempted to escape it by asserting the existence—indeed, the primacy—of conflict in the zone between total war and people's war. Between nuclear annihilation on the one hand and the exhaustion of guerrilla warfare without end on the other: this was the space in which they intended to find a renewed sense of purpose. Nor was it absurd to claim that such a zone existed. Even from the vantage point of the 1970s, the early successes of the Wehrmacht, in Poland and France, remained immensely suggestive. The unfolding history of the modern Middle East provided

American military reformers with even more recent examples, as instructive as they were fortuitous.

Even as the agony of Vietnam was playing itself out, the Arab-Israeli Wars of 1967 and 1973 provided American military officers with a template for how wars were supposed to be fought: warrior pitted against warrior in a contest whose stakes, military as well as political, were straightforward and unambiguous; commanders empowered to command and backed by political leaders who refrained from operational meddling; civilian populations that were spared direct involvement as belligerents but had no difficulty determining whose side they were on. Best of all, refuting the canard that warfare in the modern age had become synonymous with stalemate or quagmire, these conflicts ended within a matter of days and produced unequivocal decision. In the performance of the Israel Defense Forces and in the IDF's status within Israeli society (and, although less openly stated, in the performance and status of the Wehrmacht in its heyday), American soldiers found inspiration for their own recovery.

Had they examined the actual German and Israeli experience more critically, American officers might have recognized that operational excellence alone could not guarantee professional recovery. Indeed, in resolving some problems, it gave rise to others.

During the interwar period, the German army had pursued an intense military reform program aimed at rebuilding German military might, with one eye firmly fixed on recovering the social standing and prestige lost to the officer class in the defeat of 1918. The great German battlefield successes of 1939 and 1940 seemed to vindicate that program. As soon became evident, however, the upshot was not so much to restore the German profession of arms as to increase an appetite for conquest, thereby making possible a monstrous criminal enterprise. The officer corps became shamefully complicit in that enterprise and in so doing guaranteed its own well-deserved destruction.

For its part, through a string of remarkable victories, the Israeli army frustrated repeated Arab attempts to destroy the Jewish homeland. But if these demonstrations of military prowess permitted Israel to survive, they did not produce peace and security. Indeed, they encouraged tendencies that made peace and security even more remote. In 1967, the heady vapors of battlefield success fueled dreams of creating a Greater Israel and resulted in the fateful decision to annex the West Bank. In 1982, excessive confidence in Israeli arms led to the reckless and counterproductive invasion of Lebanon. In the meantime, Israel's enemies adopted irregular tactics to which the IDF, optimized for high-tech, high-intensity conventional warfare, found itself hard-pressed to reply. The result for Israel was increasing political isolation and something akin to a state of permanent and psychologically debilitating hostilities.

The history of the United States military after Vietnam offers a variation on these themes. From the perspective of the officer corps itself, great and worthy achievements gave rise to results other than anticipated and in some cases altogether perverse.

The immediate problem was one of adapting the style of warfare practiced by the Israelis to fit American strategic requirements. For the United States, the "threat" was not Arabs but the Soviet empire. The critical battlefield was not (then) the desert. Jungles or rice paddies might figure on the periphery, but the main contest lay elsewhere. From the very outset of the Cold War, the confrontation between East and West had centered on the expanse of industrialized and democratic Europe extending from Denmark south to Switzerland, from the Iron Curtain west to the Atlantic ports—in allied parlance, the so-called Central Region.

Since 1945, this Central Region had seen no battles. It had instead become the scene of an armed standoff between the North Atlantic Treaty Organization (NATO) and the Warsaw Pact, a standoff that the Soviets had respected even as the Vietnamese quagmire sucked the Americans in and held them there. The defining quality of the Central Region by the 1970s, in other words, had come to be stability—a wary and heavily armed stability, but no less real for all that. Anyone who was in the know—even the most hawkish hawk—understood that war along the dividing line between East and West had "dwindled to negligible likelihood" and that a Warsaw Pact offensive was "plainly a loony alternative."[20] The Eastern Front bristled with arms but for decades had been, and seemed quite likely to remain, quiet.

This stability, the need for vigilance, and, not least of all, the widely shared assumption that maintaining the status quo required the fielding of large and powerful armies all made the Central Region the ideal venue in which to begin undoing the effects of Vietnam. By reestablishing its bona fides as a force that with its allies could handily defeat a (theoretical but highly improbable) Warsaw Pact attack, the American military establishment might begin to recover the stature and legitimacy lost in Southeast Asia. That it might do so without fighting—indeed, the overriding political objective was to avert a fight—made the opportunity all the more attractive.

Thus disposed, American officers returned to what they viewed as real soldiering. Beginning in the mid-1970s and continuing through the 1980s, the Soviet "other" provided both focus and a sense of urgency to their campaign of military revitalization. Leaving few parts of the armed forces untouched, this effort manifested itself most prominently in the realm of doctrine, particularly in the AirLand Battle doctrine unveiled by the Army in 1982 and formally endorsed by the Air Force as well.[21] AirLand Battle offered the formula according to which U.S. forces would turn back a full-scale nonnuclear Warsaw Pact attack, relying on superior technology, superior tactics, and superior training to compensate for the enemy's superior numbers. Quality would render the adversary's enormous quantitative advantages moot.

With most Americans still persuaded even after Vietnam that the danger posed by the Soviet Union (as opposed to the now largely discredited threat of Communism per se) remained real, the mission of defending the Central Region could command critically required public support. In other words, finding that Europe, despite decades of stability, faced an imminent threat demanding urgent attention provided a plausible answer to the question left hanging in the air after Vietnam: why does the United States even need a military? By extension, gearing up to deflect that threat would generate requirements for a very large army supported by large naval and air forces, from the perspective of the armed services an agreeable prospect. AirLand Battle also implied the adoption of a distinctively new American style of warfare, one that (in the words of one of the doctrine's architects) "draws adroitly on advanced technology, concentrates force from unprecedented distances with overwhelming suddenness and violence, and blinds and bewilders the foe."[22] Developing such dazzling new capabilities required modernization, which provided a rationale for purchasing new equipment and funding the exercises needed to test new concepts and sharpen soldierly skills.

Senior military leaders advertised this as a sharp departure from the past.

Indeed, as a blueprint for how U.S. forces intended to fight future wars, AirLand Battle did contain certain innovative elements, for example, the radical decentralization implied by the doctrine's vision of "nonlinear" maneuver warfare. On the nonlinear battlefield, weapons of exceptional range and lethality promised to blur old distinctions between front lines and the rear areas; everyone would be in the fight. Meanwhile, fast-moving, self-contained units would be freed from old requirements to carefully guard their flanks and to gauge their movement to the pace of their neighbors on the left and right. But this was an idea that never made it off the printed page. Both in exercises and in subsequent combat, U.S. forces operated in ways consistent with traditional military precepts: hierarchy maintained, orders coming from the top down, forces arrayed in linear fashion. In truth, despite all the claims made on its behalf, AirLand Battle as implemented contained little that qualified as genuinely original. At its core, the new U.S. doctrine was a throwback. It was blitzkrieg, invented decades earlier by the Germans, more recently refurbished by the Israelis, now dressed up with somewhat longer range, somewhat more accurate, and somewhat more lethal weapons.

But there was more. All of the planning and preparation entailed in gearing up to defend Western Europe assumed and legitimated a specific—and, despite the trappings of novelty, inherently counterrevolutionary—conception of warfare. In the latter part of a century in which war as actually experienced had repeatedly slipped its traces, AirLand Battle presumed to impose limits and boundaries on the notional wars of the future. The clash of opposing armies, not the mobilization of entire societies, would determine the fate of the Central Region. Out of that clash would come not stalemate but decision, achieved promptly, at tolerable cost, and without widespread collateral damage or incidental slaughter. (Assuming that the Warsaw Pact would refrain from using nuclear weapons at least initially, American military planners expected any war to defend Western Europe to be a conventional one.) In the course of gaining that decision, American commanders would necessarily enjoy a high level of autonomy and be permitted to fight the war consistent with the logic and grammar peculiar to their profession. In short, the next war would find the generals back in the driver's seat; even if that war never came—again, the overriding criterion of success was to ensure that it did not—as long as the prospect of such a conflict remained central to U.S. national security concerns, then American military professionals could expect a substantial degree of deference and respect, certainly more than they had enjoyed in the wake of Vietnam.

To emphasize: the chief explanation for the U.S. military's inordinate preoccupation with a prospective Warsaw Pact invasion in the late 1970s and 1980s is to be found not in expectations that the Soviets were about to renounce the postwar division of Europe but in the imperative of reconstituting an autonomous military profession. The war that the officer corps prepared itself to fight was the war in which the prospects of actually having to fight were most remote. This made perfect sense. The whole idea, after all, was to restore and preserve, not to rebuild and then deplete.

The officer corps also had a profound interest in curtailing any inclination on the part of civilian policymakers to commit U.S. forces to contingencies other than the defense of Europe, especially any contingency in which the likelihood of gaining a rapid and favorable decision appeared problematic. As the process of recovery gained momentum, the officer corps had little appetite for putting the gains it had made at risk. It had no appetite at all for situations likely to involve protracted fighting for peripheral interests, situations, in short, that might mire the armed services in anything resembling a repeat of Vietnam.

In this regard, the officer corps sought not simply to reassert its primacy on matters relating to the planning and conduct of operations; it also wanted to have a strong say in determining when and where U.S. forces might be called upon to fight. Only influence there—prior to any actual decision to intervene—could prevent feckless civilians from committing the nation to wars or quasi-wars not to the military's own liking.

In conceiving the Total Force policy, Abrams had taken one large, if somewhat oblique, step in the direction of tying the civilians' hands. By the 1980s, the effort became more forthright and more determined, eventually finding expression in the so-called Weinberger Doctrine.

Commentators at the time attributed this doctrine, enunciated by Secretary of Defense Caspar Weinberger in November 1984, to then existing tensions within the Reagan administration, an effort by a secretary of defense reluctant to use force to rein in a secretary of state, George Shultz, ostensibly eager to do so.[23] In fact, the Weinberger Doctrine emerged out of a larger context. To explain it in terms of personality differences and bureaucratic rivalry within a particular administration is to misconstrue its true significance.

Credited with conceiving the message, Weinberger was in fact merely the medium for its delivery. The message itself—establishing specific criteria to govern decisions regarding the use of force—was the uniformed military's. Those who actually devised it did not direct it at any particular official. Nor did they wish to confine its application to a particular moment or circumstance. They intended it as a permanent and comprehensive statement of policy, codifying the paramount lessons of Vietnam as the military itself had come to understand those lessons. The intent of having the secretary of defense promulgate those lessons was simply to invest them with greater authority, in the hope that they would become binding for all time and in all situations.

The Weinberger Doctrine created a series of tests, in essence preconditions for any policy decision that might put American troops into harm's way. Chief among those preconditions were the following: to restrict the use of force to matters of vital national interest; to specify concrete and achievable objectives, both political and military; to secure assurances of popular and congressional support; to fight to win; and to use force only as a last resort.[24]

Any decision to intervene was to require policymakers first to advance a plausible case for meeting all of these tests. The failure to do so was to constitute a de facto veto. The purpose of the Weinberger Doctrine was not to facilitate the effective use of American military power but—very much in the spirit of Creighton Abrams—to insulate the armed services from another Vietnam-like disaster.

The Weinberger Doctrine had no more passionate advocate than General Colin Powell, who as Weinberger's principal military assistant had a hand in drafting it but who as an immensely influential chairman of the Joint Chiefs of Staff at the end of the Cold War did more than any other soldier to ensure its demise. Indeed, however inadvertently, Powell more than any other military figure contributed to the conditions out of which the militarization of American policy evolved. Powell managed both to give Albright's Question weight and to deprive the officer corps of any plausible response other than to accede, however reluctantly, to its demands.

Over the course of the 1990s, Powell became in the eyes of many if not most Americans a revered figure, something of a soldier-superstar. But he has never suffered for want of critics. The rap against Powell, especially during the pivotal period from 1989 to 1993 when he served as JCS chairman, was that he was a classic political general. In the eyes of his detractors, Powell was too much the insider, too adept at the arts of manipulation, and too eager to wrap himself in the protective mantle of Reluctant Warrior, quick to distinguish his own views from those of the "so-called experts" eagerly suggesting "that all we need is a little surgical bombing or a limited attack."[25]

Federal statutes charge the JCS chairman with the responsibility for providing the president and secretary of defense with disinterested professional military advice. With Powell, things proved to be considerably more complicated. No one doubted that the general deferred in principle to the tradition of civilian control. At the same time, as one careful observer of civil-military relations noted, Powell was always "pushing the limits of military autonomy."[26] Whether the issue was post–Cold War strategy or instability in the Balkans, the general often seemed to promote his own parallel agenda (which became de facto the military's agenda). Few doubted his personal honesty. But at the same time Powell operated in ways that seemed conniving and faintly mendacious. Determined to forestall a proposed U.S. intervention in Bosnia in the 1990s, he offered not analysis but arguments for inaction. According to General Merrill McPeak, then serving as Air Force chief of staff, Powell's presentation to the White House amounted to the following: "Here's Option A, it is really stupid. Here's Option B, it is dumber than dirt."[27] By his own account, Powell believed strongly in the adage that "you don't know what you can get away with until you try"—at the very least an odd rule of conduct for a senior military professional.[28] Worse, tainted with extraneous considerations, the professional counsel that he offered frequently turned out to be defective—as proved to be the case in Bosnia—although someone else always ended up taking the fall.

The liberation of Kuwait in 1991 that seemingly redeemed the military profession was also the event that vaulted Powell to the status of national hero. There was irony to this, for in the debates within the administration about how to respond to Iraqi aggression, Powell had argued against the use of force and in favor of relying on economic sanctions to pressure Saddam Hussein into withdrawing. With the Cold War just ending (and with a recent intervention in Panama having produced a gratifyingly easy success), he was not eager to expose unnecessarily a military machine rebuilt at such enormous cost and effort. As far as Powell was concerned, Iraq's invasion of Kuwait came nowhere close to satisfying each of the Weinberger Doctrine's several preconditions.

When Powell lost that argument, he made himself available for a series of off-the-record interviews with the journalist Bob Woodward, thereby establishing a record of his opposition to the war. If things went sour, he could count on the first draft of history to absolve him of blame.[29]

In the event, things did not go sour. As Abrams had intended, mounting a major campaign in the Gulf required that President George H. W. Bush first order the largest mobilization of part-time soldiers in a generation.[30] With more than seventy-five thousand Air and Army Guardsmen serving in the conflict in addition to reservists from each of the services, the country as a whole did seem to rally to the cause. Of equal or greater importance, developments on the battlefield went swimmingly well, so well, in fact, that with the Iraqi army in full flight Powell pressed for an early termination of hostilities lest the appearance of gratuitous killing besmirch the honor of America's armed forces. Powell wanted to see the war neatly concluded with no loose ends and no lingering complications. So he exerted his considerable influence to minimize civilian involvement in efforts to arrange the ceasefire ending the conflict, insisting that the battlefield commander, General H. Norman Schwarzkopf, enjoy a free hand.

On each of these two issues, Powell prevailed. Each proved to be a monumental blunder. The premature ceasefire allowed large portions of the Iraqi Republican Guard to escape intact. For his part, Schwarzkopf, perhaps confusing his role with that of Grant at Appomattox, used his free hand to grant his Iraqi counterpart generous concessions, permitting the Iraqi army the continued use of its armed helicopters, for example. Saddam Hussein responded to this magnanimous gesture by employing the helicopters along with his Republican Guard to brutally suppress an internal uprising that threatened his hold on power. Defying American expectations that defeat made Saddam's overthrow all but inevitable, the Iraqi dictator survived. To deter him from further mischief, the United States found itself obliged to retain substantial forces in the Gulf, thereby putting in train a series of events that led ultimately to 9/11 and yet another major war whose ambiguous outcome led to still deeper U.S. military involvement in the region.[31]

In the warm afterglow of a seemingly historic victory, little of this was apparent. Powell quickly seized upon that mood. Deftly capitalizing on his suddenly outsized reputation, he wasted no time in promulgating his (and the military's) own "lessons of Desert Storm" to take their place alongside the now familiar lessons of Vietnam. But the chief purpose of these lessons was to support the military's institutional agenda, nurturing conditions in which the armed services would be highly esteemed, lavishly supported, and rarely used, except in circumstances that met with the prior approval of the officer corps. The question that generals wanted to hear from their civilian masters after Desert Storm was not "What are you doing for us?" but "What can we do for you and the troops?"

The underlying premise was a simple one: for Powell and his military contemporaries, the just-concluded campaign to liberate Kuwait constituted the paradigmatic "good war." Having spent the previous fifteen years preparing to fight a theoretical war in the plains, woodlands, and cities of Central Europe, they finally got an actual war, albeit in the desert against a third-rate Third World adversary. The war's aftermath found the officer corps at peace with itself, held in high regard by the American people, and presiding over a well-honed military machine. Measured in terms of the military's own long-standing institutional goals—restoring the prestige and prerogatives of the profession of arms—Desert Storm qualified as a resounding success. Hence Powell's inattention to the sparseness of the war's political and strategic payoff. Hence too his determination to establish Desert Storm as a model for the future rather than as a one-time event.

One expression of this determination took the form of a new doctrine regarding the use of force, one this time explicitly, rather than implicitly as was the case with the Weinberger principles, the handiwork of the military itself. The Powell Doctrine supplemented, modified, and ultimately transcended the Weinberger Doctrine from which it derived. Vital interests, concrete objectives, the prerequisite of popular support: all of these stayed. But Powell added two additional considerations. The first was the requirement for an "exit strategy"—having a clear idea of when and how to extract

U.S. forces even before intervening (thereby avoiding open-ended commitments). The second was an emphasis on "overwhelming force"—approaching the task with preponderant rather than merely sufficient combat power at hand (thereby making possible a rapid end to the fighting and an equally rapid departure). Notably, however, the purpose of the Powell Doctrine remained consistent with that of the Weinberger Doctrine. It aimed not to facilitate but to impede intervention. If Powell got his way, future American wars would look very much like Desert Storm—brief, economical, operationally (if not politically) decisive, and, above all, infrequent.[32]

There was a second expression of Powell's determination to enshrine Desert Storm as definitive, this one producing results inherently at odds with the first. When it came to charting basic post–Cold War/post–Desert Storm military policy, he wanted to have his fellow generals calling the shots. "I was determined to have the Joint Chiefs drive the military strategy train," he later recalled, "rather than have military reorganization schemes shoved down our throat."[33]

For the officer corps, preserving the now fully restored profession of arms required the preservation of the force actually on hand in 1991 or of something quite like it. Not surprisingly, Powell's paramount objective coming out of Desert Storm was to maintain the status quo, to deflect any efforts to tamper with the structure, arrangements, and routines existing at the moment when the Iraqi army went down in defeat.

To permit civilians to meddle—shoving military reorganization schemes down soldiers' throats—posed a direct threat to all that the officer corps had accomplished over the previous fifteen years. In the worst case, it held out the possibility of reviving something like the situation that had existed prior to World War II, when the American military profession was a marginal institution and senior military officers figures of marginal importance. To Powell and his military contemporaries, such a prospect was anathema; hence the imperative of the Joint Chiefs rather than elected or appointed civilian officials determining military strategy.

Lending an element of plausibility to Powell's expectations that the Joint Chiefs might be able to do so was the fortuitous relationship between the fall of the Berlin Wall in October 1989 and the Iraqi invasion of Kuwait that followed so closely on its heels in August 1990. The near simultaneity of these two events—the former one of world historical importance in which military power played a decidedly ambiguous role, the latter puny by comparison but swiftly resolved by the sword—made it more difficult for Americans to take the true measure of each.

By all rights, the end of the Cold War ought to have triggered a thoroughgoing reconsideration of the size and appropriate role of America's armed forces. After all, the United States, a nation not in the habit of maintaining a large "standing army" in peacetime, had raised up those forces in response to a specific threat: totalitarian regimes possessing the wherewithal to threaten the United States and its vital interests. With the end of the Cold War and the collapse of the Soviet Union in December 1991, such threats ceased to exist. The rationale for the sprawling establishment created in the aftermath of World War II and maintained ever since had vanished. More specifically, the force that officers of Powell's generation had labored so long and so hard to create now faced the prospect of being deemed superfluous.

From this point of view, too, the timing of Desert Storm could not have been more opportune. Hardly had talk of possibly claiming a post–Cold War "peace dividend" begun when Saddam Hussein obligingly preempted that debate. Given the brief attention span of the American people, the liberation of tiny Kuwait eclipsed the fall of the Berlin Wall as a historical turning point. The resulting display of U.S. military prowess and advanced technology beguiled Americans. To those who had ignored the military since Vietnam, images of precision bombs heading unerringly to their targets and of Patriot missiles (ostensibly) intercepting incoming Scuds came as an epiphany of sorts. A seemingly easy victory also predisposed them to accept the argument that Powell, his own stature now greatly enhanced, proceeded to advance: in the new age just dawning, military might promised to be not less but more useful, even essential, as Desert Storm itself had ostensibly demonstrated. The war also showed that with the end of the Cold War, the responsibilities of global leadership were greater than ever. Those responsibilities meant that the United States could not relinquish the global military presence that it had acquired during the 1940s nor the global power projection capabilities that it had perfected after Vietnam. (In the realm of national security, "global" had emerged as a favored adjective.) In short, the United States could not stand down; it could not return to normalcy. The American soldiers scattered around the world in Europe, the Far East, Latin America, and now the Persian Gulf could not return home; their work was not yet done—indeed, was unlikely ever to be done.

Powell and the other Joint Chiefs expected future American wars to replicate Desert Storm—large-scale conventional conflicts with the United States, consistent with the dictates of AirLand Battle and the Powell Doctrine, bringing to bear overwhelming force and thereby securing a quick decision and rapid exit. Pointing to the assemblage of warships, fighter squadrons, and ground formations that had defeated the Iraqi army, they argued on behalf of the United States henceforth maintaining—at a minimum—forces sufficient to fight and win two such wars *concurrently*.

And their argument carried the day. In the aftermath of Desert Storm, the idea that the nation's well-being was contingent upon maintaining an instant readiness to fight two simultaneous large-scale conventional wars—or major regional contingencies (MRCs), as they came to be called—achieved the status of a strategic first principle.

This was a prescription for making permanent an enormous Cold War–style defense establishment—despite the absence of any Cold War–equivalent threat. By no means incidentally, a national security strategy based on the prospect of fighting multiple MRCs also promised to make permanent the clout that senior military leaders once again enjoyed within the inner circle of the policy elite. For decades, the Defense Department had accrued influence at the expense of the State Department. More recently, the generals had been accruing influence at the expense of the civilians who were their nominal masters. Maintaining in peacetime a large and highly professional standing army charged with global responsibilities seemed likely to affirm these trends, which from the outset had been the intent of the post-Vietnam military reform project.

But the implications of gearing basic strategy to the two-MRC requirement went even further. It made the use or threatened use of armed force, as never before, central to the American conception of international politics. In war, it seemed, lay America's true comparative advantage. Thus, at a time when elsewhere in the West—whether correctly or not—skepticism about the utility of force was rising and defense budgets were in free fall, the United States embarked upon a radically different course. Afflicted with fears and resentments brought back from Vietnam and determined to press on with the agenda that Abrams had begun, Powell and fellow soldiers sold their countrymen on a proposition fraught with unforeseen consequences. Without giving the matter all that much thought, Americans decided that it was the nation's destiny to remain a military leviathan. Permanently possessing dominant power, irrespective of the conditions existing beyond the nation's borders, had become an unconditional prerequisite. In the military's rush to codify the "lessons of Desert Storm," larger questions about just what it was the Defense Department ought to be defending simply never came up for serious discussion.

Powell and his uniformed contemporaries counted on their newly refurbished authority—to which the very existence of a "Powell" Doctrine testified—to provide a check against the prospect of irresponsible civilians misusing America's unprecedented military advantage. In this regard they badly miscalculated. Unanticipated developments on the international stage soon confronted the United States with situations for which a Desert Storm–style response was inappropriate if not altogether counterproductive. The new world disorder of the 1990s offered the officer corps an unwelcome choice: either soldiers could improvise a response to these highly unconventional contingencies (thereby abandoning the MRC as operational model) or they could persist in refusing to venture beyond the realm of conventional operations (thereby admitting their own irrelevance to actually existing security concerns and inviting a diminution of their status and prerogatives).

But to improvise a response was to move into territory in which the fiction of crisp divisions between war and politics was impossible to sustain. Events of the 1990s made it even more difficult to preserve a clear distinction between the world of the warrior and the world of the politician. As the two merged, Vietnam-induced prohibitions on civilian policymakers intruding in military affairs eased. And the incentives for some generals to venture into the political penumbra surrounding war increased. As a consequence, the fifteen-year-long effort to restore an autonomous military profession standing apart from (and even above) politics—which seemed for a brief moment in Desert Storm to have triumphed—began to unravel.

In the years that followed America's first Persian Gulf War, a reluctant officer corps found itself cajoled, prodded, embarrassed, or dragged into undertaking a plethora of new interventions, a journey that started in 1991 with intervention to protect the Kurds but that led inexorably to Baghdad in 2003 with few indications of ending there. These varied operations shared only one thing in common: none of them conformed to the criteria laid out in the Powell Doctrine. In the end, the effort to rebuild American military power while restricting its use, initiated by Creighton Abrams and carried to its fruition by Colin Powell, failed. Or more accurately, because that effort generated a capacity for global power projection surpassing anything the world had ever seen, reticence about how and where to use that power soon went by the board.

As a result, over the course of the 1990s, inhibitions about actually using force eased. Hardly more than a decade after President George H. W. Bush, with considerable trepidation, led the United States into its first Persian Gulf conflict, his son, laying the groundwork for a second Persian Gulf conflict, committed the United States to a new Bush Doctrine of preventive war. In doing so, the younger President Bush buried any lingering notions of the sole superpower exercising self-restraint. But in doing so, he also put paid to any illusions held by members of the officer corps that they might be able to curb the inclination of civilian policymakers to employ force. The result was to raise the prospect of war without end and of a now highly skilled military shorn of its prerogatives and once again fearful of becoming decoupled from the American people.

The end of the Cold War and victory in the Persian Gulf War gave birth to an unwelcome legacy: not peace and stability but disintegration and disorder. In the wake of Germany's joyous reunification came the bloody and protracted collapse of Yugoslavia. After Iraq's ouster from Kuwait came Saddam Hussein's brutal repression of Kurdish and Shi'ia rebels, enabling the Iraqi dictator to survive and precluding anything like a neat American exit strategy. After the demise of the Soviet Union came Russia's war against Chechen separatists. Out of the ostensible promise of the Oslo peace process there emerged a second Intifada that roiled the Middle East. And so it went.

Ethnic cleansing, genocide, failed states, civil war, terror: these became the defining characteristics of the decade-long interval between Desert Storm and the events of 9/11. In an immediate sense, few of the disturbances marking the 1990s had any direct bearing on U.S. security. Yet the very fact that the world's greatest military power faced so few threats to its own well-being made it difficult for American leaders to turn a blind eye to injustice, famine, and mass killing elsewhere. Having won the argument for maintaining global U.S. military preeminence—or at least having pre-empted any serious inquiry into why the nation needed forces in excess of those required for its own security—the Pentagon now found itself summoned time and again to "do something" to relieve the plight of the suffering and the oppressed.

Rather than being permitted to stay in garrison until the next MRC loomed, U.S. forces found themselves pressed to take on a variety of new and burdensome missions. At the outset of the 1990s, senior military leaders, content to rest on laurels garnered during Desert Storm, resisted being drawn into these adventures. On the one hand, they argued, since "super-powers don't do windows," it was the role of the United States to shoulder the tough jobs that required heavy lifting—fighting the big wars, rather than wasting the time of American soldiers "escorting kids to kinder-garten."[34] On the other hand, involving American soldiers in the lesser tasks of peacekeeping and humanitarian intervention was likely to have all sorts of untoward consequences. At a minimum, such tasks promised to undermine the readiness of the armed services to win the next Big One, whenever and wherever it developed.

The generals' inability to rebut Albright's Question undermined that resistance. The military reform project of the 1970s and 1980s had succeeded in reversing the impression left over from Vietnam that military power was worse than useless. On the contrary, Desert Storm showed that in American hands force had become eminently useful. Now voices on the Right and on the Left called for further demonstrations of that utility. With Pentagon expenditures holding steady at approximately $300 billion per year throughout the 1990s, it was incumbent upon the military to demonstrate some tangible return on the nation's investment.

Nervously, grudgingly, expecting the worst, the officer corps found ways—especially after Powell himself retired from active service in 1993—to accommodate itself to civilian demands for a more forthcoming approach to putting American military might to work. As a result, U.S. national security policy during the 1990s became a peculiar mix of activism blended with timidity.

Throughout that decade, the hallmark of the American way of war turned out to be not "overwhelming force" but "force protection." The United States waged war on the cheap and spared nothing in its efforts to avoid American casualties. The spirit informing U.S. military operations was not audacity but acute risk aversion. To minimize the prospect of U.S. losses, the armed services relied whenever possible on air power, usually administered from afar and in limited doses. If close combat seemed likely, they recruited proxies—the unfortunate experience in Somalia suggesting that Americans had no stomach for casualties. Carefully circumscribed missions—keeping the peace in the Balkans, for example, did not extend to arresting indicted war criminals—further reduced direct American exposure.

Although it is difficult to make the case that these operations were especially effective, their cumulative effect was to reduce any residual inhibitions that Americans entertained about the use of force. Each successive episode eroded that much further the collective ability of the officer corps to stay the hand of the advocates of intervention. By the end of the decade, the Powell Doctrine looked increasingly like a dead letter.

With various members of the civilian elite, whether in pursuit of an ideological, humanitarian, or strategic agenda, nourishing an increasingly hearty appetite for intervention, the solidarity of the officer corps itself broke down. The idea of using limited force in pursuit of less-than-vital objectives—rank heresy in Vietnam's immediate aftermath—began to find favor in certain military quarters. With events of the 1990s blurring the distinction between war and politics, field commanders began to fancy themselves clever enough to straddle both worlds and to master the art of "coercive diplomacy."

One such was General Wesley K. Clark, who as Supreme Allied Commander Europe in the late 1990s occupied what he called the "cockpit of strategic command."[35] By his own account, Clark sold a doubtful (or scandal-distracted) Clinton administration on using the threat of bombing to persuade Serb strongman Slobodan Milosevic to lay off the Kosovar Albanians in early 1999 and to create the conditions for peace and democracy in the Balkans. For Clark, the logic was self-evident: "With a democratic government [in Belgrade], peaceful arrangements could be made to address the [Kosovar] Albanians' concerns."[36] Furthermore, the mere threat of bombing promised to pave the way for democratic change.

The hard part proved to be selling Washington on that logic. A skeptical James Steinberg, deputy national security adviser to Bill Clinton, argued that "we don't have any leverage to persuade Milosevic to accept more democracy in Belgrade." Clark insisted otherwise: "Of course, we do, Jim." Superior air power translated into all of the leverage that the United States and NATO were likely to need. General Joseph Ralston, vice chairman of the Joint Chiefs of Staff, wondered what might happen if the mere threat of air attack didn't do the trick. "Well, then we'll bomb," replied Clark. "We'll have to follow through." But he felt certain that the likelihood of actually having to pull the trigger was slight. "I know Milosevic," Clark assured Ralston; "he doesn't want to get bombed."[37]

In fact, the Serb dictator did call the U.S. bluff. When he did so, the coercive dimension of coercive diplomacy turned out to be more difficult than Clark had anticipated.

By the end of the twentieth century, the American military profession's claim to be a profession rested above all on two anterior claims. The first was that professional soldiers understood war as civilians could not. The second claim was that they possessed a unique set of skills enabling them to win wars quickly and decisively. Through his mismanagement of Operation Allied Force, as NATO designated its war over Kosovo, Clark called both of these claims into question. As it turned out, Clark's shortcomings as a strategist—particularly failing to accurately take the measure of Milosevic— were as nothing in comparison to his deficiencies as a battlefield general.

Clark failed to anticipate his adversary's response to the start of aerial bombing: an acceleration of the Serb campaign to ethnically cleanse Kosovo, creating a humanitarian crisis for which NATO had no ready response. He vastly overestimated the effectiveness of allied bombing, employed in less than overwhelming quantities, on Serb ground forces operating in Kosovo. Dispersing their forces and hiding in forests and villages, the Serbs continued their depredations all but unmolested. When Clark launched the campaign that he had eagerly sought, he had not devised a coherent plan for overcoming the enemy and had not assembled the forces that such an effort was sure to require. The upshot was a full-blown shooting war that turned out to be far longer, far messier, and far more expensive than anything for which the White House had bargained. The outcome of this contest between giants and a pygmy was never in doubt. After eleven weeks of progressively more intense bombing, the Serbs finally succumbed to the combined weight of U.S. and European forces.[38]

In the mountain of rubble that is twentieth-century military history, Operation Allied Force does not qualify as even a decent-sized cinder.

Once ended, the war over Kosovo immediately vanished from public view. But the campaign became a defining moment in the post-Vietnam effort of the U.S. military profession to rehabilitate itself. Through much of the "window-washing" 1990s, that effort had begun to stall. It was in Kosovo that the effort started to fall apart.

Viewed from this perspective, the Kosovo campaign matters for three distinct reasons. First, it signaled an end of the military's united front on questions of war and peace. Operation Allied Force had violated the Powell Doctrine down to the last jot and tittle. Moreover, it had done so not due to interference or second-guessing from the White House but because the general in command had chosen to fight that way. Clark refused to be bound by inhibitions left over from Vietnam. In that regard, Clark's direction of Operation Allied Force showed how far he himself had strayed from established professional military orthodoxy. Indeed, it gave rise to the extraordinary spectacle of more tradition-minded members of the Joint Chiefs actively conspiring to undermine the authority of a so-called supreme commander intent upon expanding a war that they had considered ill-advised in the first place. When the initial bombing of Serbs in Kosovo had produced little in terms of meaningful results, Clark had pressed for continuous escalation. To root Serb fighters out of their hiding places, he wanted to commit Apache attack helicopters to the fight. His brother four-stars in the Pentagon made sure that that did not happen. [39]

An officer corps internally divided over fundamentals had already surrendered its ability to exercise much influence over questions of when and how to opt for war. By the end of the 1990s, in other words, the lessons of Vietnam, affirmed by the lessons of Desert Storm, had lost their lock-hold on the collective mindset of the American army. The officer corps had not forgotten Vietnam, but some among its numbers had concluded that the memories were no longer all that relevant.

Second, Clark's performance convinced civilian national security specialists that they too were no longer bound by the ostensible lessons of Vietnam. His mishandling of the war further undermined arguments for deferring to the military once the bullets started to fly. Coming on top of unhappiness with the questionable judgments of Powell and Schwarzkopf at key points during Desert Storm (and to a lesser extent unhappiness with the botched Mogadishu operations of 1993), Kosovo helped to restore to fashion the old adage that war was too important to be left to the generals—

at least in regard to the peculiar sort of war that the United States as sole superpower found itself called upon to wage. Once again, smart, confident civilians—most of them the Republican national security "bench," hoping to get back in the game if the GOP recaptured the White House in 2000—were persuading themselves that when it came to war, the generals really weren't all that smart or all that competent.

Granted, this was an "inside the Beltway" perspective; the public view of four-star generals continued to be largely worshipful, as it had been since 1991. But among insiders—especially critics who viewed the sundry military adventures of the Clinton era with frank dismay—the Kosovo experience served to confirm suspicions that generals needed more adult supervision. That is, greater civilian oversight over the planning and execution of military operations—indeed, over all facets of military activity—was required.

The third point, one not without irony, concerned the fate of Clark himself. Having been found wanting by his peers and by senior civilians in the Clinton administration, Clark reaped few immediate rewards from his triumph over tiny Serbia. In fact, hardly had the campaign ended when he received from Washington a peremptory invitation to retire forthwith.

But the ambitious general's story did not end there. After penning a rancorous, score-settling memoir, Clark reemerged as a media personality. In the aftermath of 9/11, the impeccably groomed, trim, and articulate soldier—in manner more akin to a Westmoreland than an Abrams—made a boffo impression as a commentator on CNN. From commentator, it was a short step to critic: Clark was soon targeting the Bush administration's entire approach to policy both foreign and domestic.[40] By the summer of 2003, a grassroots "Draft Clark" movement had formed and journalists were touting the former officer as presidential timber. A general who spoke well and looked good on television, Clark made a seamless transition into national politics.

Clark's bid for the 2004 Democratic presidential nomination ended unsuccessfully, but his brief political campaign nonetheless constituted a turning point of sorts. Although Vietnam and its aftermath had politicized the officer corps as never before, and although other ranking officers—Colin Powell not least among them—had hovered on the fringes of electoral politics, Clark took matters several steps further.[41] To a greater extent than any military figure since Douglas MacArthur a half century before,

Clark embraced naked political partisanship. Clark aggressively touted his credentials as a lifelong military professional—not simply as a veteran—to advance his political ambitions. The unspoken but self-evident basis of his run for the presidency was that four-star rank constituted all the qualifications necessary for political responsibilities at the highest level. He ran for office *as* a general. In doing so Clark trampled all over the principle, reconstituted by soldiers in the aftermath of Vietnam, that the justification for a distinctive profession of arms derives in part from the fact that it inhabits a space apart from and above politics.

Even after his presidential candidacy failed, Clark, the general-as-politician, remained in the partisan arena, serving, for example, as the Democratic Party's designated respondent to President Bush's weekly radio address.[42] At least as far as Clark himself was concerned, the old requirement that military officers were to refrain from partisan activity did not apply.

Furthermore, as the 2004 presidential campaign heated up, other senior military retirees followed in Clark's footsteps. The Republican and Democratic parties engaged in a fierce head-to-head competition to see which could rally the larger and more distinguished contingent of admirals and generals to its standard. Numerous three- and four-star officers volunteered—formally endorsing one candidate in preference to the other, appearing at national conventions, even making television commercials— apparently oblivious to the way that such activities subverted the identity of the soldier as apolitical servant of the state.[43]

The bar excluding soldiers from partisan politics was the same one that delineated the area claimed by soldiers as their special sphere of authority. For senior officers to venture out of that area was to invite civilians to intrude in matters that soldiers viewed exclusively as their own. In effect, through their highly publicized dalliance with politics, Clark and the other high-ranking officers who showed their partisan colors were undermining the claims of professional autonomy that Abrams and others of the post-Vietnam officer corps had worked so hard to restore.

It had taken the officer corps fifteen years, from 1975 to 1990, to recover from Vietnam. It took another fifteen years, from 1990 to 2005, to fritter away most of what the reform project had wrought. By the time of Clark's botched Kosovo campaign, cracks in the edifice were clearly becoming visible. It was left to the administration of George W. Bush to complete the demolition.

The Republican restoration of 2000 returned to power a party that was pro-military without being unduly impressed with all that the generals had wrought during the previous decade. Appalled by the civil-military dysfunction evident during the Clinton era and by the stubbornness with which the services clung to the status quo, the leaders of the new Bush administration—most notably Secretary of Defense Donald Rumsfeld—were not inclined to indulge senior military officers any further.[44] Rumsfeld and his team came to office intent on issuing marching orders.[45] "The secretary of defense is not a super admiral or general. His task is to exercise civilian control over the department for the commander in chief and the country." So read the very first of "Rumsfeld's Rules," the list of edicts that the new secretary carried with him into the Pentagon and soon thereafter published for the edification of all concerned. Ranking number two was this: "Reserve the right to get into anything, and exercise it."[46] For Rumsfeld, getting into something was synonymous with owning it.

A quarter century after the end of the Vietnam War and a decade after Operation Desert Storm, American soldiers enjoyed widespread public esteem and respect. Beginning in 2001, it became evident that respect no longer translated into influence. As the German army had learned in 1941, the reward for excellence was a summons to greater exertions. As the Israeli army had learned after 1967, imagined supremacy invited untoward ambition and miscalculation and more wars that threatened to expose supremacy as an illusion. Although members of the Bush administration professed to hold America's fighting men and women in high regard, they evinced little patience with soldiers who counseled caution or restraint. As Michael Mann has observed, "the notion of civilian control of the military became meaningless, since civilians were the leading militarists."[47]

Thus, for the top echelon of the officer corps, 9/11 was their worst nightmare come to life. In their most basic responsibility of protecting their countrymen from attack, they had been found utterly wanting. As a consequence of that failure, they faced the daunting prospect of what President Bush described as an open-ended conflict waged on a global scale. Perhaps worst of all, as events soon made apparent, they could count on having little say in how that conflict unfolded. The crusading spirit to which 9/11 gave rise swept away the last of the barriers that soldiers had so carefully erected to guard against military adventurism.

As the field commander most immediately responsible for that conflict's first stages, General Tommy Franks initially conceived of the global war on terror as a series of Desert Storms—large-scale, deliberately planned offensives permitting the United States to bring to bear overwhelming force. This prospect did not find favor with Secretary Rumsfeld and his top civilian advisers, who advocated a bolder approach, one that placed less emphasis on large mechanized formations and greater emphasis on air power supported by special operations troops and lighter, more agile ground forces. The general offered plodding orthodoxy; the defense secretary wanted novelty and dash.[48]

So Rumsfeld overruled Franks. In the planning and execution of the campaign to overthrow the Taliban in late 2001, the secretary of defense called the operational tune, not the Joint Chiefs of Staff and not the combatant commander. Secretary of State Powell privately urged Franks to resist this intrusion of civilians into matters that Vietnam had presumably taught should remain the purview of generals, but to no avail. The service chiefs were excluded from war planning and Franks bowed to Rumsfeld's demands.[49] When in the spring of 2003 U.S. forces invaded Iraq—the closest approximation to an MRC since the previous set-to with Saddam Hussein—Pentagon officials went out of their way to portray Operation Iraqi Freedom as a radical departure from the past, not some plan based on venerable truths or lifted from well-thumbed field manuals.[50]

Despite achieving initially spectacular results, the outcome considered strictly from a military professional perspective proved to be disastrous. Getting in, both to Kabul and subsequently to Baghdad, proved to be easy. Creating conditions permitting U.S. forces to get out proved to be elusive, especially in Iraq. There, instead of a quick victory followed by an early departure—Desert Storm without the loose ends—U.S. forces got a recurrence of Mogadishu, on a much larger scale. The invasion of Iraq gave way to an exceedingly nasty unconventional campaign. The Americans found themselves fighting insurgents hidden among a population either indifferent to or unhappy with the U.S. occupation.

By the spring of 2004, a year after toppling Saddam Hussein from power, with Iraqi resistance to their occupiers intensifying, American generals might still have recourse to the lexicon of the post-Vietnam military reform project, but the words rang hollow. "We will be back in Fallujah," one such senior officer declared after the U.S. pacification campaign suffered a particularly gruesome setback. "It will be at the time and the place of our choosing. We will hunt down the criminals. We will kill them or capture them. And we will pacify Fallujah." U.S. commanders wanted it known that they had no intention of relinquishing the initiative or of abandoning the fundamental operational precepts to which they had adhered since Vietnam. The coming action would occur on American terms. When the fight came, the general insisted, "it will be methodical. It will be precise and it will be overwhelming."[51]

Many months passed before any such demonstration ensued. In the meantime, to extricate their forces from Fallujah, U.S. commanders on the scene enlisted the aid of officers from Saddam Hussein's disbanded army.[52] The American siege of the Iraqi city in April 2004 culminated in thinly disguised defeat, circumstances on the ground having rendered overwhelming force, not to mention prospects of decisive victory followed by a rapid exit, at least for a time obsolete.

But generals schooled for reasons of institutional self-preservation to think exclusively in terms of the Powell Doctrine had nothing to put in that doctrine's place. By May 2004, evidence that the war had stalemated was becoming too apparent to deny, and the generals were running out of ideas. The good news, according to General Richard Myers, chairman of the Joint Chiefs of Staff, was that "there is no way to militarily lose in Iraq." The bad news was that "there is also no way to militarily win in Iraq."[53] Implicit in this analysis was an admission that U.S. forces were stuck in precisely the sort of situation that senior officers had vowed at all costs to avoid. Reflecting on the lessons that the officer corps had taken away from Vietnam, Lieutenant General Philip Davidson, writing in 1990, found one point of "total unanimity," namely, that "the United States cannot sustain a prolonged, bloody, ambiguous, and limited war."[54] Alas, that was precisely the sort of war that Iraq had become.

So, reverting to type, senior officers responded as they had following that prior war: they put the blame for their predicament elsewhere. They railed against Rumsfeld—a new McNamara surrounded by a new generation of Whiz Kids—and turned to the press to vent their grievances. Rumsfeld and his inner circle, complained one unnamed general officer to the *Washington*

Post, "refused to listen or adhere to military advice." As a consequence, the United States had plunged into Iraq without "a clearly defined war strategy, end state, and exit strategy," something that would never have happened during Colin Powell's time in the Pentagon. Another senior officer mocked the administration's expectations about democratizing Iraq as based on "fairy dust and cultural arrogance." Yet another insisted that "Rumsfeld needs to go, as does [Paul] Wolfowitz," the deputy secretary of defense.[55] Their complaints, like their efforts to defeat the Iraqi insurgents, were ineffectual.

High-ranking retirees were even louder in their denunciations of the civilian leadership. Rumsfeld and his inner circle were "the most arrogant group that anyone can remember here," fumed General Merrill McPeak, former Air Force chief of staff. The secretary of defense had "done more damage to the country than we will recover from in 50 years" and deserved to be fired.[56] General Anthony Zinni, former commander-in-chief of United States Central Command, mocked Bush administration promises to "stay the course." The course on which the United States found itself, according to Zinni, was "headed over Niagara Falls." Ticking off the problems facing U.S. forces in Iraq, he declared, "I blame the civilian leadership of the Pentagon directly." He too wanted Rumsfeld and Wolfowitz to be axed.[57] William Odom, a former Army three-star general, cited the Bush administration for having "nearly broken the U.S. Army by overextension and overcommitment" and called for a prompt withdrawal of all American troops from Iraq.[58] Almost simultaneously, the other shoe dropped. If Fallujah was a failure to which some attributed Tet-like connotations, the Iraq War found its My Lai at Baghdad's Abu Ghraib prison. In a final irony, the reservists to whom Creighton Abrams had looked to preserve his army from the recurrence of Vietnam became the source of the greatest shame to befall the Army since Vietnam itself.

In one respect only had Operation Iraqi Freedom conformed to the military's own "lessons" of Vietnam: because Secretary Rumsfeld after 9/11 had decided to fight the global war on terror without expanding the professional army, large numbers of reservists figured in the conduct of that war, precisely as Abrams had intended when he conceived the Total Force. But not all reservists proved capable of handling the extraordinary test posed by the war in Iraq. This became all too clear in late April 2004 with the explosive revelations that members of the Maryland Army

National Guard assigned to the 800th Military Police Brigade had systematically abused, humiliated, and tortured Iraqis placed in their charge at Abu Ghraib.[59]

The resulting scandal blew a gaping hole in the Bush administration's policy in Iraq. The Abu Ghraib debacle showed American soldiers not as liberators but as tormentors, not as professionals but as sadists getting cheap thrills. As such, the scandal did untold damage to the image of competence and probity that the post-Vietnam generation of soldiers had worked so long and so hard to establish.

In August 2003, before Fallujah and before the Abu Ghraib story broke, but with U.S. forces engaged on multiple fronts of a conflict global in scope and indeterminate in duration, a cry arose for the Pentagon to "do something" about Liberia, then in the throes of a vicious and pointless civil war that had stretched on for many years.

By this time, General Myers in his capacity as chairman of the Joint Chiefs of Staff had had enough. In a last faint echo of the Weinberger and Powell doctrines, he put his foot down. "There will be no commitment of troops anywhere in the world," Myers declared at a Pentagon press conference, "without some of the essentials that we need and that is a clear mission and a clear end state and sufficient force to do the job. That's not an issue."[60]

Three days after Myers spoke, a contingent of U.S. Marines helicoptered into Monrovia—their mission a vague charge to support West African peacekeepers arriving to broker an equally vague ceasefire. An episode of no particular consequence on the ground—the Marines departed Liberia eleven days later without incident—it stands out for one reason only: as a vivid illustration of the extent to which events by 2003 had attenuated the authority of the officer corps. The truth was that when it came to deciding when and how to employ U.S. forces, no one much cared what General Myers had to say. A mere decade after Colin Powell had premiered the role of general-as-celebrity, the chairman of the Joint Chiefs of Staff, wrote one shrewd observer, found himself reduced to the status of "minor spear-carrier."[61]

The further truth was that by the time the "Myers Doctrine" made its brief, ignominious appearance the officer corps was no longer master of its own fate. Whether for good or ill, by the first decade of the twenty-first century, the effort to restore the authority of the officer corps, initiated thirty years earlier by Creighton Abrams, had collapsed. Senior officers advised and implemented, but they did not decide. Henceforth, the generals might drive the bus, but others chose the destination and picked the route. As to paying the fare, that was left to the soldiers in the ranks.

Chapter Three

LEFT, RIGHT, LEFT

AMERICAN SOLDIERS were by no means alone in coming away from
Vietnam with a bitter taste in their mouths. For politically engaged intellectuals who had supported the doomed effort to save South Vietnam, the war
years had been an unmitigated disaster. During the long decade stretching
from the assassination of John F. Kennedy to the resignation of Richard M.
Nixon, they watched helplessly as would-be revolutionaries launched a
sustained assault against allegedly repressive institutions, beginning with
the university but ultimately including the federal government and the
armed services, and by extension the premises underlying a liberal interna-
tionalist foreign policy.

As the views of this New Left infiltrated into the mainstream, elite pub-
lications and the mass media alike took on a new sensibility. Chief among
the qualities defining this sensibility were skepticism toward authority, disdain for convention, and wariness about American power and its uses. The
war had spawned a perverse and peculiarly narcissistic counterculture—at
least so it seemed in the eyes of those on the opposite side of the barricades.

For critics of the New Left, Vietnam's unhappy denouement revealed
the full scope of the crisis engulfing the United States. The events following
the fall of Saigon in April 1975—Communist North Vietnam swallowing
up a long-standing U.S. ally, droves of desperate "boat people" taking
flight, and the Khmer Rouge turning nearby Cambodia into a slaughterhouse—testified to a wholesale collapse of American nerve. "Defeatism
generated by impotence" was one morose observer's pithy description of
the condition into which the United States and the West as a whole had

fallen.[1] "Weimar Germany haunts democracies in trouble," observed the writer Theodore Draper, even as the U.S. involvement in Vietnam was still winding down. For Draper, events had made it incumbent upon Americans to ask "whether we are destined to suffer the fate of Weimar Germany."[2]

New Leftists had seen in Vietnam evidence that the exercise of American power was invariably sordid in intent and lamentable in its impact. To their critics, the consequences of defeat demonstrated just the opposite: it was the absence of American power and will that invited catastrophe. American weakness was the problem, not American might. Weakness endangered those who relied on the United States for protection; it also sowed confusion among the American people. In government, it produced paralysis and invited demagoguery.

In the wake of the sixties, contrarian intellectuals believed this weakness capable of dissolving the bonds sustaining the constitutional order. So they mounted a counterrevolution. Their aim was nothing if not ambitious: to reverse the verdict of the 1960s, to repair the political and cultural damage done by that decade, and mutatis mutandis to restore American power and assertiveness on the world stage.

"What rules the world is ideas," observed Irving Kristol, one leader of this insurgency, "because ideas define the way reality is perceived."[3] Contesting the perception of reality prevailing among elites defined the insurgents' central purpose.

Observers soon dubbed this insurgency "neoconservatism," a singularly inapt label that suggests an ideological rigor that neocons have never demonstrated nor perhaps even sought.[4] Irving Kristol is surely correct in observing that neoconservatism is best understood not as a political movement or school of thought but as a "persuasion."[5] At least initially, the spirit animating that persuasion was a negative one. United by their common antipathy for the 1960s, neoconservatives knew precisely what they were against: the nihilism, untruths, and sheer silliness to which the radical decade had given birth. And, wherever it might appear, they were opposed to Communism. By all outward appearances, neoconservatism was, as Peter Steinfels observed in 1979, "ideology as anti-ideology."[6]

Apart from Communism, the causes that roused neoconservative ire seldom bore more than a passing resemblance to the core values informing mainline conservatism. Tradition, ritual, hierarchy, small government, fiscal austerity, devotion to place, homage to the past as such—none of these elicited much enthusiasm among neocons. From the outset, that is, the neo-conservative identification with the post-Vietnam Right was a marriage of convenience rather than a union of kindred spirits.

In a sense, it could hardly have been otherwise. The conception of poli-tics to which neoconservatives paid allegiance owed more to the ethos of the Left than to the orthodoxies of the Right. Their ultimate ideological objective was not to preserve but to transform. They viewed state power not as a necessary evil but as a positive good to be cultivated and then deployed in pursuit of large objectives.

Much as the counterculture had hijacked what had once been main-stream liberalism, neoconservatives set out to infiltrate a conservative movement that for decades had languished on the margins of American politics. On the Right they hoped to find the opportunity to create that alternative perception of reality necessary for fulfilling their radical aspira-tions. The essence of those aspirations was simplicity itself: to fuse Ameri-can power to American principles, ensuring the survival of those principles and subsequently their propagation to the benefit of all humankind.

In our own time—and especially since the ascendancy of George W. Bush to the presidency—"neoconservative" has become a term of oppro-brium, frequently accompanied by ad hominem attacks and charges of arrogance and hubris.[7] But the heat generated by the term also stands as a backhanded tribute, an acknowledgment that the neoconservative impact has been substantial. It is today too soon to offer a comprehensive assess-ment of that impact. The discussion of neoconservatism offered here has a more modest objective, namely, to suggest that one aspect of the neoconser-vative legacy has been to foster the intellectual climate necessary for the emergence of the new American militarism.

From the outset, the neoconservative project had no more resolute and vig-orous advocate than Norman Podhoretz. The self-declared embodiment of the New York intellectual, Podhoretz achieved notable success as critic, writer, provocateur, and above all as editor of the influential monthly maga-zine *Commentary* during the years from 1960 to 1995. Without *Commen-tary*, it seems fair to say, neoconservatism would have been stillborn.

In a series of books and essays, Podhoretz has rendered a lushly detailed account of his life as a literary intellectual: his rise to prominence as the son of immigrants crossing the East River—"one of the longest journeys in the world"—to find success in Manhattan; his discovery of the "dirty little secret" that a thirst for money, fame, power, and social standing, rather than a passion for truth or beauty, motivated "the well-educated American soul," beginning with his own; his brief flirtation with but eventual rejection of the radical enthusiasms to which the New York literati fell victim during the course of the 1960s; and the ruptured friendships that ensued as Podhoretz broke away and took it upon himself to expose those enthusiasms as puerile and pernicious.[8]

Once his own fling with sixties radicalism ended, Podhoretz launched a "scorched-earth campaign against the New Left and counterculture."[9] From his editorial command post at *Commentary* (and through organizations such as the Committee on the Present Danger, in which he figured prominently), Podhoretz did much to create and refine the fiercely combative neoconservative style. That style emphasized not balance (viewed as evidence of timidity) or the careful sifting of evidence (suggesting scholasticism) but the ruthless demolition of any point of view inconsistent with the neoconservative version of truth, typically portrayed as self-evident and beyond dispute.

If for the elected official all politics are local, defined by bread-and-butter concerns, then for the intellectual politics tend to be cosmic, bound up with the most fundamental questions. For the intellectual of neoconservative bent such as Podhoretz, the arena in which politics, culture, and morality converge is necessarily a place of no-holds-barred conflict. Within that arena, wisdom does battle against folly, right against wrong, and good against evil. With basic values at stake, the contest does not permit the taking of prisoners. There can be no quarter. Podhoretz, the historian H. W. Brands has written, "sometimes gave the impression that he couldn't order dinner without starting a fight."[10] The same pugnacity became one of *Commentary*'s abiding characteristics. A willingness to compromise suggested a lack of conviction. Fervor, certainty, and contempt for those on the other side, meanwhile, became marks of honor.

If Podhoretz more than anyone else helped to define neoconservatism's style, he also played an exceedingly large role in formulating the neocon worldview. Both style *and* substance are important to understanding how Podhoretz (along with other neoconservatives) laid the intellectual foundation of the new American militarism.

Six propositions summarize the essence of the neoconservative persuasion. All six feature prominently among the themes to which *Commentary* paid particular attention from the 1970s until the end of Podhoretz's tenure as editor.

The first and most fundamental proposition is a theory of history. That theory finds its point of origin in the depression decade of the 1930s, a decade that for Podhoretz and other neoconservatives serves as a parable.[11] That parable conveys two large truths, applicable in all circumstances and for all time. The first truth is that evil is real. The second is that for evil to prevail requires only one thing: for those confronted by it to flinch from duty.

In the 1930s, with the callow governments of Great Britain and France bent on appeasing Hitler and with an isolationist America studiously refusing to exert itself, evil had its way. The result was horrific savagery, culminating in the Holocaust. Perhaps worst of all, that catastrophe was an avoidable one, directly attributable to the pusillanimous behavior of the democracies.

Podhoretz and other neoconservatives believed that the cataclysm that befell Europe in the 1930s could easily happen again. It was precisely because the sixties recalled the worst features of the thirties, leaving the United States weak and demoralized, vulnerable to Soviet aggression from abroad, and susceptible to a "kind of spiritual surrender" within, that Podhoretz found the latter decade so disconcerting.[12] A recurrence of the 1940s was the nightmare that the neoconservatives in the 1970s were determined to avert. Time and again, writes John Ehrman in his history of the neoconservative movement, essays by Podhoretz and his compatriots "evoked the memory of French and British behavior in the 1930s, with the refusal to face up to the growing totalitarian threat, the reluctance to shore up the democracies' defenses, failed attempts at appeasement and, worst of all, the slide into a disastrous war."[13]

The remaining five propositions defining the neoconservative persuasion offer variations on that theme of World War II as a preventable disaster, but all bear the imprint of the first.

The second proposition relates to power. Diplomacy, bribes, accommodation, sweet reason, appeals to decency, fairness, or a larger community of interests: none of these deflected Nazi Germany from the path of aggression on which it had embarked. Just as it eventually required armed might to destroy the Nazi regime, so too only the possession of—and willingness to employ—armed might could possibly have deterred Adolf Hitler. The lesson was clear: at the end of the day, in international politics there was no substitute for power, especially military power.

In emphasizing the centrality of power, Podhoretz and other writers associated with *Commentary* reflected a realist perspective. They had no patience for—indeed, viewed with alarm—schemes that looked to international law, disarmament, or anything like an "international community" as alternatives to power. They judged such ideas to be hopelessly utopian. They treated with particular disdain expectations that the United Nations might evolve into a vehicle for world peace or for the advancement of liberal values.

On this question of power the parallels between the 1930s and the aftermath of Vietnam were, for Podhoretz, self-evident. Vietnam had become the new "Munich": "the self-evident symbol of a policy that must never be followed again."[14] But whereas the old Munich had warned against the dangers of military weakness, the new Munich seemed to teach the inverse. "Not perhaps since the 1930s in England had the idea of using military force fallen into such widespread disrepute as it did in the United States in the aftermath of the American experience in Vietnam," observed Podhoretz. The one "lesson" of Vietnam that had taken "the deepest root in American culture" was that force had become "obsolete as an instrument of American political purposes."[15]

Podhoretz rejected this view. In his judgment, one widely shared among neoconservatives, military power—not merely adequate, but superior power—was for the United States a sine qua non. Military power formed "the indispensable foundation" of U.S. foreign policy, he wrote; "without it, nothing else we do will be effective."[16] Yet the realism that informed the neoconservative perception of power vanished when it came to considering America's global role and responsibilities.

Few things roused Podhoretz to greater heights of dudgeon than the suggestion, commonplace during the latter phases of the Vietnam War, that it was time for America to "come home." A centerpiece of George McGovern's 1972 presidential campaign, this slogan reflected a Vietnam-induced perception that an excessive preoccupation with problems abroad had for too long permitted domestic problems to fester. According to McGovern, U.S. disengagement from the war offered an opportune moment to redress this imbalance. For Podhoretz, however, this was a mere smoke screen. The real aim was to rationalize a revival of full-scale isolationism. In his eagerness to gain the presidency, McGovern was recklessly and irresponsibly catering to a deep-seated popular American urge to turn inward. Nothing could be more dangerous.[17]

On this issue Podhoretz did not permit dissent: America had a mission and must never "come home." This was the third proposition that defined the neoconservative position. Alternatives to or substitutes for American global leadership simply did not exist. For all that Vietnam may have been "an act of imprudent idealism," a challenge that had exceeded "our intellectual and moral capabilities," the United States simply could not allow failure there to become an excuse for turning its back on the world.[18] History had singled out the United States to play a unique role as the chief instrument for securing the advance of freedom, which found its highest expression in democratic capitalism. American ideals defined America's purpose, to be achieved through the exercise of superior American power.

Those unable to grasp that imperative—most notably, President Jimmy Carter who in acknowledging the nation's post-Vietnam "malaise" seemingly accepted it as irreversible—Podhoretz held in particularly low regard. "The survival not only of the United States but of free institutions everywhere in the world," he wrote in 1982, "depends on a resurgence of American power."[19] In such circumstances, pessimism or self-doubt could have no place; indeed, they verged on the treasonous.

Podhoretz, along with many of the foreign policy writers identified with *Commentary* in the 1970s and 1980s, such as Walter Laqueur, Michael Ledeen, and Joshua Muravchik, were staunch patriots and impassioned nationalists. They were also devout Wilsonians, dedicated to the proposition that American values are by definition universal values.[20] But they did not suffer from the delusions to which they believed Wilson had been prone, rejecting, for example, the proposition that any "covenant" of nations might secure America's safety and the world's freedom. Creating a peaceful world required power, not parchment.

Heirs to the tradition of American Exceptionalism, neoconservatives did not doubt that theirs was a nation set apart. That fulfilling America's providential mission might entail great exertions and sacrifice was a prospect that they were perfectly willing to accept. America's "ruling elites," wrote Midge Decter shortly after the fall of Saigon, had become "spoiled rotten and cosmetically greedy." They had "forgotten what evil is." But millions

of ordinary Americans, Decter continued, knew better and were "still willing to pay something, maybe even quite a lot, to see to it that they have
companions in the world, preferring... not to live in a small and weak
country in a mean and narrow world."[21] Toughness, daring, and resolve: in
American political life after Vietnam these had become scarce commodities;
Podhoretz and his fellow neoconservatives were determined to bring them
back into fashion.[22]

The fourth proposition defining the neoconservative persuasion concerns the relationship between politics at home, especially cultural politics,
and America's purpose abroad. At the center of that relationship is an
appreciation for authority.

The new radicalism, Podhoretz and other neoconservatives concluded,
promised utopia but delivered little apart from sexual license, vulgarity, and
an absence of standards. The sixties had warped the arts, cheapened intellectual discourse, corrupted universities, and spawned a host of bizarre
ideas.[23] Worse, the most ardent proponents of this variant of freedom harbored anti-democratic and even authoritarian urges. For Podhoretz, the
radicalism of the 1960s, based on the conviction that political action
might alleviate "the spiritual ailments of the age," had instead "led again, as
it had so often led in the past, either to nihilism or to... 'the totalitarian
temptation.'"[24]

As one consequence of this assault, traditional sources of authority in
American society—high government officials, the police, the clergy, even
parents—found their influence sharply curtailed. This virtual collapse of
institutional legitimacy was central to the neoconservative perspective on
domestic politics. To Podhoretz, the absence of institutions able to command broad popular support imperiled democracy at home. It also undermined efforts to fulfill America's calling abroad.

Thus, part of the task that Podhoretz set for himself was to discredit
what he saw as the various forms of nonsense to which the sixties had given
rise—prominent among them multiculturalism, affirmative action, radical
feminism, and the gay rights movement. By extension he and other neoconservatives cast themselves as forceful proponents of what came to be called
"traditional values." *Commentary*'s agenda included not only support for a
muscular foreign policy, but also the defense of beleaguered institutions
such as marriage and the nuclear family, the advocacy of law and order, and
respect for organized religion. In this sense alone did Podhoretz's cultural

interests intersect with those of the established Right. Only by ensuring order and stability at home and restoring confidence in basic institutions, he believed, could the United States fend off the Communist threat and fulfill the historical mission for which it had been created.

As an antidote to the cultural disaster of the 1960s, Podhoretz and *Commentary* promoted what he called "a new nationalism." Americans needed to revive their belief in the American enterprise. According to Podhoretz, only by urgently committing themselves to a great project of national rejuvenation could Americans avoid confronting a choice between war against the Soviet Union and the "Finlandization that an unimpeded culture of appeasement is certain in the end to yield."[25]

This sentiment captures the essence of the fifth proposition defining the neoconservative persuasion: the United States after Vietnam confronted a dire crisis; absent decisive action to resolve that crisis, unspeakable consequences awaited.

Particulars might change, but for neoconservatives crisis is a permanent condition. The situation is always urgent, the alternatives stark, the need for action compelling, and the implications of delay or inaction certain to be severe. On the one hand—if the nation disregards the neoconservative call to action—there is the abyss. On the other hand—if the nation heeds that call—the possibility of salvation exists.

By 1980, after four flaccid years of Carter, Podhoretz pronounced himself close to despair. It had become apparent, even incontrovertible, that disaster loomed. The United States was "moving beyond stage three in the culture of appeasement and into stage four where surrender or war are the only remaining choices." Surrender or war: the choice seemed inescapable absent an immediate revival of American will and American power aimed at reversing the "ten years of retreat" that the bungled war in Vietnam had begun.[26] For neoconservatives, 1980 was a year of profound crisis. But for neoconservatives, so too is every year.

According to Podhoretz—according to neoconservatives generally—the antidote to crisis is leadership. This is the sixth and last component that defines the neoconservative persuasion.

Among neoconservatives it is an article of faith that men, not impersonal forces, determine the course of history. Curbing the isolationist tendencies of the American people, steeling the nation against the lure of appeasement, summoning it to pursue its destiny: these become impossible without flinty determination, moral clarity, and inspiration at the very top. Americans, neoconservatives believe, hunger for and respond to heroic—even Churchillian—leadership. In a sort of weird homegrown variant of the Fuehrer Principle, neoconservatives themselves share that hunger.

Many neoconservatives are Jewish, many are not. Some are personally religious, others not at all. For all of them, however, America is the one true universal church, the declaration of 1776 tantamount to sacred scripture, and the District of Columbia the Holy See. In this secular faith, the occupant of the Oval Office enjoys a status comparable to that of supreme pontiff.

In neoconservative lore, 1980 stands out not only as a year of crisis but as the year when the nation decisively turned things around. For the first time in a half century Americans elevated to the presidency a man who gave every sign of sharing the neocon sense of deepening peril requiring drastic remedial action. During the campaign that year, neoconservatives had thrown their support behind Ronald Reagan, seeing him as a kindred spirit who shared their passionate anti-Communism and their distaste for the cultural detritus of the 1960s. In Reagan, Podhoretz and other neocons believed that they had found their man, a leader able to lift the United States out of its slough of post-Vietnam despond.

When Reagan succeeded in ousting Jimmy Carter from office, neoconservatives were quick to claim a share of the credit.[27] A quarter of a century later, the Reagan era remains for neoconservatives a golden moment, at least according to the mythic version of Reagan's foreign policy.

In fact, however, that is not the way that neoconservatives saw it at the time. For Podhoretz and *Commentary*, the Reagan era proved to be a massive disappointment, a continuation of the timorous Carter years.[28] As a consequence, the crisis of the preceding decade continued unabated.

Podhoretz found much to like in Reagan's rhetoric, but he warned against confusing words with actions. The two differed, often drastically. To take Reagan's famous condemnation of Moscow's "evil empire" at face value was "to fall victim to a campaign of disinformation."[29] In practice, Reagan had proven himself "unwilling to take the political risks and expend the political energy" to break with the Nixon-Ford-Carter policy of détente. Like his immediate predecessors, the president seemed obsessed with making the world safe for Communism, thus implementing "a strategy of helping the Soviet Union stabilize its empire."[30] Indeed, to Podhoretz, Reagan appeared "ready to embrace the course of détente whole-heartedly as his own."[31]

For all of his high-sounding talk, the fortieth president of the United States, Podhoretz reluctantly concluded, lacked backbone. Although he "seems to have a few strong convictions," wrote Podhoretz in 1985, Reagan "invariably backed away from acting on them" if they threatened to "cost him more political approval than he might gain by tacking and trimming."[32] As late as 1986—three years before the fall of the Berlin Wall—Podhoretz was still insisting that "'the present danger' of 1980 is still present today, and the question of whether 'we have the will to reverse the decline of American power' still hangs ominously as it did then in the troubled American air."[33] As the end of the 1980s approached, the threat posed by Communism was becoming, if anything, greater than ever. That Reagan was apparently falling victim to Mikhail Gorbachev's charm offensive was almost unbearable. In Podhoretz's eyes, to parley with the enemy was to appease him.[34]

For neoconservatives, this was to be a perennial source of disappointment. Time and again, the leader in whom they invested such high hopes turned out to be less crusader than politician.

Despite Podhoretz's premonitions of impending doom, the United States survived the Reagan presidency. Indeed, in the immediate wake of the Reagan era the fondest of neoconservative hopes found fulfillment: the Soviet empire disintegrated, followed shortly thereafter by the Soviet Union itself. By the end of the 1980s, Communism stood everywhere discredited. Neocon doubts regarding Ronald Reagan voiced by Podhoretz and others were quietly shelved. Within the neoconservative lexicon, the descriptor "Reaganite" became permanently enshrined as a term of highest approbation.

For Podhoretz and his compatriots, however, this moment of supreme triumph also posed something of a dilemma. With the sudden passing of the Cold War, the dire threat from which the insurgency had drawn much of its energy vanished.

To be sure, at home there remained the legacy of the sixties to rail against; indeed, ideas associated with that decade enjoyed a revival of sorts once Bill Clinton became president in 1993. But abroad, the collapse of Communism left neocons momentarily adrift. "Without the Cold War," muttered Rabbit Angstrom, John Updike's famous protagonist, "what's the point of being an American?"[35] Without the Cold War, what was the point of being a neoconservative?

For a time, the insurgency's founders toyed with the idea of simply declaring victory and moving on to other pursuits. The fall of the Berlin Wall left Podhoretz by his own admission "unable to make up my mind as to what...America's purpose should be now that the threat of Communism...had been decisively eliminated."[36] At one point, he even pronounced the neoconservative project dead.[37]

His eulogy proved premature. During the course of the 1990s, neoconservatism enjoyed a remarkable rebirth. The movement retooled itself, applying the propositions that had defined neoconservatism in the 1970s and 1980s to a vastly more ambitious agenda. A new second generation of neocons rose to prominence, a constellation in which William Kristol, Irving's son, supplanted Podhoretz as the most luminous star.

The aim of this second generation was to prod the United States into seizing the strategic offensive. In 1979, Podhoretz had written disparagingly that the "fondest wish" of the New Left had "been to turn the United States around altogether—from a counterrevolutionary power into an active sponsor" of revolution.[38] Within a decade, that became the fondest wish of neoconservatives—soon enough including Podhoretz himself. Neocons aimed to convert the United States into an instrument for fulfilling their own revolutionary dreams.

All of this took some time to jell. In the late 1980s, as Gorbachev began signaling that the Soviet Union was looking for ways to call off the Cold War, Irving Kristol, the neocon elder statesman, was already promoting a new foreign policy of "global unilateralism." According to this reliable bellwether of coming shifts in neoconservative thinking, though, there was a problem: "we are an imperial power with no imperial self-definition."[39]

Indeed, the very notion of an imperial conception of American statecraft took some getting used to. Although the end of the Cold War had left the United States in a favorable position, Joshua Muravchik, writing in *Commentary*, cautioned that "American preeminence is not tantamount to 'hegemony.' America's hegemonic tendencies, whatever they may have been when the country was young, disappeared as it became a mature power."[40] With few exceptions, neoconservatives in the early 1990s showed little appetite for embarking on new adventures abroad.[41] Surveying the ranks, Podhoretz found "only a handful who still advocate the expansive Wilsonian interventionism that grew out of the anti-Communist passions" of the Cold War. "Today the realists have the upper hand in the neoconservative community, or what is left of it."[42]

In an essay published in *Commentary* in 1991, Robert Kagan, who emerged during the 1990s as perhaps the most influential neocon foreign policy analyst, somewhat gingerly advanced the case for basing future U.S. policy on "the *patient* support of democracy—not forcing change when change is impossible, but waiting for conditions to ripen, nurturing promising developments, discouraging those which threaten what little hope for progress may exist."[43] Even with regard to American armed might, neoconservatives after the Cold War showed a certain ambivalence. Writing in *Commentary* in 1992, for example, Muravchik found that "everyone agrees that the disappearance of the Soviet empire allows a sharp reduction in the size and cost of our own military."[44] Things were in flux; it would take time for the situation to sort itself out.

But to neoconservatives patience does not come naturally. To assume the posture of disinterested observer entailed unconscionable risks. The neoconservative writer George Weigel put his finger on the problem in 1992: to leave the post–Cold War foreign policy debate to the newly ascendant realists and the resurgent isolationists of the Left and Right meant that—given the inherent moral defects of realism—isolationism would ultimately prevail. In that eventuality, despite victory in the Cold War, all that the neoconservatives had struggled for would be lost. Hence, wrote Weigel, the imperative of reenergizing the cause of "democratic internationalism"— an approach to U.S. foreign policy based on the old neoconservative precepts of global engagement, assertiveness, and activism backed by military power.[45]

As a practical matter, the task of reinventing neoconservatism for a post-Communist world—and of spelling out an "imperial self-definition" of American purpose—fell to a new generation. To promote that effort, leading members of that new generation created their own institutions.

The passing of the baton occurred in 1995. That year, Norman Podhoretz stepped down as editor of *Commentary*. That same year, William Kristol founded a new journal, the *Weekly Standard,* which in short order established itself as the flagship publication of second-generation neoconservatives. Although keeping faith with neoconservative principles that

Commentary had staked out over the previous two decades—and for a time even employing Norman's son John Podhoretz in a senior editorial position—the *Standard* was from the outset an altogether different publication. From its founding, *Commentary* had been published by the American Jewish Committee, an august and distinctly nonpartisan entity. The *Weekly Standard* relied for its existence on the largesse of Rupert Murdoch, the notorious media mogul. Unlike *Commentary*, which had self-consciously catered to an intellectual elite, the *Standard*—printed on glossy paper, replete with cartoons, caricatures, and political gossip—had a palpably less lofty look and feel. It was by design smart rather than stuffy. Whereas *Commentary* had evolved into a self-consciously right-wing version of the self-consciously progressive *Dissent,* the *Standard* came into existence as a neoconservative counterpart to the neoliberal *New Republic.* Throughout Norman Podhoretz's long editorial reign, *Commentary* had remained an urbane and sophisticated journal of ideas, aspiring to shape the terms of political debate even as it remained above the muck and mire of politics as such. Beginning with volume 1, number 1, the editors of the *Standard* did not disguise the fact that they sought to have a direct and immediate impact on policy; not ideas as such but political agitation defined the purpose of this new enterprise.

Better than anything else, location told the tale. *Commentary*'s editorial offices were on Manhattan's East Side; for first-generation neoconservatives, the East River on one side and the Hudson on the other defined the universe. In contrast, the *Standard* set up shop just a few blocks from the White House; for William Kristol and his compatriots, the perimeter of the Washington Beltway delineated the world that mattered.

What emerged as the hallmarks of this post–Cold War variant of neoconservatism? Unlike their elders, second-generation neoconservatives did not define themselves in opposition—to Communism, to the New Left, or to the sixties. Theirs was no longer an "ideology of anti-ideology." Rather, they were themselves advocates of a positive ideological agenda, a theology that brought fully into view the radical implications—in John Judis's formulation, the "inverted Trotskyism"—embedded within the neoconservative insurgency from the outset.[46]

Fearing the implications certain to flow from an America that was weak or tormented by self-doubt, the elder statesmen of the neoconservative movement had labored to restore to the idea of American power the legitimacy that it had possessed prior to the sixties. With American power now fully refurbished—and seemingly vindicated by the outcome of the Cold War—the second generation went a step further, promulgating the notion that the moment was now ripe for the United States to use that power—especially military power—to achieve the final triumph of American ideals. In this sense, the neoconservatives who gravitated to the *Weekly Standard* showed themselves to be the most perceptive of all of Woodrow Wilson's disciples. For the real Wilson (in contrast to either the idealized or the demonized Wilson) had also seen military power as an instrument for transforming the international system and cementing American primacy.

Efforts to promote "a neo-Reaganite foreign policy of military supremacy and moral confidence" found expression in five convictions that together form the foundation of second-generation neoconservative thinking about American statecraft.[47]

First was the certainty that American global dominion is, in fact, benign and that other nations necessarily see it as such. Thus, according to Charles Krauthammer, a frequent contributor to the *Weekly Standard*, "we are not just any hegemon. We run a uniquely benign imperium. This is not mere self-congratulation; it is a fact manifest in the way others welcome our power."[48]

However much they might grumble, the baby-boomer neocons believed, other nations actually yearned for the United States to lead and, indeed, to sustain its position as sole superpower, seeing American dominance as both compatible with their own interests and preferable to any remotely plausible alternative. Despite "all the bleating about hegemony, no nation really wants genuine multipolarity," Robert Kagan observed in this regard. "Not only do countries such as France and Russia shy away from the expense of creating and preserving a multipolar world; they rightly fear the geopolitical consequences of destroying American hegemony."[49] According to Kagan, the cold, hard reality of U.S. supremacy was sure to have "a calming effect on the international environment, inducing other powers to focus their energies and resources elsewhere."[50] Joshua Muravchik concurred; rather than eliciting resistance, American dominance could be counted on to "have a soothing effect on the rest of the world."[51] With the passing of the Cold War, wrote Charles Krauthammer, "an ideologically pacified North seeks security and order by aligning its foreign policy behind that of the United States.... [This] is the shape of things to come."[52]

Failure on the part of the United States to sustain its imperium would inevitably result in global disorder, bloody, bitter, and protracted: this emerged as the second conviction animating neoconservatives after the Cold War. As a result, proposals for organizing the world around anything other than American power elicited derision for being woolly-headed and fatuous. Nothing, therefore, could be allowed to inhibit the United States in the use of that power.

On this point no one was more emphatic than Krauthammer. "Collective security is a mirage," he wrote.[53] For its part, "the international community is a fiction."[54] "'The allies' is a smaller version of 'the international community'—and equally fictional."[55] "The United Nations is guarantor of nothing. Except in a formal sense, it can hardly be said to exist."[56] As a result, "when serious threats arise to American national interests...unilateralism is the only alternative to retreat."[57]

Or more extreme still, "The alternative to unipolarity is chaos." For Krauthammer the incontrovertible fact of unipolarity demanded that the United States face up to its obligations, "unashamedly laying down the rules of world order and being prepared to enforce them."[58] The point was one to which younger neoconservatives returned time and again. For Kristol and Robert Kagan, the choice facing Americans was clear-cut. On the one hand loomed the prospect of "a decline in U.S. power, a rise in world chaos, and a dangerous twenty-first century"; on the other hand was the promise of safety, achieved through "a Reaganite reassertion of American power and moral leadership." There existed "no middle ground."[59]

The third conviction animating second-generation neoconservatives related to military power and its uses. In a nutshell, they concluded that nothing works like force. Europeans, wrote Robert Kagan, might imagine themselves "entering a post-historical paradise of peace and relative prosperity, the realization of Kant's 'Perpetual Peace.'" Americans of a neoconservative bent knew better. In their judgment, the United States remained "mired in history, exercising power in the anarchic Hobbesian world where international laws are unreliable and where true security and the defense and promotion of a liberal order still depend on the possession and use of military might."[60] Employing that military might with sufficient wisdom and determination could bring within reach peace, prosperity, democracy, respect for human rights, and American global primacy extending to the end of time.

The operative principle was not to husband power but to put it to work—to take a proactive approach. "Military strength alone will not avail," cautioned Kagan, "if we do not use it actively to maintain a world order which both supports and rests upon American hegemony."[61] For neoconservatives like Kagan, the purpose of the Defense Department was no longer to defend the United States or to deter would-be aggressors but to transform the international order by transforming its constituent parts. Norman Podhoretz had opposed U.S. intervention in Vietnam "as a piece of arrogant stupidity" and had criticized in particular the liberal architects of the war for being "only too willing to tell other countries exactly how to organize their political and economic institutions."[62] For the younger generation of neoconservatives, instructing others as to how to organize their countries—employing coercion if need be—was not evidence of arrogant stupidity; it was America's job.[63]

By implication, neoconservatives were no longer inclined to employ force only after having exhausted all other alternatives. In the 1970s and 1980s, the proximate threat posed by the Soviet Union had obliged the United States to exercise a certain self-restraint. Now, with the absence of any counterweight to American power, the need for self-restraint fell away. Indeed, far from being a scourge for humankind, war itself—even, or perhaps especially, preventive war—became in neoconservative eyes an efficacious means to serve idealistic ends. The problem with Bill Clinton in the 1990s was not that he was reluctant to use force but that he was insufficiently bloody-minded. "In Haiti, in Somalia, and elsewhere" where the United States intervened, lamented Robert Kagan, "Clinton and his advisers had the stomach only to be halfway imperialists. When the heat was on, they tended to look for the exits."[64] Such halfheartedness suggested a defective appreciation of what power could accomplish. Neoconservatives knew better. "Military conquest," enthused Muravchik, "has often proved to be an effective means of implanting democracy."[65] Michael Ledeen went even further, declaring that "the best democracy program ever invented is the U.S. Army."[66] "Peace in this world," Ledeen added, "only follows victory in war."[67]

By their own lights, the neoconservatives of the 1990s did not qualify as warmongers, but once having gotten a whiff of gunpowder during the Persian Gulf War of 1990–91, they developed a hankering to repeat the experience. The neoconservative complaint about Operation Desert Storm was

that President George H. W. Bush and his commanders had failed to press
the attack. In their eyes, the war demonstrated that the U.S. military was a
superb instrument wielded by excessively timid officers, of whom General
Colin Powell was the ultimate embodiment. "One of the [Gulf] war's
important lessons," wrote one neoconservative, "is that America's military
leadership is far too cautious.... Now the success of that campaign has had
the effect of enhancing the prestige of our military leadership while doing
little or nothing to change its underlying attitude to fighting. Thus today
and tomorrow it may feel even less inhibited in opposing the use of force
than it did before the Gulf war."[68] Indeed, promoting the assertive use of
American military power became central to the imperial self-definition
devised by second-generation neoconservatives.

Using force to advance the prospects of peace and democracy implied
that the United States ought to possess military power to spare. The fourth
conviction animating second-generation neoconservatives was a commitment to sustaining and even enhancing American military supremacy.
Recall that throughout the 1990s, even before Osama bin Laden declared
his jihad against America, U.S. defense spending remained at Cold War levels despite the absence of the Cold War. Even so, neoconservatives assessed
the Pentagon's budget as completely inadequate and pressed for more.
Highly respected historians of a neoconservative persuasion even charged
that the United States was repeating the folly of Great Britain in the period
between the world wars: engaging in de facto unilateral disarmament.[69]
With the Cold War now history, it seemed, the world was becoming even
more dangerous, and the United States therefore needed *more* military
power than ever before.[70] Whether or not a proximate threat existed, it was
incumbent upon the Pentagon to maintain the capability "to intervene decisively in every critical region" of the world.[71]

To alarmists, the prospect of conflict without end beckoned. Surveying
the world, Frederick W. Kagan, brother of Robert, concluded in 1999 that
"America must be able to fight Iraq and North Korea, and *also* be able to
fight genocide in the Balkans and elsewhere without compromising its ability to fight two major regional conflicts. And it must be able to contemplate
war with China or Russia some considerable (but not infinite) time from
now."[72] The peace that followed victory was to be a long time coming.

The fifth and final conviction that imparted a distinctive twist to the
views of second-generation neoconservatives was their hostility toward

realism, whether manifesting itself as a deficit of ideals (as in the case of Henry Kissinger) or an excess of caution (as in the case of Colin Powell). As long as the Cold War had persisted, neoconservatives and realists had maintained an uneasy alliance, based on their common antipathy for the Soviet Union. But once the Cold War ended, so too did any basis for cooperation between the two groups. From the neoconservative perspective, realism constituted a problem. Realism was about defending national interests, not transforming the global order. Realists had a marked aversion to crusades and a marked respect for limits. In the neoconservative lexicon, the very notion of "limits" was anathema.[73] To the extent that realists after the Cold War retained influence in foreign policy circles, they were likely to obstruct neoconservative ambitions. So second-generation neocons trained their gunsights on realism and shot to kill.

The problem with realists, complained Robert Kagan, was that they were "professional pessimists." In that regard there had always been "something about realism that runs directly counter to the fundamental principles of American society." The essential issue, according to Kagan, was this: "if the United States is founded on universal principles, how can Americans practice amoral indifference when those principles are under siege around the world? And if they do profess indifference, how can they manage to avoid the implication that their principles are not, in fact, universal?" To Kagan and other neoconservatives the answer was self-evident: indifference to the violation of American ideals abroad was not simply wrong; it was un-American. Worse, such indifference pointed inevitably down a slippery slope leading back toward the 1960s or even the 1930s.[74] An authentically American foreign policy would reject amorality and pessimism; it would refuse altogether to accept the notion of limits or constraints.

As the 1990s unfolded, neoconservatives pressed their case for "a Reaganite policy of military strength and moral clarity," emphasizing the use of armed force to promulgate American values and perpetuate American primacy.[75] Most persistently, even obsessively, neoconservatives throughout the Clinton years lobbied for decisive U.S. action to rid the world of Saddam Hussein. From a neoconservative perspective, the Iraqi dictator's survival after Desert Storm exposed as nothing else the cynicism and shortsightedness of the realists who had dominated the administration of George H. W. Bush and who had prevented the American army from completing its proper mission—pursuing the defeated Iraqi army all the way to

Baghdad. Topping the agenda of the second-generation neoconservatives was a determination to correct that error, preferably by mobilizing America's armed might to destroy the Baathist regime. "Bombing Iraq Isn't Enough," declared the title of one representative op-ed published by William Kristol and Robert Kagan in January 1998. It was time for the gloves to come off, they argued, "and that means using air power and ground forces, and finishing the job left undone in 1991."[76]

Neocons yearned to liberate Iraq, as an end in itself but also as a means to an eminently larger end. "A successful intervention in Iraq," wrote Kagan in February 1998, "would revolutionize the strategic situation in the Middle East, in ways both tangible and intangible, and all to the benefit of American interests."[77] A march on Baghdad was certain to have a huge demonstration effect. It would put dictators around the world on notice either to mend their ways or share Saddam's fate. It would silence doubters who questioned America's ability to export its values. It would discredit skeptics who claimed to see lurking behind neoconservative schemes the temptations of empire, the dangers of militarism, and the prospect of exhaustion and overstretch.

Above all, forcibly overthrowing Saddam Hussein would affirm the irresistibility of American military might. As such, the armed liberation of Iraq would transform U.S. foreign policy; not preserving the status quo but promoting revolutionary change would thereafter define the main purpose of American statecraft. After all, wrote Michael Ledeen well before 9/11, stability was for "tired old Europeans and nervous Asians." The United States was "the most revolutionary force on earth," its "inescapable mission to fight for the spread of democracy."[78] The operative word was fight. According to Ledeen, Mao was precisely correct: revolution sprang "from the barrel of a gun."[79] The successful ouster of Saddam Hussein could open up whole new vistas of revolutionary opportunity.

What did all of this expenditure of intellectual energy actually yield? During the decade between the end of the Cold War and the onset of the global war on terror, the achievements of second-generation neoconservatives compare favorably with those of the anti-Communist liberals who in the immediate aftermath of World War II created the ideological foundation for what became a durable postwar foreign policy consensus. Through argument, organization, and agitation, leading liberal intellectuals of the 1940s such as the historian Arthur Schlesinger and the theologian Reinhold

Niebuhr imbued the muscular, implacably anti-Stalinist internationalism that they favored with the appearance of offering the only acceptable basis for U.S. foreign policy. To diverge from this "the vital center" of American politics, which they themselves defined and occupied, as Senator Robert Taft on the right and former vice president Henry Wallace on the left proposed to do, became almost by definition perverse.[80]

When deciding how to respond to growing Communist influence in Western Europe or to the invasion of South Korea, President Harry S Truman did not necessarily pause to consult the latest scribblings of Schlesinger or Niebuhr. The influence of intellectuals on policy is seldom that straightforward. Indirectly, however, these Cold War liberals helped to lend respectability to certain propositions that in the 1930s might have seemed outlandish—for example, the decision to permanently station U.S. troops in Europe and to create the apparatus of the national security state. In short, they fostered a climate congenial to Truman's pursuit of certain hard-line anti-Communist policies and increased the political risks faced by those inclined to question such policies.

During the 1990s, the intellectual offspring of Irving Kristol and Norman Podhoretz repeated this trick. By the end of that decade, neoconservatives were no longer insurgents; they had transformed themselves into establishment figures. Their views entered the mainstream of public discourse and became less controversial. Through house organs like the *Standard,* in essays published by influential magazines such as *Foreign Affairs,* through regular appearances on TV talk shows and at conferences sponsored by the fellow-traveling American Enterprise Institute, and via the agitprop of the Project for the New American Century, they warned of the ever-present dangers of isolationism and appeasement, called for ever more munificent levels of defense spending, and advocated stern measures to isolate, punish, or overthrow ne'er-do-wells around the world. As a mark of the growing respectability of such views, each of the three leading general-interest daily newspapers in the United States had at least one neocon offering regular foreign policy commentary—Max Boot writing for the *Los Angeles Times,* David Brooks for the *New York Times,* and both Charles Krauthammer and Robert Kagan for the *Washington Post.*[81] Neoconservative views also dominated the op-ed pages of the *Wall Street Journal.* As a direct consequence of this determined rabble-rousing, neocon views about the efficacy of American military power and the legitimacy of its use gained wide currency. On issues ranging from ethnic cleansing in Bosnia to the "rise" of China to the proper response to terror, neoconservatives recast the public policy debate about the obligations imposed upon and prerogatives to be claimed by the sole superpower. They kept the focus on the issues that they believed mattered most: an America that was strong, engaged, and even pugnacious.

Ideas that even a decade earlier might have seemed reckless or preposterous now came to seem perfectly reasonable. A good example was the issue of regime change in Iraq. On January 26, 1998, William Kristol and Robert Kagan along with more than a dozen other neoconservative luminaries sent a public letter to President Bill Clinton denouncing the policy of containing Iraq as a failure and calling for the United States to overthrow Saddam Hussein. To persist in the existing "course of weakness and drift," the signatories warned ominously, was to "put our interests and our future at risk."[82] Nine months later, Clinton duly signed into law the Iraq Liberation Act of 1998, passed by large majorities in both houses of Congress. That legislation declared that it had now become the policy of the United States government to "remove the regime headed by Saddam Hussein," with legislators authorizing the expenditure of $99 million for that purpose.[83] Clinton showed little enthusiasm for actually implementing the measure, and most of the money remained unspent. But neoconservative efforts had done much to create a climate in which it had become impolitic to suggest aloud that publicly declaring the intent to overthrow regimes not to the liking of the United States might be ill-advised. At the end of the 1940s, thanks to the Cold War liberals, no politician with the slightest interest in self-preservation was going to risk even the appearance of being soft on the Soviet Union. At the end of the 1990s, thanks to the neoconservatives, no politician was going to take the chance of being tagged with being soft on Saddam.

Still, reframing debate does not mean necessarily winning the debate. To neoconservatives in the 1990s it was obvious that Clinton was no Truman. If second-generation neocons succeeded during the 1990s in making themselves heard, they enjoyed less success in persuading those actually in positions of power to heed their counsel. As a result, the two terms of the Clinton presidency—for neoconservatives, years in the political wilderness—were filled with frustration. Writing in 2000, Robert Kagan and William Kristol, echoing Podhoretz twenty years earlier at the end of the

Carter presidency, proclaimed that a great crisis was at hand. Although Americans no longer faced a great-power adversary comparable to the Soviet Union, "there is today a present danger."

> The present danger is that the United States will shrink from its responsibilities as the world's dominant power and—in a fit of absentmindedness, or parsimony or indifference—will allow the international order that it sustains to collapse. The present danger is one of declining strength, flagging will and confusion about our role in the world.... [During the 1990s] the United States has tended toward a course of gradual moral and strategic disarmament.... American leaders have chosen drift and evasion.[84]

Nor did events during the first eight months of the presidency of George W. Bush, even with prominent neoconservatives now occupying positions of influence, do much to amend this gloomy assessment. Bush seemed too willing to adhere to the paths carved out by his predecessor. Above all, despite their unceasing agitation, neocons failed to gain explicit presidential backing for a plan to remove their chief nemesis, Saddam Hussein. Nor did they convert President Bush to their belief in the necessity of unambiguously militarized global hegemony as the basis for U.S. foreign policy. But both would come, together and soon.

Writing in the summer of 2001, a decade after the United States had donned the mantle of sole superpower, Charles Krauthammer contemplated the uniqueness of the American imperium. "Unlike other hegemons or would-be hegemons," he wrote, "we do not entertain a grand vision of a new world. No Thousand Year Reich. No New Soviet Man. By position and nature, we are essentially a status quo power."[85]

In fact, the grand vision entertained by second-generation neoconservatives demanded that the United States shatter the status quo. New conditions, they argued, absolved Americans from any further requirement to adhere to the norms that had defined the postwar international order. Osama bin Laden and the events of 9/11 provided the tailor-made opportunity to break free of the fetters restricting the exercise of American power.

The moment of decision was now at hand. "Either we act aggressively to shape the world and change regimes where necessary," wrote William Kristol and Gary Schmitt, "or we accept living in a world in which our existence is contingent on the whims of unstable tyrants."[86] According to Kristol and Lawrence Kaplan, "The alternative to American leadership is a chaotic, Hobbesian world." In such a world, "there is no authority to thwart aggression, ensure peace and security or enforce international norms."[87]

Immediately after the attacks of September 11, 2001, and despite the dearth of persuasive evidence linking Saddam Hussein's regime to the attacks on the World Trade Center and the Pentagon, neoconservatives in and out of government began pressing insistently for an all-out invasion of Iraq.[88] The key to ultimate victory in the war on terror, neoconservatives believed, lay in Iraq. "The road that leads to real security and peace," argued William Kristol and Robert Kagan, was "the road that runs through Baghdad."[89]

Neoconservatives attributed 9/11 to a sickness infecting the world of Islam. They charged governments in the Middle East—some nominally friendly to the United States, some not—with being complicit in spreading the bacillus of anti-American radicalism. The only sure way of preventing further terrorist attacks was to cure the disease, through a massive, forced injection of Western liberal values into the Islamic world. As a group of prominent neoconservatives instructed President Bush in April 2002, "the surest path to peace in the Middle East lies . . . through a renewed commitment on our part . . . to the birth of freedom and democratic government in the Islamic world."[90] And the place to begin the process of using American power to liberate and to transform the Middle East was Iraq. Why Iraq? First, because the threat posed by Saddam Hussein was "enormous" and was getting "bigger with every day that passes."[91] Second, because, having endured decades of authoritarian rule, Iraq was "ripe for democracy."[92] Third, because making an object lesson of Saddam would open the door for success elsewhere in the region. Once the Iraqi dictator was gone, the whole rickety structure of faux Arab nationalism, corrupt authoritarian government, and nihilistic Islamic radicalism would come tumbling down. For neighboring countries, the effect of democratizing Iraq was sure to be "stunning."[93]

If neoconservatives harbored any lingering doubts about the ability of U.S. military power to carry off such a bold scheme, those doubts vanished with the first skirmish of the global war on terror—the nominally success-ful U.S. invasion of Afghanistan. Victory over the Taliban in the fall of 2001 convinced Krauthammer, for example, that "the way to tame the Arab street is not with appeasement and sweet sensitivity but with raw power and victory.... The elementary truth that seems to elude the experts again and again... is that power is its own reward. Victory changes everything, psychology above all. The psychology in the [Middle East] is now one of fear and deep respect for American power. Now is the time to use it."[94]

But Afghanistan was hardly more than a preliminary bout. The main event—the contest that promised to determine the future of the interna-tional order—was Iraq. "Either it will be a world order conducive to our liberal democratic principles and our safety," argued Robert Kagan and William Kristol, "or it will be one where brutal, well-armed tyrants are allowed to hold democracy and international security hostage. Not to take on Saddam would insure that regimes implicated in terror and developing weapons of mass destruction will be a constant—and growing—feature of our world."[95] Thus, Saddam had to go; the imperative of liberating and remaking Iraq demanded immediate attention.

The "political, strategic and moral rewards" of doing so promised to be enormous, according to Kristol. "A friendly, free, and oil-producing Iraq would leave Iran isolated and Syria cowed; the Palestinians more willing to negotiate seriously with Israel; and Saudi Arabia with less leverage over policymakers here and in Europe," he told the Senate Foreign Relations Committee in February 2002. "Removing Saddam Hussein and his hench-men from power presents a genuine opportunity," Kristol emphasized, "to transform the political landscape of the Middle East."[96]

Soon enough, this line of reasoning found favor with President George W. Bush. Viewing the global war on terrorism through a religious rather than an ideological lens, Bush nonetheless found much to like about the neoconservative prescription for U.S. policy, both as it applied to Iraq and more generally.[97]

As a result, the period between the summer of 2002 and the spring of 2003—bounded on the one side by Bush's speech to graduating cadets at West Point and on the other by the Anglo-American invasion of Iraq, but with its true centerpiece the publication of the Bush administration's *U.S. National Security Strategy*—became for neoconservatives something like a dream come true. During this interval, the doctrines of preventive war and permanent military supremacy were officially enshrined as U.S. policy, with Operation Iraqi Freedom removing all doubts as to whether President Bush meant what he said. The fall of Baghdad in April 2003 presented to the United States, in the words of one neoconservative, the opportunity "to create a landscape for real revolution in the Middle East—a reordering that might prevent a future clash of civilizations."[98]

As a consequence of these developments, the younger Bush, a born-again Christian, was reborn yet again in neoconservative eyes. He became what Reagan ought to have been, not only expressing all the correct sentiments but also (unlike the real Reagan) backing up words with action.[99] Thanks to President Bush, noted an approving William Kristol just months after 9/11, "American foreign policy can be said to be at war with tyranny in general."[100] Buoyed by the shift in policy inaugurated by the Bush Doctrine, the neoconservative writers David Frum and Richard Perle declared with confidence that with the United States having "become the greatest of all powers in world history, its triumph has shown that freedom is irresistible." Looking beyond Iraq, they glimpsed a world of universal peace and freedom, "brought into being by American armed might and defended by American might."[101]

No one applauded this prospect with greater enthusiasm than did Norman Podhoretz, who saw in these developments the fulfillment of long-standing neoconservative hopes and expectations. According to Podhoretz, "the sheer audacity" of the attack that Osama bin Laden had orchestrated on September 11 could have only one explanation: the weakness displayed by Bush's immediate predecessors during the 1990s had bred "contempt for American power." Proponents of violent, radical Islam had seen Bill Clinton's administration cut and run after Mogadishu in 1993. They watched as the United States did nothing or next to nothing in response to a series of terrorist attacks, beginning with the bombing of the World Trade Center in 1993 and continuing through the near-sinking of the USS *Cole* in 2000. And they had concluded, according to Podhoretz, that "we were a nation on the way down, destined to be defeated by the resurgence of the same militancy that had once conquered and converted large parts of the world by the sword."[102] Now President Bush was giving the lie to such expectations.

Bin Laden had thrust the United States into war, which Podhoretz viewed as a wondrous opportunity. Writing in December 2001 and contemplating the approaching showdown with Saddam Hussein, he observed with anticipation that "big wars… invariably end by reshaping the world." In this case, Podhoretz expected big war to "bring about the long-delayed reform and modernization of Islam."[103] An American invasion of Iraq, he believed, was sure to "set off a benevolent domino effect throughout the entire region."[104]

In other words, as crucial as it was, Iraq itself qualified as merely a way station, an interim objective facilitating the ever more aggressive use of U.S. military power. After disposing of Saddam Hussein, "we may willy-nilly find ourselves forced by the same political and military logic to topple five or six or seven more tyrannies in the Islamic world." As if responding to Irving Kristol's complaint about an absence of imperial self-definition, Podhoretz expected the prosecution of the global war on terror to create a "new species of imperial mission for America, whose purpose would be to oversee the emergence of successor governments in the region more amenable to reform and modernization than the despotisms now in place." Podhoretz even envisioned such an imperium entailing "the establishment of some kind of American protectorate over the oil fields of Saudi Arabia."[105] Indeed, he relished that prospect.

In Podhoretz's eyes, the beauty of the Bush Doctrine was not that it promised to deny the oil weapon to those tempted to discomfit the United States but that it imparted to U.S. policy an "incandescent moral clarity."[106] As no previous statement of American policy had, the Bush Doctrine illuminated the way ahead. When James Burnham had argued in the 1940s that "the only alternative to the communist World Empire is an American Empire which will be… capable of exercising decisive world control," critics had denounced him as unhinged.[107] But with 9/11, neoconservatives had come fully to embrace this imperial vision. Waging preventive war to overthrow recalcitrant regimes and free the oppressed—this had become the definitive expression of America's calling.

As a bonus, the prosecution of this war also held out the prospect of renewal at home. "Beyond revenge" for the attacks of 9/11, Podhoretz rhapsodized, Americans "crave 'a new birth' of the confidence we used to have in ourselves and in 'America the Beautiful.'"

> But there is only one road to this lovely condition of the spirit, [he continued,] and it runs through what Roosevelt and Churchill called the 'unconditional surrender' of the enemy. If we go on dithering, our lives

will remain at permanent risk. So, too, will something deeper than the desire for physical security that has been stirred and agitated by the ferocious wound we received on September 11: a wound that is still suppurating and sore for lack of the healing balm that only a more coherent and wholehearted approach to the war will bring.

What I mean is that nothing less than the soul of this country is at stake, and that nothing less than an unambiguous victory will save us from yet another disappointment in ourselves and another despairing disillusion with our leaders. Only this time the disappointment and the despair might well possess enough force to topple us over just as surely as those hijacked planes did to the twin towers of the World Trade Center.[108]

As always, crisis loomed. As always, Americans faced a choice as stark as it was clear-cut. As always, neoconservatives saw the way out: through war, the United States might yet save the world, and in doing so might also save itself. In America's future loomed the prospect of one, two, many Iraqs, and the future at long last appeared bright.

Chapter Four

CALIFORNIA DREAMING

THE NEW AMERICAN MILITARISM draws much of its sustaining force from myth—stories created to paper over incongruities and contradictions that pervade the American way of life. The exercise of global power by the United States aggravates these incongruities.

Americans want to feel secure, in their homes and where they work. Rather than safety, however, the possession of military might without precedent has in practice yielded a heightened sense of vulnerability.

Americans see themselves as an idealistic people. But the dispatch of U.S. forces to oppose tyranny and create the conditions for peace does not evoke accolades from abroad. Instead, it fuels anti-Americanism and generates suspicion of our motives and intentions.

Americans believe in democracy. But their democracy works such that the divide between rich and poor grows ever wider. In America, the winners control an ever-increasing percentage of the nation's wealth. To be a member of the upper class is to have privileges, among them ensuring that it's someone else's kid who is getting shot at in Iraq or Afghanistan.

These are hard, uncomfortable truths, for which the existing political system does not provide an easily available remedy. So Americans concoct stories to make such truths more palatable. During the past quarter century, American politicians with their eyes firmly fixed on the main chance, assisted by purveyors of popular culture with a well-honed instinct for what sells, have promulgated a host of such stories. One result has been to contrive a sentimentalized version of the American military experience and an idealized image of the American soldier.

These myths make an essential contribution to the new American militarism. They create an apparently seamless historical narrative of American soldiers as liberators, with Operation Iraqi Freedom in March 2003 becoming a sequel to Operation Overlord in June 1944. They divert attention from the reality of U.S. military policy, now having less to do with national defense than with imperial policing. They help to sustain the willingness of American soldiers to shoulder their frequently thankless and seemingly endless burdens in places like the Balkans, Central Asia, and the Persian Gulf. Above all, they function as a salve for what remains of the American conscience. Myths offer reassurance that America remains, as Ronald Reagan put it, "still a land of heroes with all the courage and love of freedom that ever was before."[1] They enable us to sustain the belief that the soldiers whom we hire to do the nation's dirty work but whom we do not know are, in fact, bringing peace and light to troubled corners of the earth rather than pushing ever outward the perimeter of an American empire.

It is worth noting that within recent memory Americans did not rely on myths to understand soldiers or to justify U.S. military policy.

During World War II and during the early Cold War, papering over the gap between the armed services and American society, for example, was unnecessary because no such gap existed. Even members of the elite served, to include the founding fathers of neoconservatism. With his degrees from Columbia and Cambridge, and already attracting notice in the early 1950s as a talented and ambitious young writer, Norman Podhoretz, for one, served a hitch as a draftee enlisted soldier.[2]

Nor during this period—with the possible exception of the Korean War—was there any requirement to conjure up reassuring explanations of what the members of the armed forces were doing and why. The rotation of citizen-soldiers through the ranks and the leavening presence of veterans throughout American society obviated the need for myths, indeed, made it all but impossible to idealize war or military service. From firsthand experience, Americans knew better. Millions of young men like Private Podhoretz—or like Sergeant Elvis Presley, Podhoretz's cultural antipode—put in their time as members of the Cold War army not because they had imbibed militaristic fantasies, but because their understanding of citizenship included a responsibility to contribute to the nation's defense. When called upon to do so, other millions fought hot wars for much the same reason.

As the American intervention in Southeast Asia became mired in stalemate, of course, all of that changed. Vietnam demolished the notion of military obligation and brought the tradition of the citizen-soldier to the verge of extinction. And it persuaded many that war itself—especially as waged by obtuse American generals doing the bidding of mendacious civilian officials—had become an exercise in futility.

Vietnam plunged the country into a funk in which it remained long after the withdrawal of U.S. troops and the fall of Saigon. Some observers—President Jimmy Carter among them—came to view that funk as an expression of a new reality, to which Americans had little choice but to adapt themselves. To others the sour mood enveloping the country suggested opportunity. All that was required was a figure astute enough to recognize that opportunity and possessing the requisite political skills to exploit it. Ronald Reagan was such a figure.

If Carter was in some respects a 1970s version of Herbert Hoover—a decent man and competent engineer, but utterly ill-equipped for the challenges he confronted as president—then Reagan found his role of a lifetime by playing a variant of Franklin D. Roosevelt. Personal effervescence and unflagging optimism combined with a promise to end the Depression by mobilizing the full resources of the federal government helped FDR to depose the dour Hoover. An equally sunny disposition backed by an insistence that America's best days were still to come enabled Reagan to depose Carter. But a fictionalized version of the American military tradition was integral to Reagan's triumphal march to and occupation of the White House.

Reagan categorically rejected what in the wake of Vietnam had become the prevailing wisdom about war, soldiers, and the contemporary American military experience. More than anyone else, he deserves the credit for conjuring up the myths that nurtured and sustain present-day American militarism. The benefits that Reagan derived from these inventions were not lost on other astute politicians who profited by his example and who helped to keep those myths alive.

Substantively, Jimmy Carter's presidency enjoyed its share of successes (brokering peace between Israel and Egypt and securing ratification of the Panama Canal Treaty) as well as failures, at least some of which (such as Iran's Islamic revolution) were as much attributable to bad timing and lousy luck as to Carter's defective judgment. Politically, however, the Carter administration was from start to finish an unmitigated disaster. Two specific incidents, disastrous miscues from which it proved impossible to recover, not only illustrate Carter's political ineptitude but also show how Carter's failures stanched the anti-military currents to which Vietnam had given rise and produced the first inkling of movement in the opposite direction.

The first of these was Carter's heartfelt, in some respects prescient, but completely misconceived address to the nation of July 15, 1979. This was the president's "Crisis of Confidence" speech.

The context from which the speech emerged is as follows. The U.S. misadventure in Vietnam had given rise to economic woes that lingered long after the war. In 1979, the third year of Carter's presidency, economic conditions as measured by postwar standards had become dire. By midyear, inflation had reached 11 percent, with 7 percent of the workforce unemployed, both unacceptably high by postwar standards. The prime lending rate was 15 percent and rising. As a result, mortgages and consumer credit were becoming prohibitively expensive. Trends in both the federal deficit and the trade balance were sharply negative. Conventional analysis, to which the administration itself fully subscribed, attributed U.S. economic woes to the nation's growing dependence on increasingly expensive foreign oil.[3]

In July 1979, Carter already anticipated that a continuing and unchecked thirst for imported oil was sure to distort U.S. strategic priorities, with unforeseen but adverse consequences. He feared the impact of that distortion on an American democracy still reeling from the effects of the 1960s. So he summoned his fellow citizens to change course, to choose self-sufficiency and self-reliance and therefore true independence—but at a cost of collective sacrifice and lowered expectations.

Carter spoke that night of a nation facing problems "deeper than gasoline lines or energy shortages, deeper even than inflation or depression."[4] Over the previous ten days, the president had consulted at Camp David with Americans from all walks of life. In essence, the president had invited various writers, teachers, ministers, business and labor leaders, and local and state officials to instruct him in what was wrong with America, and they had happily obliged.

That painful experience had affirmed Carter's conviction that the United States was suffering from a full-blown collapse of collective self-confidence, one that expressed itself in "growing doubt about the meaning of our own lives and in the loss of a unity of purpose for our Nation." Left to fester, this crisis promised "to destroy the social and the political fabric of America." The fundamental problem, in Carter's view, was that Americans had turned away from all that really mattered.

> In a nation that was proud of hard work, strong families, close-knit communities, and our faith in God, too many of us now tend to worship self-indulgence and consumption. Human identity is no longer defined by what one does, but by what one owns. But we've discovered that owning things and consuming things does not satisfy our longing for meaning. We've learned that piling up material goods cannot fill the emptiness of lives which have no confidence or purpose.
>
> The symptoms of this crisis of the American spirit are all around us. For the first time in the history of our country a majority of our people believe that the next five years will be worse than the past five years. Two-thirds of our people do not even vote. The productivity of American workers is actually dropping, and the willingness of Americans to save for the future has fallen below that of all other people in the Western world.

This crisis had brought the United States to a historical turning point. Either Americans could persist in pursuing "a mistaken idea of freedom" based on "fragmentation and self-interest" and inevitably "ending in chaos and immobility," or they could opt for "true freedom," which Carter described as "the path of common purpose and the restoration of American values."

How the United States chose to deal with its growing reliance on foreign oil would determine which of the two paths it followed. Energy dependence, according to Carter, posed "a clear and present danger," threatening the nation's security as well as its economic well-being. Dealing with this threat was also "the standard around which we can rally." "On the battlefield of energy," declared Carter, " we can seize control again of our common destiny."

How to achieve this aim? For his part, Carter vowed to put an immediate cap on oil imports. He promised massive new investments to develop alternative sources of energy. He called upon the Congress to pass legislation limiting the use of oil by the nation's utilities and increasing spending on public transportation. But he placed the larger burden squarely in the lap of the American people. The hollowing out of American democracy required a genuinely democratic response. "There is simply no way to avoid sacrifice," he insisted, calling upon citizens as "an act of patriotism" to lower thermostats, observe the speed limit, use carpools, and "park your car one extra day per week."

Carter plainly viewed the imperative of restoring energy independence as an analogue for war. But despite his allusions to metaphorical battles and battle standards, nowhere in his speech did he identify a role for the U.S. military.[5] For Carter, the "crisis" facing the nation could not have a military solution. That crisis was at root internal rather than external. Resolving it required spiritual and cultural renewal at home rather than deploying U.S. power to create a world order accommodating the nation's dependence upon and growing preoccupation with material resources from abroad.

Although Carter's stance was relentlessly inward looking, his analysis had important strategic implications. To the extent that "foreign oil" refers implicitly to the Persian Gulf—as it did then and does today—Carter was in essence proposing to arrest the growing strategic importance attributed to that region. He sensed intuitively that a failure to reverse the nation's energy dependence was sure to draw the United States ever more deeply into the vortex of Persian Gulf politics, which could at best distract attention from but was even more likely to exacerbate the internal crisis that was his central concern.

This is, of course, precisely what has come to pass, with massive and problematic implications for the nation's security and for U.S. military posture and priorities. When Carter spoke, the United States was importing approximately 43 percent of its annual requirement for oil, and the U.S. military presence in the Persian Gulf was modest—a handful of ships and naval personnel stationed in Bahrain. Some twenty-five years later, energy imports have risen to 56 percent of annual needs.[6] Over that period of time, the energy-rich regions of the world—the Caucasus and Central Asia in addition to the Persian Gulf—have absorbed an ever-increasing amount of attention by the American military, manifested in bases and infrastructure, exercises and demonstrations, contingency plans and actual campaigns. A half century ago, the proximity of a Communist threat—to Western Europe or East Asia, for example—tended to determine the stationing of U.S. forces abroad. Today, increasingly, the profile of the American military presence abroad corresponds to the location of large oil and natural gas reserves.

But if Carter was prophetic when it came to the strategic implications of growing U.S. energy dependence, his policy prescription reflected a fundamental misreading of his fellow countrymen. Although the highly publicized speech itself produced a temporary uptick in his sagging popularity ratings, the substance of the message—a call to lower expectations—evoked little positive response.[7] Indeed, as Garry Wills has observed, given the country's propensity to define itself in terms of growth, it triggered "a subtle panic [and] claustrophobia" that Carter's political adversaries wasted no time in exploiting.[8]

Those adversaries—Ronald Reagan first and foremost—offered a different message, not of a need to cut back but of abundance without end. They assured Americans not only that compromising their lifestyle was unnecessary but that the prospects for economic expansion were limitless and could be had without moral complications or great cost. This, rather than nagging about shallow materialism, was what Americans wanted to hear. Thus did Carter pave the way for his own electoral defeat a year later.

The abject failure of the Iranian hostage rescue mission the following spring sealed Carter's fate. Of greater specific relevance to this account, Desert One—the one and only time President Carter sent U.S. forces into action—offered a plausible and reassuringly simple explanation for all of the problems that the United States was facing in the Persian Gulf and elsewhere in the world. The answer to whatever crisis afflicted the United States was to be found not in conservation or reduced expectations and surely not in spiritual renewal; it was to be found in the restoration of U.S. military might, which held the promise of enabling Americans always to have more rather than to make do with less.

Seldom has such a miniscule military setback—in the Iranian rescue operation of April 1980, eight Americans lost their lives compared, for example, to 241 killed in the Beirut bombing of October 1983—had such a seismic impact, not only politically but also on a nation's collective psyche. Gauging that impact requires a proper appreciation for the circumstances in which operational failure occurred.

The Iran hostage crisis had developed as a by-product of the Iranian Revolution of 1979. In January of that year, mounting internal opposition had forced Mohammed Reza Shah Pahlavi, viewed by his own people as a puppet of the United States, into exile. The following month, the Ayatollah Khomeini, leader of the Iranian opposition, returned from exile to declare the founding of a new Islamic Republic. In October, Carter permitted the shah, ill with cancer, to enter the United States for medical treatment. Outraged—and perhaps suspecting Washington of plotting to return the shah to the throne as it had in 1953—Iranian radicals on November 4 seized the United States Embassy in Tehran and sixty-six Americans, whom they imprisoned as hostages.

The ensuing standoff between Washington and Tehran riveted the world's attention and paralyzed the Carter administration. The suspension of Iranian oil imports, the imposition of economic sanctions, and several diplomatic initiatives succeeded only in securing the release of a handful of hostages, with fifty-two remaining in prolonged captivity.

Increasingly frustrated—and facing the prospect of a difficult election campaign—Carter ordered the Pentagon to attempt a rescue. Based on an audacious but complex plan, the operation, dubbed Eagle Claw, was launched in great secrecy on April 24, 1980, only to collapse virtually before it had begun; beset with myriad equipment failures, commanders aborted the mission well short of its objective and without having met any opposition. The subsequent collision of two American aircraft while refueling at a remote staging area in the Iranian desert resulted in the sole casualties.

For Carter, the failure of this covert mission marked the low point of his presidency. Finger-pointing began almost immediately and centered on evidence of fundamental mismanagement of the armed services. Reacting to what they described as "an embarrassing background briefing" by a high-ranking military officer who "ended up admitting that the breakdowns exceeded everybody's worst fears," reporters from the *Washington Post*, writing in a front-page story, asked pointedly:

> If this is true of a rehearsed operation, using fine-tuned helicopters with the best pilots in the military, what does that admission say about the overall readiness of the American Army, Navy, Air Force and Marine Corps to go to war?
>
> How would other weapons perform in the mud and under fire?
>
> Are the critics... correct in claiming that the Pentagon is so obsessed with buying new weapons that it does not take care of the ones it already has?

Or is it that the all-volunteer military does not pay enough money to attract and keep people skilled in operating and fixing million-dollar weapons?[9]

The Carter administration had no good answers to these questions. Indeed, with Operation Eagle Claw, U.S. forces hit bottom. This proved to be the point at which the downward spiral in overall effectiveness set in motion by Vietnam finally ended.

The failure at Desert One did not erase the memory of that earlier war or instantly repeal its ostensible "lessons." It did, however, change the political atmospherics, persuading large numbers of Americans that any recurrence of such a calamity was simply unacceptable. Something needed to be done. And whatever that something was, the current incumbent of the Oval House seemed like the wrong man to do it.

In his self-assigned role as First Preacher, Jimmy Carter had failed. Americans decisively rejected his call to end their addiction to imported oil and to mend their sinful ways. They did not look to the Oval Office for moral instruction.

In his constitutionally assigned role as commander-in-chief, Carter had also failed. But in this case, his failure proved instructive: it persuaded Americans that the enfeebled state of the armed services had become intolerable. In a backhanded way, this least militaristic of recent presidents inadvertently created the conditions for the militarization of U.S. policy that was to come.

President Carter, graduate of the U.S. Naval Academy and qualified nuclear submariner, seldom spoke at length of American military power. Nor did he make it a habit of publicly paying tribute to the American soldier. His inaugural address of January 20, 1977, for example, did not allude to the armed services.[10] His State of the Union address of 1978 noted in passing that "militarily we are very strong," but offered no specifics and did not mention the men and women in uniform constituting that strength.[11] These presentations were typical. Throughout his presidency, Carter managed to convey the impression that he took American soldiers for granted.

Ronald Reagan made a point of emphasizing that he did not. As president, Reagan, whose own military experience was confined to a stint making Army Air Corps training films in World War II Hollywood, spoke to and about soldiers with great frequency, going out of his way to convey his gratitude, respect, and affection.[12] Soldiers, Reagan let it be known, were special people.

This message was integral to the Great Communicator's overarching political strategy. As Norman Podhoretz has noted, Reagan "made free and frequent use of patriotic language and engaged in an unembarrassed manipulation of patriotic symbols; he lost no opportunity to praise the armed forces, to heighten their morale, to restore their popular prestige." As a result, "he also helped restore confidence here in the utility of military force as an instrument of worthy political purposes."[13]

In "Morning in America," the imaginary movie with which Reagan beguiled himself and his supporters, soldierly ideals and exploits offered a trove of instructive and inspiring anecdotes.[14] Celebrating the American in uniform, past and present, offered Reagan a means of rallying support for his broader political agenda. His manipulation of symbols also offered a sanitized version of U.S. military history and fostered a romanticized portrait of those who made it. These were essential to reversing the anti-military climate that was a by-product of Vietnam and by extension essential to policies that Reagan intended to implement, such as a massive boost in defense spending and a more confrontational posture toward the Soviet Union. Looking beyond the Reagan era, they helped create the basis for the reflexive militarization of U.S. policy.

That Reagan chose to construct the peroration of his first inaugural address around a parable of soldierly virtue is, in this regard, hardly incidental. Martin Treptow, the president explained to an attentive nation on January 20, 1981, had been a doughboy, a small-town barber turned intrepid warrior who was killed in action on the Western Front. On Private Treptow's body, Reagan explained, was found a diary.

> On the flyleaf under the heading, "My Pledge," he had written these words: "America must win this war. Therefore I will work, I will save, I will sacrifice, I will endure, I will fight cheerfully and do my utmost, as if the issue of the whole struggle depended on me alone."

Treptow's determination and spirit of self-sacrifice exemplified Reagan's understanding of America. The nation's freshly inaugurated leader now summoned his fellow citizens to heed the example set by this fallen hero and hence to "believe in ourselves and to believe in our capacity to perform great deeds."[15]

Within weeks of his inauguration, Reagan also pointedly signaled his determination to change the poisonous civil-military climate that had evolved out of Vietnam. Reagan's intent in presenting the Medal of Honor to a veteran of that war, according to Secretary of Defense Caspar Weinberger, was to "demonstrate to the troops that not only did the President and the Defense Department care about their welfare, but the American people as a whole also respected, honored and appreciated the importance of what our military forces were doing for the country."[16] There was more, however. Reagan also used the occasion to reinterpret the Vietnam War itself.

In presenting Master Sergeant Roy P. Benavidez with his award, Reagan broke with protocol by personally reading the accompanying citation. But the president also used the high-profile White House ceremony as an opportunity to speak directly to the "men and women of the Armed Forces." "Several years ago," he began,

> we brought home a group of American fighting men who had obeyed their country's call and who fought as bravely and as well as any Americans in our history. They came home without a victory not because they'd been defeated, but because they'd been denied permission to win.
>
> They were greeted by no parades, no bands, no waving of the flag they had so nobly served. There's been no "thank you" for their sacrifice. There's been no effort to honor and, thus, give pride to the families of more than 57,000 young men who gave their lives in that faraway war.[17]

For Reagan, it was self-evident that Vietnam had been "a noble cause."[18] Noble too were the soldiers who had endured that war. Nameless others had wronged America's fighting men, misusing and mistreating them, and denying them the victory and honors that were rightfully theirs. Reagan would not repeat these errors; he would champion soldiers, correcting the injustices done to them in the 1960s by providing the soldiers of the 1980s everything that they needed and more. "I know there've been times when the military has been taken for granted," he told an audience of sailors during his first months in office. "It won't happen under this administration."[19]

By implication, Reagan was establishing support *for* "the troops"—as opposed to actual service *with* them—as the new standard of civic responsibility. Despite the president's penchant for flag-waving rhetoric, the standard he set was notably undemanding. Reconstituting U.S. military power, Reagan tacitly promised, was not going to entail sacrifice on the part of the average American. Indeed, both as a candidate and once in office, he categorically rejected any suggestion of reviving the draft.[20] Military service was to remain strictly a matter of individual preference. To anyone making that choice Reagan granted the status of patriot, idealist, and hero; of citizens he asked only that they affirm that designation.[21]

Instead of imposing obligations, the president offered memories that uplifted and reassured. His tribute to the "the boys of Pointe du Hoc"— immortalized in Reagan's speech of June 6, 1984, at Normandy as "the men who took the cliffs . . . the champions who freed a continent . . . the heroes who helped end a war"—offers a moving example of this technique.[22] The achievements of the men who defeated Nazi Germany were not mythic; they were real. But during the Reagan presidency those achievements became suffused with nostalgia. With Reagan's decision to reactivate several mothballed World War II–era battleships, this nostalgia manifested itself in a tangible way. Returning these massive yet obsolete warships to the fleet, wrote the journalist Haynes Johnson, recalled the "mythical period of American life" that Reagan sought to restore "by reversing direction and leading America back into its past."[23]

Ronald Reagan did not invent the so-called All-Volunteer Force, which had been the handiwork of Richard Nixon. But neither Nixon nor his immediate successors invested any serious effort in making the AVF work, and through the first decade of its existence it floundered. Rather than being an elite military force, it functioned as the nation's employer of last resort and as a sanctuary for dropouts and ne'er-do-wells.[24]

The Reagan administration claimed—and Reagan's subordinates accorded to the president personally—credit for converting the AVF from a dubious experiment into a resounding success.[25] However self-serving, these claims have merit. Massive increases in military spending—the Pentagon's budget just about doubled in the Reagan years—did, in fact, contribute mightily to lifting the armed services out of their Vietnam-induced doldrums. The $2.7 trillion invested in defense during Reagan's two terms purchased huge improvements in readiness, modernization, and—perhaps most impressively—recruiting and retention.[26] Moreover, the quality of recruits also improved markedly. In 1980, for example, only 54 percent of new U.S. Army enlistees were high school graduates, while 57 percent scored below average on the Armed Forces Qualification Test and were therefore classified as Category IV. By 1986, 91 percent of new Army recruits had high school diplomas and a mere 4 percent were Category IVs.[27]

As early as the fall of 1982, Reagan professed to see things turning around. "We've improved our strategic forces, toughened our conventional forces, and—one thing that's made me particularly happy—more and more young Americans are proud again to wear their country's uniform."[28] A year later, he bragged to a meeting of newspaper editors that "we have a waiting line of people who want to enlist." [29]

For Reagan, the overall U.S. military recovery, and especially the apparent change in attitudes toward service in the armed forces, offered positive proof that America was once again "standing tall." To substantiate Reagan's claim that "as a nation, we've closed the books on a long, dark period of failure and self-doubt and set a new course," one needed to look no further than the freshly minted fighter jets, tanks, and helicopters entering the force and the eager young men and women who crewed them.[30]

Thus did military might—rather than, say, the trade balance, income distribution, voter turnout, or the percentage of children being raised in two-parent families—become the preferred measure for gauging the nation's strength.

Thus too did the soldier—now set apart from his or her fellow citizens—become the preeminent icon of the Reagan recovery. Soldiers, said Reagan, made possible the rebirth of American patriotism.[31] Soldiers refurbished the nation's ideals and embodied its renewed sense of purpose. "Who else but an idealist," the president asked rhetorically, "would choose to become a member of the Armed Forces and put himself or herself in harm's way for the rest of us?"[32]

Soldierly idealism figured prominently in the little stories with which Reagan habitually embroidered his major speeches, evidence that the spirit of Martin Treptow was indeed enjoying a revival. With Congress quibbling about defense spending, for instance, Reagan told of receiving "a letter from a hundred marines stationed over in Europe, and those marines write me...and say 'If giving us a pay cut will help our country, cut our pay.'"

"I wouldn't cut their pay if I bled to death," Reagan hastened to add.

But "the response from them, all of them, is just so remarkable.... I've never heard such pride; I've never heard such willingness to accept that this was necessary."[33]

In October 1983, with questions being raised about the U.S. military presence in Lebanon, the president found support for his policies in a letter written by a Marine corporal:

It is our duty as Americans to stop the cancerous spread of Soviet influence wherever it may be, [Reagan quoted the letter] because someday we or some future generation will wake up and find the U.S.A. to be the only free state left, with communism upon our doorstep. And then it will be too late.[34]

Attributing Lebanon's woes and the U.S. military presence there to Soviet tomfoolery represented a fundamental misreading of the situation, but by calling attention to the corporal's sturdy anti-Communism Reagan implied that further explanation was unnecessary.

Later that month, when the Marine barracks in Beirut became the scene of unspeakable carnage, Reagan cited soldierly courage and determination to find within the debacle inspiration and reassurance. The emotional centerpiece of Reagan's address to the nation after the Beirut bombing became the story of the badly wounded Marine unable to communicate to a high-ranking visitor except by writing on a pad of paper. "Semper Fi," the young Marine scribbled. For Reagan, the small incident spoke volumes. "That marine and all others like him, living and dead, have been faithful to their ideals," he said. In doing so, they "have given every one of us something to live up to.... We cannot and we will not dishonor them now and the sacrifices they've made by failing to remain as faithful to the cause of freedom and the pursuit of peace as they have been."[35]

A week later Reagan returned to this theme. "The world looks to America for leadership. And America looks to the men of its Armed Forces," he remarked. "The motto of the United States Marine Corps: 'Semper Fidelis'—always faithful. Well, the rest of us must remain always faithful to those ideals which so many have given their lives to protect."[36] Showering soldiers with praise and celebrating soldierly values provided a neat device for deflecting attention from blunders directly attributable to the White

House. Reagan understood the political utility of this device and exploited it to the hilt.

This studied regard for all things military played well in Peoria, as evidenced by the consistently high popularity ratings of the Teflon president. No less important, for our purposes, is the fact that similar (and reinforcing) attitudes also played well at the box office.

Measuring shifts in the cultural climate may be a notoriously inexact science, but there can be no doubt that prevailing attitudes toward the armed services underwent a sea-change during the Reagan era. Nowhere was this transformation more clearly in evidence than in Hollywood. After a decade of ritualistically portraying soldiers as accomplices in what one prominent film critic called "a harrowing American disgrace," some filmmakers began to evolve a more sympathetic portrayal—in essence producing celluloid adaptations of various Reaganesque motifs.[37] In the course of doing so, they made a great deal of money and—whether intentionally or not—helped to etch more deeply into the popular consciousness interpretations of war, military life, and recent U.S. military history that Reagan himself was enthusiastically promoting.

Three examples, considered in the order of their release and in ascending order of importance, illustrate the point.

The first is *An Officer and a Gentleman*, released in 1982 and that year's third highest-grossing film, earning $129 million. Starring Richard Gere, Debra Winger, and Louis Gossett Jr., the movie follows a hackneyed story line and arrives at an eminently predictable conclusion: the hero, a misfit and loner, overcomes adversity to achieve manhood and find true love.

In this particular rendering, however, the film derives its distinction from its setting: officer candidate school in the U.S. Navy. For Zack Mayo, played by Gere, completion of this grueling course is a must. If he makes it through, he will qualify for pilot training and escape a dead-end existence. With an officer's commission come expectations of status and respectability, as the movie's theme song promises, "up where we belong." In the context of the immediate post-Vietnam era, the premise is a radical one. Service in uniform, the film implied, was a worthy aspiration. It offered a way to be *somebody*.

From start to finish *An Officer and a Gentleman* pays next to no attention to what the U.S. Navy actually exists to do. Apart from its vaguely populist overtones, the movie ignores politics.

The same cannot be said for Sylvester Stallone's Rambo series. Politics saturates the entire Rambo saga, packaging for the screen the Vietnam revisionism that figured so significantly in Ronald Reagan's military mythmaking. As an example of cinematic art, the entire Rambo trilogy is pure dross. Yet it was also a phenomenon, one that among other things enshrined the term "rambo" as an enduring part of colloquial American English.

On more than a few points, the world that John Rambo inhabits bears close comparison with the world of Ronald Reagan. It is one in which soldiers embody honor and love of country but find themselves obliged to fight on two fronts. Abroad they wage war against America's enemies. At home they must contend with oily and conniving politicians. In *First Blood Part II*, for example, Vietnam vet Rambo is recruited to return to Southeast Asia in search of U.S. prisoners of war left behind after the Paris Peace Accords.[38] Slightly demented but devoutly loyal to his comrades, he accepts this dangerous mission, asking only a single question, lifted from Reagan's commentary at the Benavidez award ceremony: "Do we get to win this time?"

A cartoonlike tale of mayhem and derring-do follows, one that proved to be the surprise summer hit of 1985. *Rambo: First Blood Part II* finished as that year's number two film with a total box office gross of $150 million. But apart from making money, what, if anything, was the point of this exercise? The star himself offered a ready explanation. According to Stallone, interviewed at the time of the film's release:

> If you don't have men willing to die for their country, you don't have a country.... There was a bad time a few years ago when some people stopped waving the flag and acted as if America was second rate, as if they were ashamed of it. It was a big mistake.... I love my country. I stand for ordinary Americans, losers a lot of them. They don't understand big, international politics. Their country tells them to fight in Vietnam? They fight.
>
> I'll tell you something else. The men who fought for us in Vietnam got a raw deal. Their country told them to fight. They did their best! They come home and they're scorned. People spit at them. Men who

fight for their country deserve respect. And if you don't give it to them you're in a bad situation.[39]

The point of quoting Stallone at some length is not to credit a Hollywood "action hero" with any special insights into history, politics, or the American mind. Hollywood seldom provides insights; its real business is to echo and amplify. In this instance, Stallone and his collaborators absorbed and played back (thereby validating) perceptions about Vietnam and attitudes regarding soldiers that coincided neatly with the views and agenda of Reagan and his collaborators in Washington. As measured by the response that his film evoked, it seems fair to say that Stallone, like Reagan, had a far more accurate feel for what made ordinary Americans tick than did elite observers who dismissed Rambo, as they did Reagan himself, as either a menace or a buffoon.

Indeed, Reagan himself made a point of letting it be known that he and John Rambo were on the same wavelength. Performing a mike check prior to making a presentation, the former actor and inveterate film fan joked: "Boy, I'm glad I saw Rambo last night. Now I'll know what to do next time."[40]

Yet Rambo's influence on pop culture was as nothing compared to that of Pete "Maverick" Mitchell, fighter pilot extraordinaire. *First Blood Part II* worked because it tapped undercurrents of unresolved anger about the recent past. Due in part to its far more upbeat message, *Top Gun*, released just one year later and starring Tom Cruise as Maverick, succeeded even more spectacularly.

Whereas *First Blood Part II* picked at old wounds, *Top Gun* magically made those wounds disappear. Instead of old resentments, it offered a glittering new image of warfare especially suited to America's strengths. It portrayed this new vision of warfare and those who waged it against a political backdrop shorn of messy ambiguities, and it invested military life with a hipness not seen even in the heyday of World War II propaganda movies. The upshot: *Top Gun* became the number one picture of 1986 with a box office exceeding $176 million.

At the time of its release, unfriendly reviewers dismissed *Top Gun* as "a live action recruiting poster" and "a feature-length 'Be All You Can Be' commercial."[41] Precisely what, *New Yorker* film critic Pauline Kael demanded to know, "is this commercial selling?" Apart from a frisson of homoeroticism, she announced, nothing. "It's just selling, because that's what [the producers and director] know how to do. Selling is what they think moviemaking is about.... *Top Gun* is a recruiting poster that isn't concerned with recruiting but with being a poster."[42]

In fact, critics like Kael failed to appreciate what the film's makers (whatever their professed intentions) actually accomplished. *Top Gun* may have been a poster, but the impact of that poster was profoundly subversive, undermining reigning conceptions of war and military service. *Top Gun* was the poster of Ronald Reagan's dreams, its alluring images and pounding sound track made to order to affirm an emerging consensus about the importance and purposes of American military power.

As narrative, *Top Gun* reprises a host of hoary movie clichés. The story of Maverick's trials, tribulations, and ultimate triumph is of little enduring interest. The same cannot be said, however, about the context in which his story unfolds—the technologically sophisticated, intensely competitive, and exotic world of U.S. Navy carrier aviation. In this particular poster it is the backdrop rather than the action in the foreground that matters.

Specifically, *Top Gun*—a film made with the Navy's enthusiastic cooperation—challenged at least three then-prevailing "truths." In each instance, it substituted a new "truth" that others in the worlds of politics, journalism, and entertainment subsequently refined and repackaged, so that by the beginning of the twenty-first century all three had taken root in the American imagination and together had created a new set of expectations about war and military service.

The first of these images, strangely enough, relates to hygiene. From time immemorial, the battlefield had been a filthy, stinking place. Combat had obliged soldiers to exist in the damp and the mud, at times amidst blood and decay, with lice and flies and rats as their frequent companions. Preparing soldiers to encounter this environment had traditionally involved an emphasis on stress and deprivation. Whether in war or in peace, soldiering had been a dirty, exhausting business, in which rest, clean clothes, decent food, and bathing tended to figure as something of an afterthought.

Now, *Top Gun* suggested, all of that was beginning to change. Order, crispness, and a palpably cool sensibility characterized the world of the modern warrior, it appeared. Warm California sunshine, hot motorcycles and classic cars, leather jackets festooned with military patches and worn as fashion accessories, sleek-bodied aircraft flown by sleek-bodied men, a plentitude of beautiful women: these defined the universe of the naval avia-tor. Maverick and his comrades never missed a meal and got sweaty only when they felt like it.

Along with offering military service as an attractive lifestyle choice, Maverick's adventures as an F-14 pilot conveyed a second "truth," one that pointed to the emergence of a new and distinctive American way of war. As depicted in *Top Gun,* the hallmark of this novel approach to warfare—the element that set it apart—was a heightened emphasis on technology.

By no means did the movie intimate that the warrior himself was becoming ancillary to combat. Indeed, as rendered in *Top Gun,* modern war resembled nothing so much as a throwback to the days of knighthood—brief, violent clashes producing unequivocal results and followed immedi-ately by festive ceremonies honoring the victor. But human strength, bravery, and resourcefulness alone no longer sufficed to win these duels. Victory derived from providing the highly skilled warrior with the latest in weaponry, together producing a quantum leap in speed, agility, and lethal-ity. *Top Gun* made it abundantly clear that here lay America's decisive edge—not only in having at hand the very latest gee-whiz gadgetry but also in possessing a peculiar talent for organizing technology so as to exploit its potential.

Finally, the movie offered its own take on politics. Unlike *An Officer and a Gentleman,* which had ignored politics altogether, and unlike *First Blood Part II,* which had displayed its political cynicism as a sort of badge of honor, *Top Gun* promulgated a conception of politics congenial to this newly reconfigured formulation of U.S. military power.

Maverick and his comrades inhabited a world that permitted little room for uncertainty. Neither history nor any appreciation for interests or moti-vation figured appreciably in explaining how that world worked. Indeed, since dwelling on such concerns might compromise a pilot's ability to make instantaneous life-or-death decisions, it made sense to exclude them from the cockpit. From a fighter pilot's perspective, it sufficed to know that there were good guys and bad guys, the latter in *Top Gun* anonymous but readily identifiable thanks to their black aircraft, black helmets, and opaque visors. In the end, all that really mattered was that the good guys should prevail. By definition, Americans were good guys, and in *Top Gun,* needless to say, they did prevail.

The point is not to suggest that at the time that it was produced *Top*

Gun accurately reflected the political views prevailing in Hollywood. It did not. Nor did the profits earned by the cluster of revisionist movies described here mean that the film world subsequently surrendered to overt militarism. Studios continued to produce films skeptical of or overtly hostile to the military. Indeed, Tom Cruise soon underwent a cinematic metamorphosis, the swaggering fighter pilot becoming an embittered Vietnam vet in *Born on the Fourth of July,* a drama that did nothing to glamorize combat or justify jingoism.

Revisionist films did have an impact on the culture, however, affirming and adding weight to views all but identical to those of Ronald Reagan. They created a second competing narrative, one that depicted soldiers, military life, and war itself in ways that would have been either unthinkable or unmarketable in the immediate aftermath of Vietnam. They therefore contributed in ways not easily measured but still indisputably real to the advent of attitudes conducive to the militarization of U.S. policy in the 1980s and beyond.

Nor did movies provide the sole evidence that in the 1980s the prevailing cultural winds were beginning to shift. At approximately the same time that the films discussed above appeared, a parallel phenomenon was occurring in the realm of popular fiction. The military techno-thrillers clogging bestseller lists during that decade also made their contribution to myth-making.

During the 1980s, the acknowledged master of the techno-thriller, although by no means its sole successful practitioner, was Tom Clancy. Indeed, the genre in its contemporary form dates from the 1984 publication of Clancy's first novel, *The Hunt for Red October.* Endorsed by President Reagan as "a perfect yarn," this book sold three million copies within two years of its appearance and subsequently provided the basis for a hit motion picture.[43] More than that, along with the blockbusters that followed such as *Red Storm Rising* (1986) and *Patriot Games* (1987), it served as a blueprint for what became a flourishing and highly lucrative industry.

As Clancy himself has acknowledged, that industry exists to produce entertainment rather than literature. An action-filled plot rather than fully developed characters or literary artistry is what attracts the genre's legions of fans. That standard plot, whether conceived by Clancy or his many imitators, bears the imprint of an identifiable worldview, and that worldview, in turn, is informed by a well-developed appreciation for U.S. military power.

In any Clancy novel, the international order is a dangerous and threatening place, awash with heavily armed and implacably determined enemies who threaten the United States. That Americans have managed to avoid Armageddon is attributable to a single fact: the men and women of America's uniformed military and of its intelligence services have thus far managed to avert those threats. The typical Clancy novel is an unabashed tribute to the skill, honor, extraordinary technological aptitude, and sheer decency of the nation's defenders. To read *Red Storm Rising* is to enter a world of "virtuous men and perfect weapons," as one reviewer noted. "All the Americans are paragons of courage, endurance and devotion to service and country. Their officers are uniformly competent and occasionally inspired. Men of all ranks are faithful husbands and devoted fathers."[44] For Clancy and other contributors to the genre, refuting the canards casually tossed at soldiers in the aftermath of Vietnam forms part of their self-assigned charter. Indeed, in the contract that he signed for the filming of *Red October*, Clancy stipulated that nothing in the movie show the Navy in a bad light.[45]

As was the case with film, pop fiction as a whole did not become overtly militarized, but certain market-savvy writers correctly discerned and responded to the changing mood that Reagan had promoted. In doing so, they powerfully reinforced the mythmaking that was central to Reagan's larger purpose.[46]

Present-day observers might still argue the relative merits of Reagan's legacy for subsequent U.S. military policy. With regard to the political benefits that he accrued from identifying his own cause with that of "the troops," no room for argument exists. Reagan showed that in post-Vietnam America genuflecting before soldiers and playing to the pro-military instincts of the electorate wins votes.

Given their pronounced political utility, neither the myths that Reagan conjured up—about past American wars, about the purposes of American military power, and about those who served in uniform—nor the techniques he devised to exploit those myths disappeared when Reagan himself retired from office. Rather they became enshrined as permanent aspects of American political theater. No one did more to affirm the Californian's military mythology and to perpetuate the use of soldiers as political props than did Bill Clinton.

During the Reagan era, Clinton was a rising star in the Democratic Party and aspirant to the presidency. As such, Clinton understood that both his party and he personally had a military problem. To have a shot at becoming president, he had to overcome both.

By the time Reagan left office, Republicans had managed to brand Democrats as national security wimps. Democrats had gotten the United States into Vietnam, had made a hash of things, and then had washed their hands of the mess they had made, leaving it to Republicans to clean up. When it came to military matters, therefore, the Democratic Party was untrustworthy. Worse, among the party rank and file, undercurrents of anti-military sentiment persisted. Democrats didn't understand and didn't much like soldiers—so at least the story went.

The 1988 presidential election, which chose Reagan's successor, affirmed these impressions. The most enduring image to emerge from the campaign, which ended with Vice President George H. W. Bush clobbering his Democratic opponent, Governor Michael Dukakis, was of the diminutive and obviously ill-at-ease Dukakis peering out of the hatch of an M1 Abrams tank. The intent of the photo op had been to counter impressions that the liberal Dukakis might be suspect on defense. Instead it posed a question: would you entrust the nation's security to this man and others of his ilk? Not on your life, came the answer.

Clinton's own problem was, if anything, even more daunting. In the 1960s, he had "opposed and despised" the Vietnam War with a vehemence that, by his own reckoning, he had previously reserved for racism. The position that he had staked out as a young man was nuanced but clear: Clinton counted himself among the "many fine people [who] have come to find themselves still loving their country but loathing the military."[47] Despising the war and loathing the military, he had maneuvered adroitly to avoid military service. In a moral if not strictly legal sense he was a draft-dodger.

When Clinton's chance at the brass ring came in 1992, he knew that he had to erase the memory of Dukakis's tank ride and show that on national security Americans could count on his party to do the right thing. And without renouncing his stance on Vietnam—essential to his bona fides as a Democrat—he had to assure a majority of American voters that he shared in the now-prevailing admiration for those serving in the armed forces. In short, to be competitive against an incumbent like George Bush, himself a war hero and proven war leader, Clinton needed to make a persuasive case that when it came to military matters the Democratic Party and its candidate were sound. This was the politics of the issue. Lurking behind the politics were other implications; simply put, these extended well beyond simply determining the outcome of a particular election.

We have already noted that in terms of U.S. military posture and priorities the end of the Cold War was the great turning point that wasn't. During the administration of George H. W. Bush, General Colin Powell and the Joint Chiefs of Staff had capitalized on their just-refurbished prestige to preempt serious debate. Any reassessment of basic policy might have undermined the status quo, which the generals were determined at all costs to preserve. In the first presidential election of the post–Cold War era, Bill Clinton tacitly signaled his support of this effort. From Clinton's perspective, to invite such a reassessment—raising first-order questions about the implications of a democracy asserting the prerogatives of "world's sole superpower," of organizing statecraft around expectations of permanent military supremacy, of abandoning the tradition of the citizen-soldier in favor of a permanent class of warrior professionals—would have entailed great risk. Given the reigning political dynamic, such a debate could be expected to work to his opponent's advantage, not his own. With his eyes fixed firmly on the prize, Clinton made sure that no such debate occurred.

Instead, tearing a sheet out of the Reagan playbook, the candidate offered reassuring myths and his own variant of history with the warts removed. Proposing in December 1991 "A New Covenant for American Security," candidate Clinton began by situating himself relative to the history of his times:

> I was born nearly half a century ago at the dawn of the Cold War, a time of great change, enormous opportunity, and uncertain peril. At a time when Americans wanted nothing more than to come home and resume lives of peace and quiet, our country had to summon the will for a new kind of war—containing an expansionist and hostile Soviet Union which vowed to bury us. We had to find ways to rebuild the economies of Europe and Asia, encourage a worldwide movement toward independence, and vindicate our nation's principles in the world against yet

another totalitarian challenge to liberal democracy. Thanks to the unstinting courage and sacrifice of the American people, we were able to win that Cold War.[48]

It was an account that retrospectively designated all Americans—himself not least among them—Cold Warriors in good standing. Clinton in effect inverted Reagan, his rendering of his times excising any reference to controversy or dissension. Faced with the threat of totalitarianism, "we" had acted as one and had prevailed.

But that was the past. In the lengthy presentation that followed, the candidate outlined his views on the security challenges just ahead.

In many respects, the speech was a typically wonkish mélange of ideas, the real intent of which was to convey three reassuring messages. First, it promised that Clinton could be counted on not only to maintain but even to enhance U.S. military strength. Chock-full of references to space-based communications, strategic airlift, smart weapons, and the need for more flexible power projection capabilities, it suggested that here was a candidate possessing a keen grasp of ideas then au courant among defense specialists. In fact, few of these ideas survived contact with reality once Clinton was safely elected. But that was beside the point.

Second, the speech put to rest any doubts about the candidate's willingness to use force. On this score, Clinton was unambiguous. He was not an anti-war candidate. He forthrightly commended President Bush for ejecting the Iraqi invaders from Kuwait. Faced with a comparable threat, he would act with comparable vigor and dispatch. He was, after all, a new kind of Democrat, one who understood the value and the role of military power. "To protect our interests and our values, sometimes we have to stand and fight," he allowed. On this point, Clinton proved true to his word; as president, he intervened with greater frequency in more places for more varied purposes than any of his predecessors.

Finally, the speech made clear where Clinton stood in relation to the American soldier. On this point the candidate concluded and finally rolled Vietnam into view. He did this not by referencing the war itself but by recalling the parade that as governor he had organized in Little Rock to welcome the troops home after Operation Desert Storm. To participate in this victory celebration, Clinton had invited not only the veterans of the

Gulf War but the veterans of prior American wars as well. Attended by over a hundred thousand people, the event became for Clinton a memorable one.

> I'll never forget how moved I was as I watched them march down the street to our cheers, and saw the Vietnam veterans finally being given the honor they deserved all along. The divisions we have lived with for the last two decades seemed to fade away amid the common outburst of triumph and gratitude.

Extending to the veterans of Vietnam the honor that they had deserved all along, Clinton thereby placed himself in the camp that Reagan had inhabited all along. Thus did the candidate make clear his view of the American soldier. In his eagerness to become president, Clinton wanted it known that he stood where Reagan had stood: always and everywhere with "the troops."

Chapter Five

ONWARD

THE UNITED STATES of America remains today, as it has always been, a deeply, even incorrigibly, Christian nation. Well before 1776, Americans claimed for themselves a pivotal role in the panoramic drama of salvation achieved through the death and resurrection of Jesus Christ. Indeed, the American story begins with the forging of a special covenant. God singled out Americans to be His new Chosen People. He charged them with the task of carving out of the wilderness a New Jerusalem. He assigned to them unique responsibilities to serve as agents of His saving grace. America was to become, in John Winthrop's enduring formulation of 1630, "as a city upon a hill," its light illuminating the world. Present-day Americans beyond counting hold firm to these convictions. Even among citizens oblivious to or rejecting its Christological antecedents, widespread, almost automatic support for this doctrine of American Exceptionalism persists.

In that sense, the continuities in American history are striking and impressive. At the crossroads of religion and politics, little of consequence appears to have changed. From the age of Winthrop to the age of George W. Bush, an abiding religious sensibility has informed America's image of itself and of its providential mission.

In other respects, however, change has been pervasive and consequential. In the complex genealogy of American Protestantism, the assertive and muscular Puritanism of the seventeenth century has long since given way to something that John Winthrop would scarcely recognize. The lineal descendents of the Puritans are today's Congregationalists and Unitarian

Universalists—inclusive, proudly heterodox, dwindling in overall numbers, and politically anemic.

As these and other mainstream denominations vacated the public square that they once dominated, others have vied to take their place. In recent decades, none have done so with greater energy and effect than the churches constituting modern Protestant evangelicalism.[1] In the United States today, evangelicals are numerous, intensely devout, and politically engaged. Out of a total population of some 290 million, approximately 100 million Americans define themselves as evangelicals.[2] In comparison with the rest of their fellow citizens, they are more likely to vote, and although by no means a monolithic bloc, evangelicals—white evangelicals in particular—tend to be conservative and to vote Republican.[3] In national politics, they wield enormous clout.

The churches and related institutions constituting the contemporary evangelical movement are of particular interest to this account because of the way that their aspirations touched on matters relating to military institutions and the uses of American power. The calamity triggered by Vietnam and the 1960s—in the eyes of those who viewed that calamity as one that persisted long after the fall of Saigon—had several dimensions. It was a foreign policy crisis but also a domestic crisis. It was a cultural crisis but also a moral one. It touched on matters that were immediate and personal—family and the relationship of men to women, for example—while also raising profound questions about national purpose and collective identity. No group in American society felt more keenly the comprehensive nature of this crisis than did Protestant evangelicals. It was here, among committed Christians dismayed by the direction that the country appeared to be taking, that the reaction to Vietnam as a foreign policy failure and to Vietnam as a manifestation of cultural upheaval converged with greatest effect.

Certain in their understanding of right and wrong, growing in numbers, affluence, and sophistication, and determined to reverse the nation's perceived decline, conservative evangelicals after the 1960s assumed the role of church militant. Abandoning their own previously well established skepticism about the morality of force and inspired in no small measure by their devotion to Israel, they articulated a highly permissive interpretation of the just war tradition, the cornerstone of Christian thinking about warfare. And they developed a considerable appetite for wielding armed might on behalf of righteousness, more often than not indistinguishable from America's own interests.

Moreover, at least some evangelicals looked to the armed services to play a pivotal role in saving America from internal collapse. In a decadent and morally confused time, they came to celebrate the military itself as a bastion of the values required to stem the nation's slide toward perdition: respect for tradition, an appreciation for order and discipline, and a willingness to sacrifice self for the common good. In short, evangelicals looked to soldiers to model the personal qualities that citizens at large needed to rediscover if America were to reverse the tide of godlessness and social decay to which the 1960s had given impetus.

Militant evangelicals imparted religious sanction to the militarization of U.S. policy and helped imbue the resulting military activism with an aura of moral legitimacy. Policy options that policymakers advocated as feasible and necessary, Christians discerned as right and good. The aim of this chapter is to tell that story.

The relationship between Christianity and war has been a tangled one. Despite Christ's admonition to love one's neighbor and to turn the other cheek, Christians historically have slaughtered their fellow men, to include their fellow Christians, in breathtakingly large numbers.

Still, during the course of the twentieth century, the experience of two world wars and the prospect of a third fought with nuclear weapons had served to revive tendencies toward Christian pacifism. This was true not only in the Protestant mainstream but with regard to Roman Catholicism as well.[4] Vietnam only served to reinforce these propensities.

Even before the turning point of the 1968 Tet Offensive, the establishment church—represented in particular by the Protestant denominations comprising the National Council of Churches, but also increasingly by the hierarchy of American Catholicism—had grown weary of the war and dubious about the orthodox interpretations of the Cold War that ostensibly had made U.S. intervention necessary in the first place. More broadly, when it came to the utility of force and the importance of sustaining American military strength, these churches professed increasing ambivalence. In making the case for military action, official Washington could no longer count on the leaders of mainline churches to offer their automatic endorsement or at least to withhold judgment. By the latter stages of the Vietnam War, to the extent that the Christian voice was making itself heard in that corner of the public square reserved for national security questions, the message expressed was one of skepticism rather than support.[5] Evangelical denominations were the exception to the rule. To the very end an overwhelming majority remained steadfast in their support of the war and of those who waged it.

There was substantial irony here. Evangelicals had not always been gung ho about soldiers and armed conflict. Nor as a matter of course had they courted political controversy. Indeed, during the first half of the twentieth century, the reverse had been true. For generations, American evangelicals had cultivated a robust anti-war tradition. Furthermore, they had tended to take a rather dim view of soldiering, seeing the profanity, harsh conditions, loose women, and cheap whiskey associated with camp life in the Old Army as not especially conducive to Christian living.[6] Nor had they sought to engage in collective political action or to attach themselves to a particular political party. Indeed, as a matter of course, the several evangelical denominations had tended to keep one another at arm's length. After the humiliation of the Scopes Trial in 1925 evangelicals had steered clear of partisan politics altogether.[7]

Beginning with World War II and spurred by reform-minded fundamentalists such as J. Elwin Wright of the New England Fellowship and Will Houghton, president of the Moody Bible Institute, all that began to change. In 1942, these reformers founded the National Association of Evangelicals, intended among other things to unite and energize conservative Christians and to refurbish their public image.[8] As one historian has observed, "A generational retreat from the world was being called off."[9] A process of engaging the world—with an eye toward transforming it—had commenced.

The advent of the Cold War accelerated this process. By the 1950s, the fight against atheistic Communism drew evangelicals away from the margins of American life toward its center. Nothing more clearly testifies to evangelicalism's rising profile than does the advent of Billy Graham. Beginning in World War II as a leader of the fledgling Youth for Christ movement, Reverend Graham catapulted himself within a few short years into national prominence, becoming a spiritual counselor to presidents and leading members of Congress and something of a political power broker able, it was said, to swing millions of votes. Graham stood foursquare for the traditional evangelical values of biblical inerrancy and personal conversion, but he was also a vigorous critic of Communism and an equally vigorous and forthright defender of the American way of life. In the context of the early Cold War, this necessarily meant being pro-military, both in terms of ministering to the needs of soldiers—Graham, for example, was prominent among the clergy visiting the troops in both Korea and Vietnam—and in terms of supporting government policies when it came to building up the U.S. arsenal or using force.[10]

In the 1950s, that is, evangelicals were conservative in the sense that they endorsed the status quo.[11] Graham and other leading evangelical preachers such as Harold John Ockenga and Charles E. Fuller sought to affirm rather than critique. In the Cold War against the Soviet Union and in the hot wars fought in Korea and Vietnam, Graham provided Christian Americans with authoritative assurances that the United States was doing the Lord's work, a message warmly welcomed in the corridors of power.[12]

Yet as Graham and other evangelical leaders were busily courting politicians and being romanced in return, the country as a whole suddenly veered away from Zion and lunged headlong toward Babylon. At least so it appeared from a conservative Christian perspective.

In November 1960, Richard Nixon, Graham's favorite politician, lost the White House to a Catholic, in evangelical eyes not an auspicious development. In August 1974, that same Nixon, who in eventually gaining the presidency had won favor with conservative Christians by instituting weekly religious services in the White House, resigned his office in disgrace. Sandwiched in between these two signal events were other developments that evangelicals could only view with consternation: a sexual revolution occurring amidst an atmosphere of growing permissiveness; new campaigns for "women's lib," homosexual rights, and the promotion of "alternative lifestyles"; Supreme Court decisions legalizing abortion and banishing prayer from public schools; *Time* magazine's authoritative pronouncement that "God Is Dead"; and, of course, the widespread protest and attacks on authority fueled by the Vietnam War.[13]

As seen by conservative Christians, all of these developments testified to a nation turning away from God. The upshot was to send evangelicals into political opposition. The old-time religion became the new counterculture. Returning the United States to the path of righteousness became the professed aim of a new generation of politically astute and organizationally adept evangelical leaders. For a time, perhaps the most prominent among them was the Reverend Jerry Falwell, founder in 1979 of the Moral Majority, and the evangelical equivalent of Norman Podhoretz as energizer, point man, and lightning rod for critics. Others included Jim Bakker, Jim Dobson, Tim LaHaye, Pat Robertson, and James Robison, each possessing a knack for mobilizing Christians disenchanted with the direction in which the country was headed. As they saw it, the national trends that evangelicals deplored reflected the machinations of a minority—a New Class of liberal elites—rather than the considered preferences of the people as a whole.[14] "We have enough votes to run the country," Robertson boasted in 1980. "And when the people say, 'We've had enough,' we are going to take over."[15] Robertson and other evangelical leaders aimed to rouse the mass of God-fearing Christians to say "enough" and to take the country back.[16]

"Pro-life, pro-family, pro-moral, pro-American": these, according to Falwell, were the movement's watchwords.[17] In an operational sense, however, there was much more. A secondary but still consequential aspect of their campaign addressed specifically military concerns. "These evangelicals set down precise requirements that they find spelled out in the Bible," reported Kenneth A. Briggs of the New York Times in evident amazement. "None is more vigorously preached than the lesson on military preparedness to combat Communism."[18] Briggs was indulging in a bit of journalistic hyperbole, but was not entirely off the mark. Although a determination to reclaim America for Christ best explains the evangelical thrust into politics, the back story had distinctively military overtones.[19]

Never wavering in their support for the Vietnam War, Christian conservatives saw the rise of anti-war sentiment, popular disparagement of the armed services, and the wasting away of American military strength as combat in Southeast Asia dragged on as indicators of the path down which the United States was headed.[20] Vietnam was persuading the nation's best and brightest to turn their backs on America's soldiers. For their part, when the war began evangelicals "regarded military service as not only compatible with Christian belief and practice but as an obligation of American citizenship," and they did not budge from that conviction.[21] As late as 1969, Falwell was still touting the GI fighting in Vietnam as "a champion for Christ," a judgment, it seems fair to say, not in accord with the views then prevailing on campuses of the Ivy League.[22]

The divide could hardly have been clearer, nor from the evangelical point of view could the stakes have been greater. All the evidence suggested that America's ability to stand up to the threat posed by atheistic Communism and even its willingness to make such a stand were waning. Were this not bad enough, at least as evangelicals saw it, military weakness and anti-militarism itself were also symptomatic of the nation's larger moral affliction. Thus Falwell, elucidating in 1980 on "the grim truth that America, our beloved country, is indeed sick," pointed his finger first at "the tide of permissiveness and moral decay that is crushing in on our society from every side," but he also argued that decay had specifically military manifestations.

> The United States is for the first time in my lifetime... no longer the military might of the world....We are not committed to victory. We are not committed to greatness. We have lost the will to stay strong.... Because of the overwhelming conventional and nuclear strength of the Soviet Union, it is now possible that the Soviet government could demand our capitulation. Our unwillingness to pay the price of a nuclear conflict could well force our leadership into lowering our flag and surrendering the American people to the will of the Communist Party in Moscow. [23]

The essential response to this crisis required both moral and military restoration. "I believe," Falwell continued,

> that Americans want to see this country come back to basics, back to values, back to biblical morality, back to sensibility, and back to patriotism.... Communists know that in order to take over a country they must first see to it that a nation's military strength is weakened and that its morals are corrupted so that its people have no will to resist wrong. ...Our enemies know that when we are weak morally, and when we have lost our will to fight, we are in a precarious position for takeover. ...By militarily disarming our country, we have actually been surrendering our rights and our sovereignty and, as the Soviets would soon like to see—our freedoms and our liberties.... America [today]... is at the threshold of destruction or surrender....Our faltering defenses... [show that we are] permitting a godless society to emerge in America [and that] we are sowing corruption in our own land and are reaping instability in our nation....A political leader, as a minister of God, is a

revenger to execute wrath upon those who do evil. Our government has the right to use its armaments to bring wrath upon those who would do evil by hurting other people.[24]

Other conservative Christian writers were, if anything, even more strident, emphasizing that it was incumbent upon evangelicals to rescue not only their country but also its beleaguered military. The believing Christian was called upon to wage two wars at once—not only against the godless enemy abroad but also against those at home intent on dragging the country down into sinful ways. The problem was all of a piece.

In his 1979 book *America at the Crossroads,* the evangelical writer John Price characterized the decline in U.S. military power after Vietnam as "virtually unprecedented in world history." During the 1970s, the United States had been "disarming on the installment plan" and in doing so had set in motion a series of events "literally leading to America's last days as a free nation." Communism was everywhere on the march, whereas the United States was "beset by disorder, weak in spirit, and unsure of itself," and thus "an ideal captive state." As a result, "Soviet occupation of America before the end of this century" loomed as a real possibility. This American vulnerability was a direct consequence of American society having fallen upon sinful ways. "When we forgot God," wrote Price, "we lost our national strength. If we refuse to repent, we may lose our freedom." To avoid the ultimate divine "chastisement" of foreign occupation required a reconciliation with God and a revival of Christian values. Only then might "aroused Christians... motivate an aroused Congress to adequately provide for our defense."[25]

Echoing this assessment was Rene Noorbergen and Ralph W. Hood's 1980 book *The Death Cry of an Eagle,* which found abundant evidence that a decadent America was in an accelerating spiral of decline. Turning away from God and toward corruption and licentiousness, the United States was in danger of suffering the same fate as Babylon, Greece, Rome, and other great civilizations of the ancient past. Not least among the symptoms pointing toward collapse, according to the authors, was "the shocking discovery that global power, once thought to be the monopoly of the United States, is fast slipping from this country's grasp." With American military power "rapidly dwindling," they described "Soviet supremacy [was] already a reality." Only a comprehensive program of moral and cultural renewal could stave off disaster.[26]

In a similar vein, the Christian conservative policy analysts G. Russell Evans and C. Greg Singer began their 1982 book *The Church and the Sword* by declaring that "the day of reckoning is upon us." On the one hand, there loomed a Soviet Union that "is armed to the teeth, is now militarily superior, is continuing her buildup, has repeatedly stated her intentions of dominating the world, and is threatening America's interests and security on every front—and even more important, is gravely and perniciously imperiling Christianity itself." On the other hand were American liberals and especially liberal Protestant churches whose objectives "have closely paralleled those of the Communist Party." It was liberals who by promoting "pacifism, disarmament, the Equal Rights Amendment, abortion on demand, more welfare spending, the Panama Canal treaties, dump Taiwan, and more school busing" had brought the country to the brink of ruin. For Evans and Singer, the solution was self-evident: it was necessary to rebuild America's defenses while also reviving traditional values, the one being all but synonymous with the other.[27]

Evans and Singer also linked the revival of U.S. military power to the nation's fulfillment of its larger providential mission. Unlike the Soviet army, which "supports revolution and the control and enslavement of peoples," they noted that "America's might is for self-defense and defense of freedom and, in many respects, for the defense of the faith—never for conquest or aggression."[28] In fact, however, from an evangelical perspective, defending freedom and defending the faith could easily fuel military ambitions as grandiose as anything that the leadership of the Kremlin had ever entertained.

In *One Nation Under God,* another critique of post-Vietnam policy written from an evangelical perspective, Rus Walton made plain the transcendent context in which Christian America wielded military power. "This world is engaged in a death struggle," wrote Walton.

We, as Christians, cannot ignore the battle any more than we can ignore the criminal on our streets. To ignore is not to keep the peace; it is to entertain the enemy, to thrust the world into darkness.... Our Savior and our King instructs us to love our enemies. Yes! But nowhere in Scripture, nowhere, does the Lord God tell us to love His enemies or to make covenant with them in any way.... [Today's enemy is] *atheistic communism.* It poses the severest threat, the most sustained threat, this nation and the free world has ever known. . . . Let others seek to remove that great old hymn "Onward Christian Soldiers" from their hymnals. Let us go forth, the Cross of Jesus going on before. In the final analysis, He must lead us against the foe, at home and abroad. The battle is His. It has been; it is now. And *His* will be the victory! In the meantime we go forth—commissioned, instructed, inspired—to seek dominion in His name and for His holy sake.[29]

To emphasize further the desirability of a resurgent America seeking dominion, Walton cited the work of Charles W. Lowry, a clergyman who chaired the Foundation for Religious Action in the Social and Civil Order. In his book *Communism and Christ,* Lowry had described the United States as "a strategic agent in continuing God's recreative [*sic*] work in Christ." According to Lowry, the Cold War had handed Americans "the mightiest opportunity in history."

It is not merely the chance to throw back the forces of reaction and to repel the evil and demonic dream of a single, man-governed totalitarian world. Nothing negative will suffice. . . . The opportunity of our great country . . . is to lead faltering mankind beyond the twilight and the hovering darkness into the sunshine of a larger, happier day. . . . It is to extend and ever-more to consolidate in the affairs of men the Christian Revolution.[30]

The scholar Michael Lienesch has credited Walton and others with articulating for evangelicals "a crusade theory of warfare." This theory took precedence over the established just war tradition, which mandated that force be used for defensive purposes only. In the circumstances that existed after Vietnam, it would not do for God's strategic agent to remain passive, waiting on events. According to Lienesch, conservative Christian analysts found scriptural sanctions for striking the first blow. As they saw it, "preventive war has biblical precedents."[31] God was literally on America's side, and He had empowered Americans to act on His behalf.

In a pre-9/11 era, this seemed like a radical if not outlandish proposition, one completely at odds with American tradition—proof that when it came to national security strategy evangelicals tended to be slightly deranged. In fact, in their advocacy of preventive war, Christian conservatives were merely a little ahead of their time.

As the writings of Walton and others suggest, many evangelicals view the requirements of U.S. national security in the here-and-now and the final accomplishment of Christ's saving mission at the end of time as closely related if not indistinguishable. How, exactly, are these two seemingly separate things connected?

At the very point where national security and eschatology converge lies Israel, both as nation-state and as promise of the imminent fulfillment of biblical prophecy. Conservative Christians in the United States have an obsession with the Jewish state.[32] In 1997, Prime Minister Benjamin Netanyahu told a gathering of three thousand American evangelicals that "we have no greater friends and allies than the people sitting in this room." The "roars of approval, multiple standing ovations and shouts of 'amen' and 'hallelujah'" that the Israeli prime minister's remarks elicited suggested that he knew whereof he spoke.[33]

Underlying this preoccupation with Israel is the doctrine of premillennial dispensationalism, to which numerous (but by no means all) American evangelicals subscribe. In essence, this theology finds in scripture the foretelling of a spectacular—indeed, horrific—sequence of events culminating in the last days: a period of great tribulation giving rise to the Antichrist but leading to his destruction in a great battle at Armageddon and finally to Christ's Second Coming and the inauguration of a thousand years of peace and justice. Crucial to this sequence is the return of Jews to the Holy Land. In that sense, the founding of the state of Israel in 1948 started the clock ticking—this was a central premise of Hal Lindsey's 1970s mega-bestseller *The Late Great Planet Earth*—and suggested to many evangelicals that the end days are indeed fast approaching.[34]

Dispensationalists, who themselves number in the millions, welcome this prospect and want to do their part in keeping events on track.[35] As one consequence, the Religious Right has been unflinchingly loyal to the Jewish state, eager to support Israel in the performance of its prescribed role (although according to the most commonly accepted script, before the Millennium arrives all Jews will either convert to Christianity or be killed off).[36]

In the context of what Washington can or should do to advance the Middle East peace process, much has been made of these Christian Zionists—their pronounced affinity for Israeli hard-liners and their purported ability to prevent any U.S. administration from compelling Israel to make concessions it does not care to make.

Our interest here is of a different order. It is to suggest that as a result of the Religious Right's fetish for the Jewish state, the distinctive Israeli strategic style—the way that Israelis conceive of military power and its uses—has colored conservative Christian thinking about these same subjects. By extension, this evangelical appropriation of Israeli strategic precepts has altered the terms of religious discourse about war and the use of force in ways that have contributed to the militarization of U.S. policy.

For reasons rooted in geography, demographics, and history, when it comes to security, Israelis perhaps prudently are inclined to put their trust in guns rather than expressions of good will. Furthermore, from the founding of the Jewish state onward, the Israeli way of war has placed a premium on early offensive action. Small and outnumbered, Israel in the first decades of its existence could ill afford to let its enemies dictate the terms of any armed conflict. Survival, therefore, mandated a forward-leaning military posture with an eye toward eliminating threats before they could fully develop.[37]

In June 1967, that meant preemption, getting in the first blow against Arab armies massing to invade Israel. Victory in the Six Day War marked Israel's emergence as the Middle East's strongest military power. Despite this position of dominance, the Israeli preference for shooting first remained deeply ingrained.

In June 1981, for example, Israel struck without warning to destroy a partially constructed Iraqi nuclear reactor that might someday have produced fissile materials for an Arab bomb. A year later, in an act of calculated aggression, Israeli mechanized forces invaded Lebanon, a militarily insignificant neighbor whose very weakness the government of Menachem Begin deemed a threat to Israeli security.

These were highly controversial episodes. Evaluated in terms of the just-war tradition, Israeli military actions defy easy moral justification. The argument that Israel in either instance acted in self-defense is at best a stretch. Claims that Israel resorted to force only as a last resort do not withstand close scrutiny. Most egregiously, in clear violation of the *jus in bello* dictum of noncombatant immunity, Operation Peace in Galilee, the Israeli incursion into Lebanon, resulted in widespread civilian casualties.

Whether or not pragmatic considerations justified the use of force against Iraq and Lebanon is not at issue. Indeed, one can make a plausible case that full compliance with every aspect of just-war requirements would compel Israel to accept a level of risk that no other nation would tolerate.

What is of interest here is the response that Israel's disregard for the just-war tradition evoked from American evangelicals. That response was to insist upon the unqualified righteousness of Israeli military actions.[38] In 1967, evangelicals delighted in Israeli territorial gains made as a result of the Six Day War, particularly the seizure of East Jerusalem from Jordan. Believing that the restoration of the Old City to Jewish control is a precondition of the Second Coming, dispensationalists were not inclined to quibble over the legality of annexation; this was conquest in service of a larger cause.[39] Similarly, in bombing Iraq's nuclear reactor and invading Lebanon, Israel enjoyed uncritical support from the preponderance of American evangelicals.[40] More recently still, conservative Christians have adamantly rejected any criticism of the measures that Israel has employed in its efforts to suppress the Palestinian uprising.[41]

In effect, American evangelical support for Israel created loopholes in the just-war tradition. For some countries—those designated for special roles in God's program of salvation—the usual rules do not apply. Israel is one such special country. When it uses force to advance its own interests, it is in fact operating within what conservative Christians see as a far wider framework. Wittingly or not, a militant Israel is advancing the cause of a militant, even militaristic Messiah not at all shy about using the sword to complete His saving mission.[42]

Thus when it comes to war evangelicals grant Israel a special dispensation. Confronted with violence between Israel and its neighbors, writes one scholar, "the Christian Zionist does not have to rework the ethical arithmetic ... in order to reckon whose side he is on." To support Israel "cannot, by definition, ever be incompatible with the will of God."[43] But conservative Christians clearly believe that the United States is another special country—perhaps the only other. For both Israel and the United States, therefore, restrictions on the use of force become less stringent.

For conservative Christians after Vietnam, the prerequisite for fulfilling America's mandate as divine agent was the immediate reconstitution of U.S. military power. In this regard, evangelicals saw rearmament not simply as a prudential matter but as akin to a religious imperative. In his sequel to *The Late Great Planet Earth*, Hal Lindsey made this point emphatically. In *The 1980s: Countdown to Armageddon*, which spent twenty-one weeks on the *New York Times* bestseller list, he surveyed the "crisis of internal decay" and the "crisis of military weakness" confronting the country and found the antidote to both in rearmament. Lindsey believed that "the Bible supports building a powerful military force. And the Bible is telling the U.S. to become strong again." It was incumbent upon Americans "to use our vast and superior technology to create the world's strongest military power."[44]

Lindsey intended his reflections—published in the election year of 1980—to do more than simply educate. *Countdown to Armageddon* was a call to action. "If you are a Christian reading this book," he concluded, "then it is up to you to get involved in preserving this country." Involvement meant political activism. "We need to elect men and women who will have the courage to make the tough decisions needed to insure out nation's survival.... We need people who see how important a strong military is to keeping peace for us and what remains of the free world."[45]

Ironically, the unnamed target of Lindsey's slings and arrows was himself a devout evangelical.

Jimmy Carter's defeat of Gerald Ford four years earlier had for the first time ever elevated a born-again Christian to the White House. In the eyes of political observers, the victory of this Baptist Sunday school teacher affirmed that evangelicals had indeed arrived and were now a force to reckon with. *Newsweek* even declared 1976 "the Year of the Evangelical."

Once in office, however, Carter disappointed his coreligionists, failing to stand up for core evangelical convictions. Carter was chief among the "godless, spineless leaders" who, according to Jerry Falwell, had "brought our nation floundering to the brink of death," leaving "America depraved, decadent, and demoralized."[46] Other Christian conservatives might not have endorsed the overheated language, but they shared the sentiment. As a consequence, well before 1980 most white evangelicals had abandoned Carter and in doing so cut their remaining ties to the Democratic Party.

Disillusionment with Carter did not cause evangelicals to withdraw from politics. It did mean that henceforth the great majority—African Americans excepted—saw the Republican Party as a more likely venue through which to achieve their political ends.[47] Thus was born the Religious Right.

In 1980, Ronald Reagan, although twice married, an indifferent parent, and an irregular churchgoer, presented himself to evangelicals as one who understood their message and embraced their cause. In private conversation with Falwell, Reagan let it be known that he too believed that "we are approaching Armageddon...maybe not in my lifetime or yours, but in the near future."[48] Campaigning against the incumbent Carter in August 1980, Reagan told the Religious Roundtable's National Affairs Briefing, "I know that you can't endorse *me*. But...I want you to know that I endorse *you*."[49] The stratagem worked, to great effect.[50] While Norman Podhoretz and his doughty band of literary intellectuals fancied that they had elected Reagan president in 1980, Jerry Falwell and his far larger evangelical following could make a much stronger claim for actually doing so.

What did Christians get in return for that support? In many respects, as was the case with Reagan's neoconservative followers, the answer is, not much. When it came to rhetoric, evangelicals could always count on Reagan to say the right thing and to say it with evident sincerity. When it came to translating words into action, however, they soon discovered that they could count on very little. Whether or not Reagan himself actually believed that abortion was murder, that the alternative to the nuclear family was societal collapse, and that promiscuity, pornography, and the absence of prayer in public schools posed dire threats to the nation, he and his chief aides proved unwilling to expend any serious political capital on behalf of those causes. The so-called Reagan Revolution offered Christian conservatives access without influence. Leaders of the Religious Right got handsome Oval Office photos suitable for framing but essentially no substantive help on the family-values agenda that was their highest priority.[51]

To the extent that Reagan did repay evangelicals for their support—enabling them to avoid the conclusion that they had been completely taken—that repayment came on the military front. Reagan's increases in defense spending, his emphasis on patriotism and appreciation for soldiers, and his counteroffensive against the "evil empire" all found favor with the Religious Right.

As a result, although privately grousing about the White House dragging its feet on social issues, conservative Christians praised Reagan's military policies and thus helped to sustain them. "We have a president who
wants to build up our military strength. But he is catching it all from all
sides," complained Falwell, citing "the 'freeze-niks,' 'ultra-libs' and 'unilateral disarmers,'" who opposed the president's plans for rearmament. It was
incumbent on evangelicals, he concluded, to let Reagan and his team "know
that you are with them."[52] Here is the one place the evangelical campaign
against the prevailing culture bore substantive fruit: millions of believing
Christians provided the core political constituency on which Reagan could
count to support both his overall military build-up and even his most controversial national security initiatives.[53]

On matters related to war and peace, the post-Vietnam opinions offered
by the mainstream churches, including the Roman Catholic Church, came
in various shades of gray—the implication being that making moral judgments was a complex and difficult matter. In contrast, evangelical discourse
emphasized black-and-white. With leaders like Falwell shouting down contrary views, questions of right and wrong were easily discerned and easily
settled.

As a result, when Reagan urged the National Association of Evangelicals, which in the 1980s already had four million members, "to speak out
against those who would place the United States in a position of military
and moral inferiority," that organization and its adherents took heed.[54] In
the 1980s, to counter the views expressed on national security issues by
mainstream churches, the NAE instituted a "Peace, Freedom, and Security
Studies" program. It scoffed at calls for nuclear disarmament and threw the
weight of evangelical opinion behind Reagan's interventionist foreign policy in places like Central America.[55] In 1983, Falwell's Moral Majority was
running full-page ads in major newspapers proclaiming that "we cannot
afford to be number two in defense. But, sadly enough, that's where we are
today. Number two. And fading!" The ads derided those who questioned
the rationale and need for the Reagan defense buildup.[56]

Most significant in this regard was the campaign that evangelicals
mounted on behalf of the Strategic Defense Initiative, President Reagan's
vision of a defensive shield to protect Americans from the threat posed by
long-range ballistic missiles. SDI became the ultimate expression of the
post-Vietnam divide between hawks and doves. Just as the abortion contro-

versy was freighted with larger cultural implications, so too did the wrangling over Star Wars, as opponents dubbed it, involve much more than questions about cost and technological feasibility. Implicit in Reagan's proposal, unveiled in March 1983, was a reassertion of national innocence; it was simply wrong, he believed, that Americans should go to bed each night contemplating the prospect of nuclear annihilation. The logic of Mutual Assured Destruction that tried to make a virtue of this perverse circumstance was, in Reagan's view, unconscionable. SDI promised to void this immoral strategy by placing America beyond the reach of any would-be adversary. By extension, the restoration of invulnerability would reaffirm America's uniqueness among all the world's nations and among all nations in history. Star Wars, in other words, would revalidate American Exceptionalism. Innocence, invulnerability, uniqueness: all of these stuck in the craw of the left. All evoked sustained applause from the right, in particular from evangelicals.[57]

Thus Jerry Falwell, along with Jimmy Swaggert, Jim Bakker, and an assortment of other evangelical leaders, formed a "Religious Coalition for a Moral Defense Policy" to promote ballistic missile defense. According to Falwell's coalition, SDI was the "only moral strategic nuclear military policy." For its part, the Coalition for the Strategic Defense Initiative organized a statement of support from 2000 conservative clergy who flatly declared that SDI was "morally obligatory." As one scholar has aptly noted, Star Wars became for evangelicals a "powerful symbol of deliverance." By erecting this military shield, the nation would reclaim and reshape its destiny, an aim dear to the heart of conservative Christians.[58]

This military history of the Religious Right contains a second theme that overlaps with and even in some respects anticipates the first. That theme concerns the tacit alliance between evangelicals and the armed services, paralleling the overt alliance between evangelicals and the GOP.

Evangelical awareness of the potential value of such an alliance—and recognition of the potential role of soldiers in facilitating moral renewal at home—dates back to the first half of the Vietnam experience. As early as 1967, for example, an editorial in *Christianity Today*, the leading evangelical periodical, took the National Council of Churches to task for "imply[ing] that men in the armed forces are rather to be pitied than prayed for and supported." When "leftist churches pray for their servicemen," the editorial continued, "these prayers are burdened by an apparent solicitation of God's aid in the fulfillment of a presumably non-Christian vocation." *Christianity Today* rejected this condescending attitude, arguing that

if the churches were really interested, a new type of American layman could be shaped. Servicemen could be moved to earnest participation in the arenas of private morality, social concern, and evangelistic engagement.... [In Vietnam] liberal optimism about human nature and history, and sentimental notions about Communist benevolence and about the dispensability of force in the promotion of peace, do not long survive.... Evangelical churches must shoulder their responsibility in this hour. They can help sons of the Church to rise to new awareness of the claims of the Gospel and of social justice upon every man. And men who have carried those concerns through the jungles of Viet Nam can—when God crowns their devotion to peace—help lead a nation to a better day for both the citizenry and the churches.[59]

More so than other quarters of American life at the time, the evangelical camp also appreciated the dangers of allowing a cleavage to develop between soldiers and society. With "the press and the liberal intelligentsia of America show[ing] less and less respect for the intellect and the activity of men in the armed forces," wrote one contributor to *Christianity Today,* "the Viet Nam veteran is more likely to find his military service a source of embarrassment" than a matter of pride. But scapegoating those who had fought the war promised only to create a class of "lonely, defensive, alienated men." This was not only unjustified but also ill-advised.

We do our church a disservice to condemn a whole body of citizens, creating in them a sense of isolation and helplessness and of shame while flattering ourselves in our fake innocence.... [Instead] we as Christians should seek to create a rapport with the members of that group, for our sake as well as theirs.... We don't want to be left with an army of muscle-flexing killers, a subsidized Mafia for our defense.

If the nation hoped to have an army officered by "responsible, moral, Christ-like leaders," it was incumbent upon Americans to remain engaged with that army. With others in their Vietnam-induced aversion to all things military turning away from that task, it now fell to evangelicals to pick up the slack.[60]

It did not take long for the military itself to recognize the potential benefits of making common cause with conservative Christians. As one scholar has concluded, "the Vietnam War facilitated a dramatic change in evangelicals' image and status within the military. Formerly regarded with skepticism, if not suspicion, evangelicals gained respect and influence within the armed forces as a result of the support they demonstrated for the military services, the war, and the men who fought it."[61]

As a consequence, in very short order the leadership of the armed services began to reciprocate the friendly gestures made by evangelicals. Indeed, ratification of the entente between evangelicals and the officer corps can be dated with some precision: it occurred on May 1, 1972, when the U.S. Military Academy bestowed on Billy Graham its Sylvanus Thayer Award, conferred annually on a citizen who exemplifies the academy's ideals of duty, honor, and country.

To collect his award, the nation's preeminent evangelical journeyed to West Point, the spiritual seat of American military professionalism and an institution whose physical remoteness in the Hudson highlands was then matched by a psychic distance from a country in the throes of great turmoil. By 1972, with many Americans dancing to strange new rhythms, the military academy was finding itself increasingly out of step with society. Eager not to be left marching alone, West Point and the armed services more generally saw evangelicals as a group that marched to a drumbeat not unlike their own. Thus the citation accompanying Graham's award praised him for many things but in particular singled out his firm defense of "traditional values," in the context of the time a phrase loaded with political connotations.[62] Here lay the moral terrain that Christian conservatives and the U.S. Army shared (or fancied that they shared) in common.

The remarks that Graham prepared for the occasion mapped the contours of this ground jointly occupied by good soldiers and good Christians. Warning the assembled cadets that they were beginning their military careers at a moment when "the very survival of the American democratic way of life is at stake," Graham made it clear that the primary threats to that way of life came from within. The "demonstrations, pickets, marches, protests and bombings" of recent years, he said, imperiled the "delicate balance between freedom and order." To save the country from self-destruction, he looked to those who foreswore picketing and protest, to "the men and women who believe in duty, honor, and country—and have a strong faith in God." Graham believed that the values of West Point fused to the values of religious traditionalism might "become the beacon lights to guide our nation through this perilous period."[63]

In the aftermath of Vietnam, evangelicals came to see the military as an enclave of virtue, a place of refuge where the sacred remnant of patriotic Americans gathered and preserved American principles from extinction. (Lending this notion a veneer of plausibility was the fact that the just-created All-Volunteer Force was in the process of rebranding itself as "family friendly." In order to expand the pool of potential recruits and improve retention rates, the armed services were emphasizing childcare centers, youth programs, and better housing for young married soldiers. During the 1970s, senior military leaders were themselves quite literally on the cusp of discovering "family values.")

For their part, the armed forces, feeling themselves to be prime targets in the ongoing culture war, came to see the evangelicals as allies—sharing the same enemies and sharing at least to some degree in a common mission of restoration.

Therefore, just as the politics of the officer corps took on a distinctly conservative (and Republican) hue as a result of Vietnam, so too did its sectarian leanings undergo something of a transformation. Since time immemorial, the unofficial church of the American officer corps had been the unofficial church of the American establishment: Episcopalian.[64] This had not reflected actual religious conviction so much as the collective perception of military professionals about where they fit (or aspired to fit) in the American social hierarchy. Now the officer corps shed its Episcopal coloration, the change having less to do with religious conversion than with recognition that the relationship between the U.S. military and American civilian elites had changed radically.

This evangelical tilt expressed itself in several ways, not least among them in the changing composition of the military chaplaincy. Beginning in Vietnam, as the number of chaplains provided by mainline Protestant denominations dwindled, evangelicals volunteered to make up the difference, an offer that the services were happy to accept.[65] Programs that tended to fall within the purview of the chaplaincy took on an evangelical flavor. Commanders extended a warm welcome to Christian performers who came to entertain and inspire the troops while also opening military installations to teams of evangelical lay ministers who organized programs for soldiers and their families.

After Vietnam, that is to say, on U.S. military posts at home and abroad, evangelicals came to enjoy a privileged place.[66] As the leading student of the military-evangelical entente concludes, those who ministered to the armed forces "succeeded in winning thousands of military men and women to evangelical religion, and through the influence they gained among the military leadership, exerted a significant impact on the armed forces as an institution."[67] As a serving officer in 2004 put it more bluntly, "Christian fundamentalism was the hidden hand that changed the military for the better."[68]

The contemporary observer should be careful not to read into this evangelical alignment with the armed services more than it deserves. Angst-laced descriptions of "soldiers who literally equate being an officer in the U.S. military with duty in God's Army" and who "envision themselves as training for the coming battles of Armageddon" may find occasional affirmation, but do not describe the politico-religious worldview of the officer corps taken as a whole.[69] In the aftermath of 9/11, Lieutenant General William G. Boykin garnered unwanted headlines by telling an audience of evangelicals that "the battle that we're in is a spiritual battle." According to Boykin, "Satan wants to destroy this nation ... and he wants to destroy us as a Christian army."[70] Whatever Satan's actual intentions, it would be a gross error to consider Boykin's views as representative.

A preoccupation with institutional well-being rather than religious fervor informs the collective temperament of the present-day American officer corps. To explain or justify military actions already under way, soldiers reflexively advert to the language of ideals rather than of interests. During and after the invasion of Iraq in 2003, for example, U.S. commanders routinely described their purpose in terms of liberating the oppressed and supporting human rights. But with few exceptions, generals do not view America's providential mission as a sufficient basis for *initiating* hostilities.

They are too cautious for that—or perhaps, from the perspective of a devout evangelical, too lacking in faith.

Even within the conservative Christian camp, moreover, militaristic fevers eased a bit once the Cold War ended. When facing off against the evil empire or against those fellow citizens who after the confusions of the 1960s had lost their stomach for resisting that empire, conservative Christians had considered it critically important to show that America was reasserting itself. Following the collapse of Communism, evangelical foreign policy priorities became more diffuse. The afflictions of the underdeveloped world became the new focus of attention. In the 1990s, evangelicalism's foreign policy agenda began to place greater emphasis on alleviating poverty, fighting AIDS, ending the trafficking in human beings, and above all responding to the plight of persecuted Christians around the world.[71] When it came to solving these sorts of problems, carrier battle groups and ballistic missile defenses had little to offer.

This is not to say that evangelicals questioned the advisability of the United States remaining a superpower. Still, with the demise of the Soviet evil empire, military matters as such lost much of their former urgency. In 1996 the National Association of Evangelicals approved a "Statement of Conscience" that put religious persecution and human rights at the top of the conservative Christian foreign policy agenda. Evangelical leaders took U.S. officials to task for putting trade ahead of torture.[72] High levels of military spending offered little in terms of preventing children from being forced into the sex trade. National missile defense wasn't going to do much to help embattled Christians in Sudan or China. After the Cold War, according to Richard Cizik, NEA vice president for governmental affairs, evangelicals became "more interested in making a difference than in making a statement."[73]

When it came to the use of force, therefore, the knee-jerk bellicosity that Christian conservatives had manifested in the late 1970s and 1980s waned. Operation Desert Storm in 1991, for the United States the first major armed conflict since Vietnam, found evangelicals for the most part (and in sharp contrast to the U.S. Catholic bishops and leaders of mainline Protestant denominations) unequivocally in the pro-war camp.[74] Thereafter, evangelical views became more nuanced, perhaps prompted by the fact that the commander-in-chief ordering U.S. troops into action throughout most of the 1990s was Bill Clinton, detested by the Religious Right as fervently as Ronald Reagan had been admired. When Clinton ordered the bombing of Serbia in 1999, for example, Charles Colson, the former Nixon political operative who after being born again founded the Prison Fellowship Ministries, was sharply critical not only of U.S. policy but of "the almost total silence of the Christian Church." Assessing the Kosovo war against just war requirements, Colson found that the administration's case for initiating hostilities fell "woefully short."[75] A decade earlier such a stringent application of just war standards by a leading member of the Religious Right would have been unheard of.

Evangelicals did remain protective of soldiers and vigilant in their determination to insulate the armed services from corrupting influences. This the newly elected Clinton discovered to his chagrin in 1992 when he casually announced his intention of issuing an executive order permitting gays to serve openly in the military. The proposal evoked a storm of protest. Conservative Christians joined the generals in opposition and forced Clinton to back down. But as soon as this controversy passed, it was all but forgotten. As an expression of defense for traditional moral values, the victory proved to be a hollow one.

In truth, the issue that by the 1990s determined how the armed services figured as a battleground in the ongoing culture war was not sexual orientation but gender. Whether measured in terms of numbers, roles, or responsibilities, women in uniform achieved hitherto unimaginable prominence after the Cold War. Many of the same generals and admirals who had threatened mass resignation if forced to serve with gays were complicit in "feminizing" the force. Whether they acted out of principle or in response to political pressure is beside the point; when it came to defining the role of women in American life, the men who led the armed forces parted company with the men dominating the Religious Right. As one result, the identity of the American warrior shed much of its traditionally masculine character. With senior officers unable to stanch a never-ending string of military scandals related to sexual misconduct and the abusive treatment of women, but keen to show that they "got it" on all matters relating to gender, evangelicals began to get an inkling that their partnership with the armed forces in the defense of a conservative Christian agenda had from the outset been illusory. Evangelicals wanted to put women on a pedestal, not in a cockpit or a turret.

Indeed, more astute evangelicals recognized that the problem was not to preserve the military from contamination from without but to prevent soldiers from becoming too distant from the American people. As Colson observed with regard to the fully mature All-Volunteer Force, "many in the military no longer care to protect our way of life—because they regard civilian life in America as degenerate and corrupt." The armed services were "drifting farther and farther away from America's mainstream." To permit this trend to continue was to invite trouble.[76] By the turn of the twenty-first century, at least some conservative Christians were coming to realize that a military establishment fancying itself morally superior to the society it was charged with defending might not be such a good idea.

Still, in the aftermath of 9/11, evangelicals reverted almost immediately to their old bellicosity, uniting behind the Bush administration with as much enthusiasm as they had behind the Reagan administration twenty years before. The Manichean worldview to which many evangelicals subscribed reasserted itself, with familiar figures such as Jerry Falwell and Pat Robertson rehearsing old lines in which Islam now substituted for Communism.[77] Appearing on *NBC Nightly News*, Franklin Graham, son of Billy and himself a prominent preacher, went so far as to denounce Islam as "a very evil and wicked religion."[78] Confronted with evil, the God-fearing had no alternative but to overcome it.

"This is a war between Christians and the forces of evil, by whatever name they choose to use," announced Jack Graham, president of the Southern Baptist Convention. "The ultimate terrorist is Satan," Graham said, echoing language emanating from the White House.[79] That the president was himself a born-again Christian obviously mattered, and as the global war on terror heated up, believers stood by their man: when it came to how Americans assessed George W. Bush's war, churchgoers were more supportive than nonchurchgoers and evangelicals were the most supportive of all.[80]

Perhaps most notably, evangelicals after 9/11 revived their accommodating interpretation of just-war theory and thereby put their imprimatur on the so-called Bush Doctrine. Thus, when the National Association of Evangelicals declared in the run-up to the 2003 Iraq War that "most evangelicals regard Saddam Hussein's regime—by allegedly aiding and harboring terrorists—as already having attacked the United States," it was putting just-war precepts at the service of what was in fact a preventive war.[81] Even more than had been the case during the Cold War, just-war principles after

9/11 became not a series of stringent tests but a signal: not a red light, not even a flashing yellow, but a bright green that relieved the Bush administration of any obligation to weigh seriously the moral implications of when and where it employed coercion. In effect, the NAE was extending to the United States the same immensely elastic permission to use force previously accorded to Israel.

This is not to say that during the controversy surrounding the invasion of Iraq conservative Christian views commanded universal assent; indeed, plenty of American churches and religious groups weighed in with contrary opinions.[82] In practical terms, however, those dissenting opinions did not count for much. Given their numbers and political clout, evangelicals at the very least canceled out the views of those who opposed the war.

The result was ironic: in the developed world's most devoutly Christian country, Christian witness against war and against the dangers of militarism became less effective than in countries thoroughly and probably irreversibly secularized. Thus, in the words of the leading religious scholar Martin Marty, did fervent followers of Jesus Christ become the Americans who were "most ready to sing the battle hymns of the republic and to support warfare in its name."[83]

This, then, gets to the essence of the evangelical contribution to the rise of the new American militarism since the end of Vietnam. Conservative Christians have conferred a presumptive moral palatability on any occasion on which the United States resorts to force. They have fostered among the legions of believing Americans a predisposition to see U.S. military power as inherently good, perhaps even a necessary adjunct to the accomplishment of Christ's saving mission. In doing so, they have nurtured the preconditions that have enabled the American infatuation with military power to flourish.

Put another way, were it not for the support offered by several tens of millions of evangelicals, militarism in this deeply and genuinely religious country becomes inconceivable.[84]

Chapter Six

WAR CLUB

THE BUSH DOCTRINE of preventive war represents the clearest articulation to date of the new American militarism. As a statement of intent, the doctrine is unambiguous: in an age when deterrence "means nothing" and containment "is not possible," the United States will exercise the prerogative of striking first. "In the world we have entered," George W. Bush has declared, "the only path to safety is the path of action. And this nation will act."[1]

Underlying that statement is an assumption: that the United States possesses the means to make good on Bush's promise. The aim of preventive war is not to warn or wound. It is to kill, quickly and efficiently. When it acts in pursuance of the Bush Doctrine, therefore, the United States must do so with decisive effect. The only acceptable standard of performance is a first-round knockout.

Even passing familiarity with modern military history suggests that this is a very high standard indeed. Since the beginning of the industrial age, war has time and again proven itself to be all but ungovernable. The shattered reputations of generals and statesmen who presumed to bring it under their control litter the twentieth century. On those rare occasions when war has yielded a seemingly decisive outcome, as in 1918 or 1945, it has done so only after exacting a staggering price from victor and vanquished alike. Even then, in resolving one set of problems, "good" wars have fostered resentments or created temptations, leading as often as not to further conflict.

Present-day U.S. policymakers are undaunted by that historical record. When it comes to warfare, as in so many other realms, they are intent on transcending history. "By a combination of creative strategies and advanced technologies," President Bush has confidently declared, "we are redefining war on our terms."[2] Still, the assertion, with its implication of making war as never before an efficacious instrument of policy, is nothing short of extraordinary.

Whence does such a claim originate? Not from George W. Bush. President Bush can no more claim credit for "redefining war" than President Bill Clinton in his day could claim credit for "reinventing government." In each case, the most powerful man in the world was functioning as a mouthpiece, appropriating ideas not his own.

However one evaluates his accomplishments as war president, the fact remains that Bush succeeded to his office possessing only the most rudimentary grasp of the military arts and sciences. Prior to his election, all Bush knew about war was what he learned some thirty years earlier as an unblooded National Guard fighter pilot. Granted, during his service in Massachusetts, Georgia, and Texas, the young Bush had adduced his own lessons of Vietnam, carefully enumerated in his campaign autobiography. These included various banalities, some self-evident, others highly dubious. Given "proper training and adequate personnel," wrote the then Governor Bush, "the military can accomplish its mission." The responsibilities of the commander-in-chief were simple; he "must define the mission and allow the military to achieve it." Of one thing, Bush professed to be absolutely certain: "We can never again ask the military to fight a political war."[3] Moreover, there is little to suggest that upon becoming president or even after 9/11 he embarked upon a meticulous study of military affairs. All Bush knows about war is what he learned through an intensive course of on-the-job training, supplemented by such information as his staff and subordinates funneled his way.

In fact, the American attempt to redesign war, a project of monumental scope and ambition, was conceived well before Bush's arrival in the White House. Ironically, at the time of its inception some sixty years ago, the declared purpose of this project was not to refashion war to suit American needs but to avert war altogether—or, more specifically, to avert a third world war commonly expected to be even more calamitous than the first two. To achieve that end, the project's founders—not soldiers or statesmen, but bright young civilian academics eager to put their stamp on public policy—set out to reconstitute the relationship between war and politics, which the events of 1945 had seemed to rupture. In an age of nuclear weapons, what relevance, if any, did armed force retain for the pursuit of basic national interests? This was the question that they claimed as their own. In assaying an answer, they established themselves in short order as the high priests of U.S. national security strategy.

In Vietnam, one large wing of the edifice that they had erected collapsed, raising doubts about the integrity of the entire enterprise and calling into question the credibility of its architects. Undaunted and unchastened, the project's guiding spirits set out in hot pursuit of a still bolder aim. Rather than limiting themselves to matters of strategy, they now trained their sights on war itself. This second burst of creativity culminated in the discovery of a putative military revolution, promising a quantum leap in the effectiveness of American arms. It is belief in the imminence and potential of this revolution that imbues the Bush Doctrine with the appearance of plausibility.

Reading news reports of the bombing of Hiroshima in early August 1945, Bernard Brodie, a young University of Chicago–trained student of military affairs, then teaching at Yale, and for a time the priesthood's animating spirit, remarked to his wife, "Everything that I have written is obsolete."[4] Everything that Brodie had written up until then had stemmed from the hallowed conception of war as simply the continuation of politics by other means, in the famous formulation by Carl von Clausewitz. This Clausewitzian conception of war had seemingly vanished in the fireball that consumed Hiroshima.

So, with a handful of collaborators, Brodie set out to reconceptualize war's relationship to politics. Within a matter of months, having located the point from which to begin his search for an answer, he enunciated the dictum for which history would remember him. "Thus far the chief purpose of our military establishment has been to win wars," Brodie wrote in 1946. "From now on its chief purpose must be to avert them. It can have almost no other useful purpose."[5] War had long been a bane of human existence; now, with the coming of the nuclear age, it had also become impermissible. Henceforth, the essence of strategy was to forestall Armageddon. To expect anything more was to indulge in a dangerous and retrograde illusion.

How to derive from that insight specific guidelines of use to policymakers was the tricky part. Hiroshima had evoked widespread calls for world government or the complete abolition of arms. "One World or None" was the battle cry heard in such quarters.[6] Brodie and his compatriots had little patience with emotion-charged assertions that "war and obliteration are now completely synonymous."[7] Preventing the recurrence of war required not utopian schemes but realism, dispassion, and cool-headed analysis. Alas, within the upper echelons of the United States government—and especially within the United States military—these qualities were in short supply. At least so Brodie believed.

Heretofore, standard American practice had been to treat strategy as ancillary to the actual conduct of war, which soldiers had always claimed as their exclusive preserve. Until 1945, strategy had been more or less synonymous with campaign planning, taught (if at all) to military professionals attending war colleges and pretty much ignored by civilians as a subject remote from the concerns of everyday life. Now nuclear weapons had invested strategy with an importance that was as immediate as it was urgent. But as Brodie had concluded from firsthand observation, when it came to thinking through the implications of those weapons, soldiers—especially very senior ones—were sadly ill-equipped.[8] In practice, their entire conception of strategy boiled down to a single principle: bringing the maximum destructive power to bear against the enemy in a decisive battle. Although soldiers were slow to acknowledge the fact, the Bomb had rendered this principle politically counterproductive and morally unconscionable.

Brodie proposed an alternative principle, one that promised henceforth to subordinate war to strategy. That principle was deterrence—*threatening* force in order to persuade would-be adversaries to forego misbehavior, with success making the actual *use* of force unnecessary.

Not so incidentally, organizing strategy around the principle of deterrence meant wresting control of strategy away from soldiers, thereby circumscribing traditional military prerogatives. After Hiroshima, as Brodie saw it, it no longer made sense that the color of a man's tunic or the number of stars on his collar should determine the weight assigned to his opinions on compelling issues of war and peace. Real influence ought to devolve to those equipped with the appropriate analytical tools. Strategy, that is, should become the purview not of generals like the crude, cigar-chomping Curtis LeMay who had presided over the firebombing of some sixty Japanese cities and the utter destruction of Hiroshima and Nagasaki without losing a night's sleep, but of highly-trained, cutting-edge academics—men like Brodie, with his preference for bow ties, his unquestioned brilliance, and his basic decency. Henceforth, tweed should tutor khaki.

This became Brodie's calling: to counter the One Worlders touting unworkable schemes for global disarmament, but more urgently to keep in check the LeMays who were hankering to incinerate Moscow as they had incinerated Tokyo, and as a consequence of both to restore order and rationality to a world turned upside down by the invention of nuclear weapons.

With others joining Brodie, that calling formed the basis of a new profession, its members known as defense intellectuals. It gave birth to new institutions such as the RAND Corporation, the federally funded research facility founded in Santa Monica, California, in 1946, with Brodie as one of its first hires. RAND assembled a circle of mathematicians, economists, and political scientists that in addition to Brodie included such luminaries as Charles Hitch, Herman Kahn, and John von Neumann. The defense intellectuals produced a vast literature, most of it highly classified and bristling with jargon—"not incredible counterforce first-strike" and "Doomsday Machine," "overkill" and "mutual annihilation," "MAD" and "N+1." Although ostensibly of enormous importance to the survival of humankind, these arcane writings were accessible only to a few.

As charter members of the new postwar national security elite, Brodie and the other high priests of nuclear strategy came to wield great influence, without the burden of actual responsibility. Members of this priesthood remained largely hidden from public view and thus unaccountable. By comparison, the curia of the Roman Catholic Church seemed a model of openness and transparency.

There was, however, a problem. Brodie's Dictum—the text from which the priesthood drew its raison d'être—rested on an utterly false premise. Hiroshima had not, in fact, robbed violence of its political utility. It had certainly not made war obsolete. The events of August 1945 had at most blocked up the channel through which military history had coursed during the previous several decades—toward the Somme, Sedan, and Stalingrad—and diverted it in the direction of Inchon, Dien Bien Phu, and the Sinai.

Moreover, even before the battlefields of the 1950s and 1960s made the point self-evident, members of the priesthood already grasped that Brodie's

Dictum was in error. But they persisted in pretending otherwise, for the Dictum provided useful camouflage, concealing the priesthood's actual purpose. The Pentagon was not, in fact, funding the research undertaken by Brodie and his colleagues in a high-minded search for ways to prevent the recurrence of Hiroshima. From the outset, the object of the exercise was entirely pragmatic: to perpetuate the advantages that had accrued to the United States as a consequence of Hiroshima and to use those advantages to advance vital American interests, without triggering World War III. This was the challenge that imbued nuclear strategy with excitement and allure.

In that regard, the really interesting arguments were not with the hopelessly naive One Worlders or the hopelessly simple-minded generals but with the economists, mathematicians, and political scientists across the corridor or down the hall, whether at RAND or any of the other institutions such as Harvard, MIT, and the University of Chicago where members of the priesthood congregated. To inhabit the world that Brodie and his compatriots created was to engage daily in the cut and thrust of high-level intellectual combat, where the issue at hand was not truth as such—the nuclear strategist's world contained few fixed truths—but the honing of alternatives, trade-offs, and risks, conceived and evaluated in a context of political uncertainty and rapid technological change.

Nobody engaged in this combat with greater gusto and effectiveness— or had more fun in the process—than did Albert Wohlstetter.[9] By the time of his death in 1997, Wohlstetter had long since been acknowledged as the dean of American nuclear strategists, renowned among those in the know as a powerful intellect and relentless critic of the conventional wisdom.[10] In the words of Richard Perle, a protégé and lifelong admirer, Wohlstetter brought "clarity and wisdom to everything he studied."[11] Trained at Columbia University as a mathematical logician, Wohlstetter joined RAND in 1951. His first major project—a study of Strategic Air Command (SAC) basing policies ostensibly demonstrating that a Soviet attack could destroy virtually the entire U.S. long-range bomber force before it even got off the ground—vaulted him into the front rank of defense intellectuals.[12]

As a result of the basing study, Wohlstetter concluded that "strategic-retaliatory-force vulnerability" was "*the* problem of nuclear war."[13] The United States needed to ensure against any would-be adversary entertaining the slightest inkling that it could attack the United States and survive to tell the tale. This was the ultimate strategic imperative and the theme to which Wohlstetter repeatedly returned. For Wohlstetter and those he influenced, vulnerability became an obsession and eventually a fetish.[14] The apparent simplicity of deterrence as a strategic principle, it turned out, was an illusion. In fact, the effective management of what Wohlstetter subsequently termed the "balance of terror" was a dynamic and difficult business, requiring great exertions and continuous refinement. To pretend otherwise was to invite disaster.[15]

Indeed, by the end of the 1950s, Wohlstetter had concluded that disaster loomed just ahead. The problem was one of complacency. Although momentarily roused when a large Soviet rocket in 1957 put the first satellite in orbit around the earth, Americans had soon thereafter returned to what Wohlstetter called their "deep pre-Sputnik sleep," oblivious to the "terribly dangerous" situation that they faced "in a world of persistent danger." The Soviet arsenal was growing in size and sophistication; Soviet defenses were also becoming more formidable, making it impossible to guarantee that a U.S. retaliatory strike would get through. Looking to the decade ahead, Wohlstetter assessed the prospects of avoiding nuclear war to be iffy at best, largely dependent upon the willingness of Americans to engage in an "urgent and continuing effort," one certain to involve "hard choices" and necessarily entailing sacrifice. Whether or not the American people would rise to the occasion was, in his judgment, "by no means certain."[16]

Few historians today find such alarmism about trends in the then-existing strategic balance to be justifiable.[17] In actual fact, that balance favored the United States. But at the time, with worries of a "bomber gap" giving way to concerns about a "missile gap" and a presidential election just over the horizon, Wohlstetter's argument—a barely concealed attack on the defense policies of the Eisenhower administration—was exquisitely timed to have the maximum political impact. The threats that he so persuasively conjured up constituted something akin to a grave national emergency—a theme that Senator John F. Kennedy placed at the center of his presidential campaign.

When it came to spelling out the specifics of what needed to be done, Wohlstetter articulated a set of requirements that presaged Kennedy's policy of "Flexible Response," shifting attention away from mere deterrence toward a more activist posture. The real imperative was to enhance the ability of the United States to fight, whether all-out wars or limited ones, whether brief or protracted, whether employing nuclear or conventional weapons. A wider range of robust military capabilities (necessarily requiring increases in defense spending), more options available to decision makers, and a blunt willingness to go to the mat: these alone could keep the Red menace at bay.[18]

The interest here is not in the extent to which Wohlstetter's writings informed the subsequent actions of the Kennedy administration but in what his views portended for the ongoing evolution of American thinking about strategy. In that regard, the impact of the argument upon the strategic illuminati at RAND and elsewhere was profound. Safety, it turned out, was to be found not as Brodie had asserted in 1946 in a single-minded focus on averting war; rather, safety lay in devising more effective ways of actually using force. To remain passive was to court great danger. Only through action—deliberate and carefully controlled—could there be a chance of avoiding the ultimate catastrophe. Defensive ends required the use of offensive means. Indeed, collapsing what Wohlstetter saw as the arbitrary distinctions between strategy and tactics on the one hand and between offensive and defensive weapons on the other held the promise of opening up a host of new and potentially viable options.[19] Thus at the end of the 1950s did Wohlstetter's fallacious (even fraudulent)[20] case for vulnerability nudge the strategic priesthood around a corner and down a path ending some four decades later in a fully developed argument for preventive war as the cornerstone of U.S. strategy.[21]

In a nuclear era, how exactly could the United States respond to the futurist Herman Kahn's 1960 call for devising "more reasonable forms of using violence," in essence salvaging something from the old Clausewitzian view of war?[22] To this question too the priesthood of strategists offered an answer—or two answers, really. For the first answer failed, and out of that failure came the second, whose validity remains at issue.

The first answer was to derive a new logic for the conduct of war, incorporating into thinking about strategy and military affairs precepts drawn from economics and from "game theory," which sought to understand the logic of competitive interaction among opposing "players," each engaged in the pursuit of objectives to which each assigns a certain value.

The central idea was to abandon the old tendency to see war as a contest that produced winners and losers—"a zero-sum game." Better to conceive of war as an exercise in suasion and the use of armed force, whether force actually expended or force threatened but withheld, as a form of bargaining. The aim was not to crush the enemy but to bring him to the realization that ending the war on your terms served *his own* interests. The object of the exercise was not to achieve total victory, which in most cases was likely to be too costly, too risky, and probably unnecessary. Rather it was, through the calibrated application of force, to affect the enemy's own internal cost / benefit analysis and by extension his commitment to continued struggle.[23]

No one pretended that this was going to be easy. Americans had traditionally tended to see their wars as great crusades, waged to achieve the noblest of ends and therefore justifying a maximum effort to achieve total victory. Limited wars in the nuclear era were sure to demand an altogether different temperament and a different approach. They would be wars fought for finite purposes and in cold blood. They would be shrouded in ambiguity, in all likelihood long, drawn-out affairs, testing American patience and resolve. Deciding when, where, and how to punish would demand the utmost perspicacity lest intended signals go awry and warnings be misinterpreted. Understanding the enemy's frame of reference would be crucially important.

But if decision makers could overcome these challenges, the payoff promised to be large. The theory of limited war offered the prospect of enhancing the direct political relevance of American military power. Intelligently employed, force could enable the United States to dispose of garden-variety irritants, thereby reducing the likelihood of having to confront the big problem of an all-out nuclear showdown with the Soviet bloc. And it could accomplish all this at an acceptable cost.

Furthermore, in the eyes of the nuclear strategists, the challenges inherent in managing limited wars did not seem insurmountable. Wohlstetter, for one, thought that protracted wars might actually work to the U.S. advantage. Ever the critic of the conventional wisdom, he questioned the assumption that "the best way for the West to fight a limited war is that way that promises to end it quickest." Instead, Wohlstetter argued that "the greater economic resources of the West offer many advantages in a war of attrition."[24] In a limited war, the indisputable fact of the West's greater wealth would overshadow the entire bargaining process to the disadvantage of the materially inferior Communists. Long wars could actually be good wars.

Moreover, by the early 1960s Wohlstetter detected promising signs that senior authorities in Washington had begun to assimilate and implement the rigorous, meticulously cerebral approach to thinking about war that he and others had been promoting. In the ways that they addressed the complexities of strategy, high-ranking Pentagon officials had begun to "grow in professional competence." Wohlstetter praised their new sophistication and took satisfaction from the signs that "the application of the method of science to the analysis of political-military strategic alternatives" was now beginning to take root.[25]

Indeed, by 1963, the Wohlstetter style was meeting with notable favor in the upper echelons of the Defense Department. The passing of the stodgy old Eisenhower era had put paid to Ike's unimaginative approach to national security policy; "the old order had been overthrown and the new one installed."[26] When members of the strategic priesthood mounted their pulpit, a Washington eager for fresh ideas listened attentively and believed. True on the apocalyptic questions of nuclear strategy—Secretary of Defense Robert S. McNamara tied himself in knots trying to apply the latest theoretical permutations of deterrence—this was true also with regard to lesser matters.[27] Especially pressing among those lesser matters was deciding what to do about the Communist insurgency threatening the U.S. ally and quasi-dependency of South Vietnam. In conceiving U.S. strategy in Southeast Asia, McNamara and his chief lieutenants—several of them RAND veterans—drew heavily on the precepts of limited war devised by Wohlstetter and his colleagues.[28]

The disastrous results that ensued from this effort are too well known to require detailed documentation here. Suffice it to say that the Vietnamese Communists did not subscribe to American theories of limited war; indeed, they viewed their struggle for unification under the banner of revolutionary socialism as the very inverse of limited. They did not fight with an eye toward negotiating a compromise settlement but to achieve complete victory. They did not respond to and may not have comprehended U.S. attempts to use force as a means to "signal" or to "bargain." Of even greater importance, they proved to be far more willing to die for their cause than were Americans to die for theirs. In Vietnam, the United States did indeed get the lengthy war of attrition that Wohlstetter had fancied to be an American strong suit and that war turned out to be an unmitigated nightmare.

Vietnam appeared to be, in Fred Kaplan's aptly chosen words, "the Waterloo for the entire enterprise of strategic analysis." The war, Kaplan continues, "exposed something seamy and disturbing" about the very project in which the defense intellectuals had engaged. "It revealed that the concept of force underlying all their formulations and scenarios was an abstraction, practically useless as a guide to action."[29]

So indeed it appeared to a legion of critics, who frequently lumped the whole class of defense intellectuals among those held accountable for the war's mismanagement. For their part, the nuclear strategists themselves refused to accept that adverse judgment about the value of their enterprise, just as they refused to accept any responsibility for the war's conduct and outcome. Apart from the odd exception like Daniel Ellsberg, the former RAND analyst and Defense Department official who in 1971 leaked the Pentagon Papers and became an anti-war activist, few in the priesthood were inclined to recant, confess their sins, or perform acts of contrition.

During the formative phases of the Vietnam War, Wohlstetter himself had remarkably little of use to contribute. Once the dimensions of the debacle became apparent, he offered little in terms of finding a way out. Instead, he acted with almost unseemly haste to put Vietnam in his rearview mirror.

"Of all the disasters of Vietnam," Wohlstetter warned in 1968, when the war still had four and a half more years to run, "the worst may be the 'lessons' that we'll draw from it." Among the prospective lessons that disturbed him most was the prospect of future administrations backing away from the nuanced strategic concepts to which he had contributed and reverting instead to archaic notions like vintage-1950s massive retaliation. But Wohlstetter worried more still about a generalized reaction against military power. He fretted over the possibility of Americans, singed by Vietnam, coming to view intervention abroad as inherently problematic rather than searching for new ways "to use our power discriminately and for worthy ends." He was concerned that when it came to force his countrymen might decide "we are better off reducing the choices available to us" rather than seeking to expand them. As Wohlstetter saw it, such tendencies were already in evidence by 1968 and they pointed to the onset of a "new isolationism" sponsored by an "odd coalition...of the old defenders of Fortress America and the New Left."[30]

In effect, Wohlstetter feared that Vietnam might induce a populist challenge to elite control of strategy. Elites—David Halberstam's "best and brightest"—had made the case for war in a very far-off place and as a consequence the United States had squandered strength, legitimacy, lives, and treasure to no purpose. That outcome raised at least the theoretical possibility that the American people—those comprising the "odd coalition" to which Wohlstetter referred—might in the future be less inclined to defer to elites on matters related to war and strategy. Allied with an officer corps with plenty of reasons to recoil from the prospect of more Vietnams, they might draw their own intuitive conclusions about the war. Adherents of what Wohlstetter scornfully termed "a kind of SAC-SDS position"—the all-or-nothing airmen of Strategic Air Command allied with student radicals instinctively suspicious of U.S. military power per se—might, for example, view force as something to be employed with considerable reluctance and only when truly vital national interests were at stake.[31] They might develop a bias against mucking about in places of little or no immediate importance to the United States. They might reject as nonsense ornate theories for fighting limited wars. When it came to force, they might evolve a preference for constraining policymakers rather than permitting them to select from an ever wider range of choices and options. This prospect Wohlstetter viewed as intolerable: that in a nuclear world requiring American assertiveness, the United States might pursue policies of self-restraint and self-abnegation and might reduce the emphasis it placed on military power.

Like the leaders of the U.S. military, Wohlstetter and his fellow strategists embarked after Vietnam upon a great project of military reform. But whereas the generals' underlying aim was reactionary—to revive traditional conceptions of conventional war while erecting barriers to the actual use of force and restoring their own prerogatives—Wohlstetter's purpose was genuinely radical. He wanted not to reestablish conventional notions of war but to transcend them—to invent methods of waging war suited to the priesthood's strategic imperatives, namely, to prevent World War III while facilitating U.S. efforts to secure its vital national interests.

Soldiers took from Vietnam the lesson that it made no sense to fight unless you were willing to go all out to win. From the perspective of the officer corps, the big problem in Vietnam was outside interference: politicians hadn't allowed them to do what needed to be done. According to Wohlstetter and other members of the priesthood, the big problem lay within the military profession itself: it had not adapted itself to the imperatives of war in a nuclear age. The military instrument was ill suited to the actual requirements of U.S. national security. The big lesson that Wohlstetter took from Vietnam was that soldiers needed new and better ways to fight.

Wohlstetter's advocacy of activism to shore up deterrence and thereby reduce U.S. strategic vulnerability had assumed an ability to use force with dexterity and discrimination. In practice, the way that the U.S. military had fought the Vietnam War, both the bombing of the North and the counterinsurgency campaign in the South, had been arbitrary, inconsistent, and heavy-handed. Waging limited war called for a scalpel in the hands of a skilled surgeon; in Vietnam, the generals had wielded a club and paid too little attention to who they hit and with what effect.

The new challenge facing defense intellectuals after Vietnam was to create that scalpel. Moreover, the American experience in Indochina had offered them a preliminary glimpse at a solution, for Vietnam had seen the first efforts to introduce precision weapons to the battlefield. In the war's latter stages, the first such weapons—munitions designed with expectations of a near 100 percent probability of hitting their intended target—had made their appearance. Although the introduction of these novel devices, such as bombs that could be steered to their aim point, had made no difference in the war's outcome, and although in the general revulsion against Vietnam they had attracted no particular public notice, they did catch the attention of Wohlstetter and his colleagues. Here was the technological breakthrough that held the promise of permitting the United States to use force on its own terms.

In considering the strategic implications of this idea, Wohlstetter pursued two distinct but interrelated lines of development. The first of these concerned the possibility of tapping the potential of these new technologies to render harmless the Soviet strategic threat. The second concerned the possibility of exploiting many of these same technologies to devise a form of highly discriminate nonnuclear warfare.

From the 1960s onward, Wohlstetter was an ardent advocate of ballistic missile defenses (BMD)—designed to destroy or disable attacking missiles—touting them as essential to a comprehensive effort to protect the U.S. strategic deterrent.[32] To ensure that the United States possessed the ability to retaliate after absorbing an attack by the Soviet Union or any other adversary was, in his judgment, to decrease the likelihood of any such attack in the first place. That is, missile defenses enhanced overall stability and permitted an escape from the bind of Mutual Assured Destruction, which Wohlstetter condemned as "a dangerous and repugnant doctrine."[33] In this regard, he considered the Anti-Ballistic Missile (ABM) Treaty, nego-tiated by the Nixon administration in 1972, to be a blunder of the first order and thereafter lobbied for its repeal.

Wohlstetter rejected out of hand assertions that American efforts to shield its deterrent might provoke an arms race or induce an adversary to strike before effective defenses were fully in place. Although elsewhere quick to disregard distinctions between offensive and defensive weapons as illusory, when it came to BMD Wohlstetter was adamant that they qualified as purely benign, both in inspiration and prospective effect. He refused even to countenance the notion that the protection offered by missile defenses might permit or encourage the United States to employ its own forces, nuclear and nonnuclear alike, offensively. "In spite of dark hints by the con-spiratorial Left in the West," he wrote, "preventive war has never been seri-ously considered by responsible U.S. leaders"—a statement whose accuracy even during the Cold War depended on the definition of "responsible."[34]

In point of fact, reliable strategic defenses would provide policymakers in Washington with greater discretion in deciding when, where, and how to employ force. A functioning BMD system would widen the range of avail-able options, always in Wohlstetter's view a useful outcome. Ballistic mis-sile defenses were like condoms: whatever the intent of their designer, their practical effect could well be to encourage promiscuous behavior.

At this point Wohlstetter's obsession with vulnerability crossed the boundary between defensive and active measures. Regardless of how leakproof any conceivable ballistic missile defense system might appear to be, it made little sense, in his view, to risk everything on a thin layer of pro-tection. Why rely solely on a condom to prevent sexually transmitted dis-eases if it were also possible to identify and inoculate or altogether remove from circulation carriers of STDs? Properly protecting America's safety and well-being required the ability to eliminate threats before they fully developed—an ability that the first-generation precision weaponry

deployed in the latter stages of the Vietnam War was now seemingly bringing within reach.

This prospect of precision attack was the key conceptual breakthrough.
Throughout the 1970s and 1980s, Wohlstetter (supported by other members of the priesthood) campaigned vigorously—and in the face of what he
called the "enormous inertia" of the armed services—to make "more carefully modulated and precisely limited military force" the centerpiece of a
distinctive new conception of warfare.[35] As Deputy Secretary of Defense
Paul Wolfowitz recalled in 2003, Wohlstetter was the first major figure "to
understand what a dramatic difference it would make to have accurate
weapons." Wolfowitz, who as a graduate student had studied with
Wohlstetter at the University of Chicago, credited his mentor with being
the first to grasp the crucial point that "accuracy translates into a whole
transformation of strategy and politics."[36]

As early as 1974, Wohlstetter was touting the potential of an "expanding
family of precision guided munitions" to permit the "much more effective
and discriminating application of force in an increasingly wider variety of
political and operational circumstances."[37] By exploiting what he called the
"revolution in microelectronics" along with the promise of "less expensive,
small packages of reliable sensors, powerful data processors, and communications," he wrote, the United States could substantially reduce the ineffi-
ciencies and uncertainties that had plagued large-scale industrial-age
combat: the huge expenditures of material, the needless destruction, the
incidental killing and maiming of noncombatants, and the indeterminate
duration and outcome of operations.

Making force less wasteful and its effects more predictable held the
promise of enhancing the efficacy of American striking power. In a 1983
essay, Wohlstetter posited that "a tenfold improvement in accuracy is
roughly equal in effectiveness to a thousand-fold increase in the explosive
energy released by a weapon."[38] Increase accuracy by a factor of one hundred and the payoff would equal in effectiveness a millionfold increase in
destructive power. This prospect in turn opened up whole new vistas for
the application of force. At a minimum it promised to make war more readily available as an instrument for advancing U.S. security objectives. "We
should be prepared to use discriminating offensive strategies, tactics, and
precise weapons," Wohlstetter argued in the mid-1980s. The idea was to
transcend notions of war as gratuitous murder "and to direct our weapons

at the military rather than at bystanders—to select targets of a sort, number and location that will accomplish an important military purpose and yet contain the destruction."[39] *Discriminating offensive strategies*: here was the distilled essence of the nuclear priesthood's efforts to discern the right lessons of Vietnam and to shake the United States loose from the wrong ones to which politicians, the media, and especially soldiers remained devoted.[40]

The high point of Wohlstetter's efforts to reconceptualize warfare and to promote a more expansive approach to thinking about force came in 1987 when he cochaired the bipartisan Commission on Integrated Long-Term Strategy.[41] Under the guise of reinforcing deterrence, this panel candidly advanced the case for a national security strategy incorporating the anticipatory use of force, eliminating threats before they could mature.

The commission's report *Discriminate Deterrence*, published in January 1988, stands as an important milestone on the road to the Bush Doctrine. In their report, Wohlstetter and his colleagues credited technological advances such as radar-defeating designs and materials ("stealth"), extremely accurate long-range weapons, and improved targeting and communications achieved by exploiting outer space with having unleashed "revolutionary changes in the nature of war." The Soviet Union fully appreciated the potential of these changes; the Pentagon, in the commission's view, did not. Yet if the United States awoke to the opportunity at hand, it might acquire "a more versatile, discriminating and controlled capability" to employ violence for political purposes. Ultimately, this technology-driven revolution held out the prospect of "the strategic use of non-nuclear weapons," meaning that the United States could accomplish through conventional means and at tolerable costs the same objectives assigned since 1945 to (essentially unusable) U.S. nuclear forces. Wohlstetter and his fellow commissioners treated this contingency as if it were a grim necessity. "In the changing environment of the next 20 years," they predicted, the United States was going to require the ability "to bring force to bear effectively, with discrimination and in time to thwart any of a wide range of plausible aggressions."[42]

Bringing force to bear to thwart plausible aggression: this was the ultimate promise contained within the new American way of war that Wohlstetter advocated. The scalpel was seemingly now at hand, making it possible to eliminate threats with near-antiseptic efficiency. Gone for good were the old discredited notions of using limited force to bargain or signal.

The new methods could enable the United States to use carefully calibrated force to win outright.

Gone too were the last of the distinctions that Wohlstetter had always bridled against as arbitrary and confining. Deterrence had now collapsed into warfighting. Strategically, the two had become indistinguishable.

But would the priesthood's innovative ideas for warfighting work any better this time around than they had in Vietnam?

In short order, the opportunity to find out presented itself. In August 1990, with the Cold War over and the Soviet Union teetering on the edge of oblivion, Saddam Hussein's legions invaded Kuwait.[43]

For the U.S. military, the Persian Gulf War of 1990–91 came as a not altogether welcome test. The restoration of orthodoxy that had preoccupied soldiers for the previous fifteen years had been an end in itself, which they were not eager to put at risk. In marked contrast to Wohlstetter, their aim had never been to devise new ways to employ force. Indeed, with the Soviet threat at long last disappearing, the last thing that the officer corps wanted was to get tangled up in a protracted and ugly brawl, as many observers feared that a fight with Iraq's ostensibly seasoned and very large Soviet-style army might turn out to be.

For his part, Albert Wohlstetter dismissed out of hand predictions of a long, drawn-out slugfest. In his judgment, the crisis offered a made-to-order chance to show that orthodoxy had outlived its moment and, once and for all, to put paid to Vietnam's invidious "lessons."

Within ten days of Iraq's invasion of Kuwait, well before the Bush administration had decided on the course of action that culminated in Operation Desert Storm, Wohlstetter had rushed into print an editorial in the *Wall Street Journal* calling for bold offensive action to turn back Iraqi aggression. All the tools to permit a quick, decisive, economical victory were at hand. With its arsenal of "precise weapons, stealth and other advanced techniques for penetrating defenses," the United States could conduct "highly effective and discriminate air attacks against key military targets—including Iraq's air and missile forces, and stocks and production facilities for chemical or nuclear weapons." Relying in particular on high-tech air power, U.S. forces "could avoid indiscriminate collateral damage to civilians." Indeed, Wohlstetter insisted that preserving the Iraqi people from harm was "a political as well as moral necessity."[44]

The swift and certain unfolding of the ensuing campaign seemed to vindicate Wohlstetter's estimate, ending in what appeared at first blush to be a victory of staggering proportions. Awe-struck observers were quick to declare that Operation Desert Storm marked a watershed in the history of modern warfare. According to a preliminary analysis prepared by RAND, the campaign constituted "a remarkable milestone in military history."[45] The United States and its allies had achieved "an unprecedented military victory," one that "gave the world a peek at the twenty-first century, at the power of precision-guided weapons, at the speed of combat."[46] American arms had achieved a success that had been "literally unimagined" beforehand.[47] Something genuinely extraordinary had occurred.

Yet that victory had actually solved very little. A dismayed Wohlstetter could hardly believe that President Bush had allowed large parts of the Iraqi army to escape intact and the Baathist police state to survive. Although precision warfare had restored the independence of Kuwait, the political harvest produced by Desert Storm turned out to be meager indeed. Even handed a finely honed implement, the chief surgeon had managed to botch the operation.

Bush, it seemed, had failed to grasp the central issue. In Iraq, Wohlstetter explained in exasperation shortly after the war, "the durable problem is a dictatorship sitting on the world's second largest pool of low-cost oil and ambitious to dominate the Gulf and the Mediterranean." Wohlstetter publicly chided the strategically obtuse Bush administration for repeating in the Persian Gulf the same error that the strategically obtuse Johnson administration had made in Southeast Asia. "In the long drawn-out war in Vietnam, U.S. political leaders never challenged the rule of the totalitarian government in North Vietnam," he wrote.[48] Throughout the Gulf crisis, Bush had gone to great lengths to show that he was not Johnson and that he had fully absorbed the correct lessons to be drawn from Vietnam. That the war ended with Saddam Hussein still in power, no doubt plotting revenge and rebuilding his arsenal, was enough to convince Wohlstetter to the contrary. True victory—and an end to the threat posed by Iraq—required the installation in Baghdad of a suitably liberal alternative to the existing tyranny.

Here was the final piece in the evolving logic that pointed toward a strategy of preventive war: *by their very existence dictatorships constituted an unacceptable threat.* The only sure remedy to the problem of vulnerability—the true application of the strategy of deterrence in a nuclear age—was to bring despotic regimes into full compliance with American norms, using force if necessary to do so. Cleansing the world of tyrants like Saddam Hussein was the overriding strategic imperative. For his part, Wohlstetter believed that precise and discriminating U.S. military capabilities now made a policy of regime change feasible, if only responsible political authorities had the wit and the gumption to act.

For all of the elder Bush's mismanagement of the war, Operation Desert Storm seemingly affirmed Wohlstetter's contention that big changes were afoot in military affairs. In that regard, Wohlstetter stood in relation to the events of 1991 as Brodie stood in relation to the events of 1945: he was among the first to divine the implications and gained acclaim as the first to articulate them.

In his preliminary sketch of the new American way of war and of its proper application, Wohlstetter had employed very broad strokes. He left to others the task of refining the design, drawing up the detailed blueprints, and cajoling the officer corps into full compliance with his vision, all steps necessary to put the United States into a position where it could as a matter of routine employ force proactively to thwart plausible aggressors and overturn regimes that refused to abide by American norms.[49]

Foremost among those who took up that task was a contemporary of Wohlstetter's and fellow veteran of RAND, although since 1972 a senior civilian working in the Office of the Secretary of Defense. His name was Andrew Marshall.

In terms of personal style, Marshall was Wohlstetter's polar opposite. Wohlstetter basked in the role of the flamboyant intellectual freelancer beholden to no one.[50] By contrast, Marshall was the ultimate insider, a colorless, self-effacing bureaucrat. "In a government where leaking is an instrument of policy, he shuns publicity," *Newsweek* reported in an admiring profile. "At briefings, he drones and mumbles; the military brass have nicknamed him Yoda," an allusion to the ancient Jedi Master of Hollywood's *Star Wars* saga.[51] Circumspect when it came to venturing opinions that might find their way into the public domain, Marshall was also shrewd and astonishingly durable. The founding director of the Pentagon's Office of Net Assessment, devoted to long-range strategic analysis, he remained in that job for over thirty years, making himself invaluable to administrations of whatever ideological stripe. But however much the famously reticent and even inscrutable Marshall appeared to differ from the opinionated and pro-lix Wohlstetter, he too was a true believer: in military activism as the anti-dote to American vulnerability and in the imperative of enhancing the utility of force, by extracting the full measure of advantage from the tech-niques unveiled in Desert Storm. As a result, during the course of the 1990s, Andrew Marshall eclipsed Wohlstetter as the leading proponent of what Marshall himself now dubbed the (not "a") Revolution in Military Affairs. Marshall was certain not only that there was a revolution afoot but that he had deciphered the true nature of that revolution.

The first measure of Marshall's influence is that the label stuck. By the mid-1990s, the Revolution in Military Affairs, or RMA, had established itself among specialists as the authoritative frame of reference within which the debate over the future of warfare unfolded. Although few remarked upon the fact, the earlier revolution of 1945—the one that had supposedly made war itself obsolete—now shrank to seeming insignificance. The RMA promised war a brand-new lease on life.

During the 1990s, Marshall himself saw this revolution less as an accom-plished fact than as a prospect. This was a crucially important point. How-ever impressive their battlefield performance in Desert Storm, U.S. military forces as configured at the end of the Cold War possessed only in limited and rudimentary forms the capabilities suggested by the RMA.[52] General H. Norman Schwarzkopf's army with its thousands of armored vehicles and mammoth supply train and his campaign plan with its several weeks of aerial bombardment preceding a deliberate and carefully choreographed ground attack still looked more "old" than it did "new." Military revolu-tions did not happen overnight. They took time to mature and required far-reaching, expensive, and frequently painful institutional change.

The scalpel unsheathed in the desert had been at best a usable prototype. America's armed services circa 1991 bore comparison to the British army of 1918: primitive tanks and squadrons of wood-and-canvas fighter planes were a portent of things to come, but Great Britain in the latter stages of World War I had neither embraced full-fledged mechanization nor fully recognized what the mechanization of warfare entailed. And as subsequent

British experience in the 1920s and 1930s suggested, hesitancy in exploiting a potential revolution was to forfeit the opportunity to others, with potentially fatal consequences.[53]

Marshall believed that the United States had entered a new interwar period, comparable in his mind to the interval between the two world wars. Determined not to repeat the mistakes that Britain had made during the interval between the world wars when the British officer corps had briefly toyed with but then lost interest in the chief technological innovations of the Great War, Marshall set for himself a threefold agenda.[54] First and most urgently, he sought to spell out in great detail the full implications of the RMA. Second, he sought to build among political elites a consensus on behalf of fundamental military reform. Third, he hoped to whittle away at the resistance to such reforms from soldiers chary about giving up old habits and routines that seemingly worked well enough—indeed, by their own estimation, during Desert Storm had worked almost flawlessly. To return to the 1918 comparison, Marshall had to derive from primitive tanks and airplanes all of the technological, doctrinal, and organizational concepts integral to blitzkrieg; to persuade politicians with other immediate priorities to invest in mechanization; and then to persuade officers still enamored with horses and swagger sticks that their future lay with internal combustion engines and tracked vehicles. By and large, over the course of the decade, he accomplished his first two objectives, while achieving mixed success with the third.

What exactly was Marshall's vision of the RMA? In the broadest sense, it meant adapting warfare to specific technological changes that in the closing third of the twentieth century were sweeping through developed societies around the world. The essence of the RMA was to move war out of the industrial age and into the information age.[55]

The Western style of warfare throughout the machine age had relied on armies that were large, heavy, and replaceable. When these armies collided with one another in immense, vastly destructive battles, they killed large numbers of soldiers and civilians alike, leveled cities, and turned the surrounding countryside into wasteland, all in the name of what was termed "military necessity." In the computer age, Marshall believed, such armies and such methods were rapidly becoming obsolete. In their place, he advocated the creation of forces that were lean, nimble, and, above all, "smart."

As Marshall explained in a rare published expression of his views, tapping the military potential of the information revolution had two immedi-

ate implications. First, he said, "long-range precision strike weapons coupled to systems of sensors and to command and control systems will fairly
soon come to dominate much of warfare." Second, "the information
'dimension' increasingly becomes central to the outcome of battles and
campaigns." As a consequence, Marshall predicted that protecting "one's
own information systems and being able to degrade, destroy, or disrupt the
functioning of the opponent's information systems will become a major
focus of the operational art." In essence, the RMA promised ultimately
both to render the battlefield and the enemy's order of battle transparent
and to make it possible to hit and kill anything anywhere on the planet at
any time. Protracted struggle and gratuitous slaughter would become a
thing of the past. "Defeat will occur," Marshall wrote, "due to disintegration of command and control capacities, rather than due to attrition or
annihilation." In determining the outcome of future wars, the size and
weight of your arsenal was likely to matter less than the speed, capacity, and
durability of your computer networks. "Obtaining early superiority in the
information realm will become central to success in future warfare," Marshall concluded.[56] Indeed, to achieve information dominance even before
the fight began—thereby controlling the conditions that would determine
war's outcome—was to secure military preeminence on a permanent basis.[57]

This was not war waged with a scalpel; it was laser surgery. In the years
following Desert Storm, Marshall's vision of future warfare captured the
imagination of the small community of people, mostly politicians, journalists, and members of the strategic priesthood, who attend to such things.
RMA enthusiasts found the vision a mesmerizing one less because it
responded to a proximate threat—although inside the Pentagon Marshall
pressed hard to cast China as the new archenemy—than because it meshed
neatly with a host of other notions that were fashionable in the years immediately following the Cold War.[58] The RMA both drew upon and affirmed
the zeitgeist of the 1990s.

Nor was this a phenomenon without precedent. Again, comparisons
with blitzkrieg are instructive. In the Germany of the 1920s and 1930s, as
one scholar has noted, a "close affinity existed between the radical visions
of machine warfare... and the cultural and intellectual currents partaking
of the proto-fascist and fascist outlook, or 'mood.'" Advocates of mechanized warfare "were searching for a comprehensive outlook, interpretation
of history and the direction it was taking, and view of the current state of

humanity."[59] Tying their vision of war to such a comprehensive outlook promised to invest their proposals for radical military reform with greater legitimacy. But doing so also offered a way of tapping hitherto unrecognized synergies, incorporating into thinking about war ideas and concepts drawn from beyond the realm of military affairs. German fascists saw the creation of new methods of elite, mechanized warfare not only as the means to reverse the verdict of 1918 but also as the vehicle to fulfill their dreams of world mastery and to validate their theories of racial superiority.

That blitzkrieg was not a particularly humane approach to warfare did not concern German authorities in the 1930s, since humanitarian considerations did not figure in the fascist hierarchy of values. Their aim was conquest and intimidation.

Similarly, in 1990s America, there existed a pronounced affinity between Marshall's vision of a Revolution in Military Affairs and the cultural and intellectual currents emblematic of the postindustrial or postmodern mood. The RMA was peculiarly suited to the outlook, interpretation of history, and expectations of the future then au courant among American elites. The amalgam of ideas informing this zeitgeist included the "end of history," globalization, virtual reality, the CNN effect, the New Economy, the discovery of gender as mere social construct, and the role of the United States as "indispensable nation." Together, these seemingly disparate ideas suggested the onset of a historical era characterized by unprecedented transparency and connectivity. Mankind had embarked upon an age in which technology promised very rapid change, while also bringing total mastery of the human environment more closely within reach. In all sorts of enterprises, technology held the key to power and the United States was indisputably the technologically most advanced nation on the planet.

The RMA both anchored war to these perceptions and simultaneously drew on them to enrich the new thinking about the organization and employment of military forces. For example, when *New York Times* columnist Thomas Friedman declared in 1999 that globalization had become "the international system that has replaced the cold-war system," he also declared definitively that it had become incumbent upon the United States to police that system. According to Friedman, "the emerging global order needs an enforcer. That's America's new burden."[60] In a system based upon the free flow of goods, capital, people, and ideas across borders, the enforcer's job was to not break things. It was rather to ensure compliance with rules sustaining progress toward ever-greater openness. The RMA, with its emphasis on measured force producing little collateral damage, was ideally suited to the task of policing without disrupting. At the same time, for military planners to contemplate the security implications of a globalized world, in which, for example, a computer virus could pose as great a problem as an atomic bomb, was to gain useful insights about emerging threats and the capabilities needed to counter those threats.

Or consider the issue of gender. Combat through the ages had placed a premium on qualities commonly associated with young males—strong backs and a taste for mayhem; on the information-age "battlefield" those qualities lost much of their salience. In the world of the RMA, interpreting or manipulating data was becoming at least as important as the ability to tote a rucksack or willingness to charge a hill. As a result, automatically "coding" soldiers as masculine no longer made sense. Now women too could be warriors. This development suited those who viewed distinctions based on gender as inherently invidious and who wished to advance toward a society that treated men and women as interchangeable. At the same time, it made available as potential recruits that half of the population traditionally seen as possessing limited military utility.

In this regard, that the RMA seemed in particular to herald a more humane approach to warfare mattered quite a lot. In the American hierarchy of values, humanitarian considerations did figure. In reserving to itself the prerogatives of global leadership—prerogatives it intended neither to relinquish nor to share—the United States nonetheless wished to see itself as a benign, liberal, and progressive hegemon. Americans in the 1990s did not entertain dreams of dominating through brute force as had the fascists of the 1930s, but they did wish to perpetuate their nation's status as world's sole superpower. Indeed, they were intent on doing so. In this regard, Marshall's promise of techniques for using force in ways that avoided massive physical destruction and spared the lives of innocents was exquisitely well suited to both America's post–Cold War purpose and its self-image.

In short, although the Revolution in Military Affairs offered a way of reconceptualizing warfare, its importance extended well beyond that sphere. In fact, the RMA was one expression of a larger effort to formulate a new vision of the world itself and of America's proper place in (and astride) that world.

*   *   *

As viewed from a vantage point midway through the first decade of the twenty-first century, many of the ideas that achieved prominence during the last decade of the twentieth century appear preposterously foolish. Once the dot-coms collapsed in the late 1990s, the New Economy no longer looked like the sure road to easy riches. In the aftermath of 9/11, globalization's promise of a world without borders lost much of its luster. Nor at least not for the foreseeable future does the universal triumph of democratic capitalism seem foreordained. History, alas, continues in full swing.

In retrospect, that is, we can see that in the 1990s irrational exuberance was by no means confined to the stock market. During the interval between the end of the Cold War and 9/11, irrationality also infected the mood prevailing among American elites on a variety of other issues. What passed in many cases for sober, empirically grounded analysis amounted to little more than speculation, fueled by the intoxicating vapors given off by successive American triumphs over the Soviets and then Iraq.

Much the same observation could be made with regard to what in the 1990s passed for the latest thinking about war. There too exuberance created expectations that became increasingly uncoupled from reality. War's ancient power of seduction was reasserting itself. Winston Churchill referred to this phenomenon as the "the romance of design"—the alluring belief that sufficient diligence could bring the perfect weapon within reach and that, once realized, that weapon was sure to make short work of all sorts of nagging difficulties.[61] At the time about which Churchill wrote, the years leading up to World War I, the Royal Navy dreamed of perfecting the battleship, thereby enabling Great Britain to deflect the challenge of German seapower and maintain its empire. In the 1990s, dreamers inspired by the RMA conjured up images of a radically transformed U.S. military equipped not only to deflect any and all challenges to American security but also to promote American values around the world.

Although Marshall himself was circumspect about the prospects of bringing the RMA fully to fruition, others were not so reticent. The ideas embodied in the RMA kindled enthusiasms that blurred the distinction between actually existing U.S. military capabilities and mere aspirations. Those converted to Marshall's vision (or at least willing to pay it lip service) churned out documents limning the Pentagon's plans to achieve within a decade what it called "full-spectrum dominance"—complete and uncontestable ascendancy in every form of warfare.[62] Journalists eager to clean up the world's ills contemplated the implications of "virtual war" and beat the drums for a new era of interventionism on behalf of the persecuted and oppressed.[63] Other analysts, including recently retired four-star generals, speculated on the possibility of achieving victory not through physical destruction but by relying on "shock and awe" to stun the enemy into sub- mission, "quickly if not nearly instantaneously."[64] With various observers thus resurrecting ideas that had last enjoyed favor in the run-up to Vietnam, the mind of the adversary was reemerging as the *Schwerpunkt* of the Amer- ican way of war.

Such ideas did not find automatic favor with serving officers, many of whom groused that in Marshall's RMA Abrams tanks, carrier battle groups, and piloted aircraft figured only on the periphery, if at all. Soldiers had no gripe as such with advanced technology, but in the eyes of many military professionals, the technological package known as the RMA threatened their soldierly way of life much as the Soviet Union had once threatened the American way of life. To reorganize the Army, Navy, and Air Force consistent with all that the revolution implied would produce entities no longer recognizable in the traditional sense as an army, a navy, or an air force. So soldiers resisted this new enemy within the Pentagon with the same fervor and determination that they had resisted the prior enemy on the other side of the Iron Curtain.

Thus throughout the 1990s, presidents and would-be presidents regu- larly issued grand pronouncements calling for radical military reform. Blue-ribbon commissions issued thick reports warning that U. S forces urgently needed to get on with reconfiguring themselves to meet the chal- lenges of a new era, and various and sundry secretaries of defense unveiled plans for military transformation—all to little or no avail.[65] Foot-dragging soldiers found ways of postponing or at least limiting the scope of Mar- shall's revolution, adorning old orthodoxies with new labels reading "RMA," mobilizing congressional allies with a stake in avoiding change, or just studying a problem to death.

This pattern has persisted into the present decade. In a campaign speech laced with allusions to the RMA, Governor George W. Bush in 2000 prom- ised if elected to empower his secretary of defense with "a broad mandate— to challenge the status quo and envision a new architecture of American defense for decades to come."[66] Once that November's disputed election made him the forty-third president, Bush tried dutifully to make good on that commitment. With notable fanfare, he directed Secretary of Defense Donald Rumsfeld to move out smartly on transforming the military. To advise him on this project, Rumsfeld immediately turned to Andrew W. Marshall, at eighty years of age still firmly ensconced in the Pentagon and with Wohlstetter's passing in 1997 now the undisputed high priest of American strategists.[67]

All but lost in the turbulent aftermath of 9/11 is the fact that Rumsfeld too got almost nowhere in his efforts to reform the armed forces. By September 10, 2001, military transformation appeared to be dead in the water. With the "military brass made up of generals and admirals wedded to existing weapons systems, troop structure and strategy," the *Washington Post* reported, the new administration's plans to implement big change had been "doomed from the start." The generals had been "content to let Rumsfeld talk about transformation as long as his plans didn't interfere with their own priorities."[68] In short, the defenders of military convention had seemingly prevailed yet again.[69]

Or so it seemed. In fact, President Bush's decision after September 11 to wage a global war against terror boosted the RMA's stock. After 9/11, the Pentagon shifted from the business of theorizing about war to the business of actually waging it. This created an opening for RMA advocates to make their case. War plans—not for some remote theoretical contingency but for real campaigns—became the means for demonstrating once and for all the efficacy of ideas advanced by Wohlstetter and Marshall and now supported by policymakers such as Rumsfeld and his deputy Paul Wolfowitz. Rather than acceding to the risk-averse inclinations of the officer corps, Rumsfeld and Wolfowitz pushed for options that relied on precision air power supplemented by small, lean, and agile ground forces.[70] Operation Enduring Freedom, the invasion of Afghanistan in the fall of 2001, and Operation Iraqi Freedom, the invasion of Iraq in the spring of 2003, were the result.

Aficionados of the new American militarism attributed to these two brief episodes significance comparable to that which military historians previously assigned to Poland in the fall of 1939 and France in the spring of 1940: lightning campaigns demonstrating beyond all doubt one nation's total mastery of a radically new conception of warfare.

For his part, Richard Perle, long an advocate of removing Saddam Hussein by whatever means necessary, was quick to credit the immediate result to his mentor Albert Wohlstetter. "This is the first war that's been fought in a way that would recognize Albert's vision of future wars," remarked Perle. "That it was won so quickly and decisively, with so few casualties and so little damage, was in fact an implementation of his strategy and his vision."[71] Reflecting Wohlstetter's vision in its design and execution, the invasion of Iraq also bore his imprint in its rationale and in the scale of ambition that inspired the Bush administration to undertake the war in the first place. Above all, in engaging in a war of choice against Iraq, the Bush administration signaled that the United States no longer felt itself constrained when it came to the use of force. This ultimate rejection of the conventional wisdom was also the ultimate expression of all that Wohlstetter had wrought.

But if Operation Iraqi Freedom was Wohlstetter's war, it was also Marshall's war and even, in a sense, the priesthood's war. The forcible ouster of the Baathists from Baghdad in 2003—undertaken with expectations that such a demonstration of American power offered the shortest route to a democratic Iraq and a more peaceful Middle East—represented the culmination of the project that had absorbed Wohlstetter and his colleagues since 1945. The enterprise launched as an effort to forestall war by reinventing strategy ended up providing a rationale for war launched in a spasm of strategic irrationality.

In the end, the priesthood had turned out to be a war club.

Chapter Seven

BLOOD FOR OIL

IN THE EYES of its most impassioned supporters—few if any of whom would acknowledge the existence of a new American militarism—the ongoing global war on terror constitutes a de facto fourth world war.[1] That is, the conflict that erupted with such fury with the attacks on the World Trade Center and the Pentagon is really a sequel to three previous conflicts that, however different from one another in terms of scope and duration, have defined contemporary history.

According to this interpretation, the long twilight struggle between Communism and democratic capitalism qualifies as the functional equivalent of World War I (1914–18) and World War II (1939–45). In retrospect, we can now see the East-West rivalry commonly referred to as the Cold War for what it really was: World War III (1947–89). After a brief interval of relative peace, corresponding roughly to the 1990s, a fourth conflict, comparable in magnitude to the previous three, commenced on September 11, 2001. This fourth world war promises to continue indefinitely.

Classifying the war on terror as World War IV offers important benefits. It fits the events of September 11 and those that have followed into a historical trope familiar to almost all Americans. In that regard, it offers a reassuring sense of continuity: we've been here before; we know what we need to do; we know how it ends. By extension, the World War IV construct facilitates efforts to mobilize popular support for U.S. military actions undertaken in pursuit of final victory. It also ratifies the claims of federal authorities, especially those in the executive branch, who insist upon exercising "wartime" prerogatives, expanding the police powers of the state and circumscribing constitutional guarantees of due process. It makes available a stock of plausible analogies to help explain the otherwise inexplicable—seeing the dastardly events of September 11 as a reprise of the dastardly surprise of December 7, for example.[2] It thereby helps to preclude awkward questions. It disciplines.

But, at least as originally conceived, it also misleads. Lumping U.S. actions since 9/11 under the rubric of World War IV can too easily become an exercise in sleight-of-hand. Among other things, it tacitly endorses the ever more militaristic cast of U.S. policies—or, if finding fault with those policies, suggests that the problem has been one of being insufficiently proactive. In this reading, the chief defect of U.S. policy prior to 9/11 has been an excess of timidity.

Worse still, to the extent that some Americans might be cognizant of their country's drift toward militarism, the declaration of World War IV permits them to suppress any latent anxiety about such tendencies. After all, according to precedent, a world war—by definition a conflict thrust upon the United States—changes everything. Responsibility for world wars lies with someone else—with Germany in 1917, Japan in 1941, or the Soviet Union after 1945. Designating the several U.S. military campaigns initiated in the aftermath of 9/11 as World War IV effectively absolves the United States of accountability for anything that went before. Blame lies elsewhere: with Osama bin Laden and Al Qaeda; with Saddam Hussein and his Baath Party thugs; with terrorists or with radical Islam. America's responsibility is to finish what others started.

The previous several chapters showed how the reaction to Vietnam produced radical changes in American thinking about soldiers, the armed services, and war itself. Out of defeat, that is, emerged ideas, attitudes, and myths conducive to militarism. But this militaristic predisposition alone cannot explain the rising tide of American bellicosity that culminated in March 2003 with the invasion of Iraq. For that we must look also to interests and, indeed, to the ultimate in U.S. national interests, which is the removal of any obstacles or encumbrances that might hinder the American people in their pursuit of happiness ever more expansively defined.

During the 1980s and 1990s, the U.S. strategic center of gravity shifted, overturning long-established geopolitical priorities that had appeared sacrosanct. A set of revised strategic priorities emerged, centered geographically in the energy-rich Persian Gulf but linked inextricably to the assumed prerequisites for sustaining American freedom at home. A succession of administrations, both Republican and Democratic, opted for armed force as the preferred means to satisfy those new priorities. It was, in other words, a new set of strategic imperatives, seemly conducive to a military solution, that combined with a predisposition toward militarism to produce the full-blown militarization of U.S. policy so much in evidence since 9/11.

This convergence between preconditions and interests suggests an altogether different definition of World War IV—one that did not begin on 9/11, does not have as its founding purpose the elimination of terror, and does not cast the United States as an innocent party. This alternative conception of a fourth world war constitutes not a persuasive rationale for the exercise of U.S. military power in the manner pursued by the Bush administration but the definitive expression of the dangers posed by the new American militarism—for waiting in the wings are World Wars V and VI, inevitably to be justified by the ostensible demands of freedom.

Providing a true account of World War IV requires first placing it in its correct relationship to World War III, the Cold War. Doing that requires briefly reexamining the Cold War itself.

As the great competition between the United States and the Soviet Union slips further into the past, scholars work their way toward an ever more fine-grained interpretation of its origins, conduct, and implications. Yet as far as public perceptions of the Cold War are concerned, their diligence goes largely unrewarded. When it comes to making sense of recent history, the American people, encouraged by their political leaders, have shown a demonstrable preference for clarity rather than nuance. Even as the central events of the Cold War recede into the distance, the popular image of the larger drama in which they figured paradoxically sharpens.

As if compressing world history into a single phrase, "Cold War" serves as a sort of self-explanatory, all-purpose label, encompassing the entire period from the mid-1940s through the late 1980s. And since what is past is prologue, this self-contained, internally coherent, authoritative rendering of the recent past is ideally suited to serve as a template for making sense of events unfolding before our eyes.

From a vantage point midway through the first decade of the twenty-first century, the commonly accepted meta-narrative of our time consists of three distinct chapters. The first, beginning where World War II leaves off, recounts a period of trial and tribulation lasting several decades but ending in an unambiguous triumph for the United States. The next describes a short-lived "post–Cold War era," a brief, dreamy interlude abruptly terminated by 9/11. The second chapter then gives way to a third, still in the process of being written but expected to replicate in broad outlines the first, if only the United States will once again rise to the occasion.

This narrative possesses the virtues of simplicity and neatness, but it is fundamentally flawed. Perhaps worst of all, the narrative does not alert Americans to the full dimensions of their present-day predicament. Instead, it deceives them.

Far more useful from our present perspective is to admit to a different and messier parsing of the recent past, beginning with the Cold War itself. For starters, we should recognize that far from being a unitary event, the Cold War occurred in two very distinct phases.

The first—defined as the period of Soviet-American competition that could have produced an actual rather than apocryphal World War III— essentially ended by 1963. In 1961, by acquiescing in the erection of the Berlin Wall, Washington affirmed its acceptance of a divided Europe, any lingering chatter about the United States liberating "captive nations" notwithstanding. In 1962, during the Cuban Missile Crisis, Washington and Moscow contemplated the real prospect of mutual annihilation, more or less simultaneously blinked, and tacitly agreed to preclude any recurrence of that frightening moment. This recognition of a vital common interest did not open the way to brotherhood and harmony between the two nuclear superpowers. Yet a more predictable, more stable relationship ensued, incorporating a certain amount of ritualistic saber-rattling but characterized by careful adherence to a well-established set of routines and procedures.

Out of stability came opportunities for massive stupidity. During the Cold War's second phase, from 1963 to 1989, both of the major protagonists availed themselves of these opportunities by pursuing inane adventures on the periphery. In the 1960s, of course, the Americans plunged into Vietnam with near-fatal results. Beginning in 1979, the Soviets impaled themselves on Afghanistan with results that did ultimately prove fatal. Whereas the inherent resilience of democratic capitalism enabled the United States to repair the wounds that it had inflicted on itself, the Soviet political economy lacked recuperative powers; thus an already ailing Soviet empire during the course of the 1980s became sick unto death.

Crucially, the key developments hastening the demise of the Soviet empire came from within. When the whole ramshackle structure came tumbling down, Andrei Sakharov, Vaclav Havel, and Karol Wojtyla, the Polish prelate who became Pope John Paul II, could claim as much credit for the result as Ronald Reagan, if not more. At the end of the day, the Helsinki Accords probably made a greater contribution to undermining the Soviet Union than did the reconstitution of U.S. military power in the 1980s. In short, the most persuasive explanation for the final outcome of the Cold War is to be found in Soviet ineptitude, in the internal contradictions of the Soviet system, and in the courage of the dissidents who dared to challenge Soviet authority.

In this telling of the tale, the Cold War remains a drama of compelling moral significance. Shorn of its triumphal trappings, though, that tale has next to nothing to say about the present-day state of world affairs. In a post-9/11 world, it possesses little capacity either to illuminate or to instruct.

To find in the recent past a useful explanation for the present requires an altogether different narrative. Indeed, the materials from which to assemble such an alternative narrative are readily available. All that is required is to resurrect the largely forgotten or ignored story of America's recent use of military power for purposes unrelated to the Soviet-American rivalry or having implications extending beyond that rivalry.

For the fact is that even as the Cold War was slowly winding its way to its denouement World War IV was already under way—indeed, had commenced two full decades before September 2001. World Wars III and IV, that is, consist of parallel rather than sequential episodes. Rather than one preceding and one following the transitional decade of the 1990s, they evolved more or less in tandem, with the former overlaid on top of and therefore obscuring the latter.

The real World War IV began in 1980, and Jimmy Carter of all people declared it.

To be sure, Carter acted only under extreme duress, prompted by the irrevocable collapse of a policy to which he and each of his seven immediate predecessors had adhered, specifically the arrangements designed to guarantee the United States a privileged position in the Persian Gulf. For Cold War–era U.S. policymakers, preoccupied with Europe and East Asia as the main theaters of action, the Gulf prior to 1980 had figured as something of a sideshow. Jimmy Carter now changed all that, thrusting the Gulf into the uppermost tier of U.S. geopolitical priorities.

From 1945 through 1979, the aim of U.S. policy in that region had been twofold: to ensure stability and American access, but to do so in a way that minimized overt U.S. military involvement. In February 1945, Franklin Roosevelt had laid down the basic lines of this policy at a now famous meeting with King Ibn Saud of Saudi Arabia on an American warship anchored in the Great Bitter Lake. Out of this meeting came an understanding: henceforth, Saudi Arabia could count on the United States to guarantee its security; and the United States could count on Saudi Arabia to provide it preferential treatment when it came to exploiting the kingdom's vast, untapped reserves of oil.[3]

In implementing this commitment, the United States opted whenever possible to keep its forces over the horizon and out of sight. For religious reasons, the Saudis considered this essential. As huge wartime U.S. troop deployments in Europe and the Pacific gave way after 1945 to onerous Cold War–mandated requirements to continue garrisoning Europe and the Pacific, the limitation suited Washington as well.

In military parlance, U.S. strategy in the Middle East from the 1940s through the 1970s adhered to the principle known as economy of force. Rather than establishing a large presence in the region, Roosevelt's successors sought to achieve their objectives in ways that entailed a minimal expenditure of American resources and especially of U.S. military power. From time to time, when absolutely necessary, Washington might organize a brief show of force—for example, in 1946 when Harry Truman ordered the USS *Missouri* to the eastern Mediterranean to warn the Soviets to cease meddling in Turkey, or in 1958 when Dwight D. Eisenhower sent U.S. Marines into Lebanon for a brief, bloodless occupation—but these modest gestures proved to be the exception rather than the rule.

The clear preference was for a low profile and a hidden hand. Although by no means averse to engineering "regime change" when necessary, Washington preferred covert action to the direct use of force; the CIA coup that in 1953 overthrew Mohammed Mossadegh in Tehran offers the best-known example.[4] To police the region, Washington looked to surrogates—through the 1960s British imperial forces and, once Britain withdrew from "East of Suez," the shah of Iran.[5] To build up indigenous self-defense (or regime defense) capabilities of select nations, it arranged for private contractors to provide weapons, training, and advice—an indirect way of employing U.S. military expertise. The Vinnell Corporation's ongoing "modernization" of the Saudi Arabian National Guard (SANG), a project now well over a quarter century old, remains a prime example.[6]

By the end of 1979, however, two events had left this approach in a shambles. The first was the Iranian Revolution, which sent the shah into exile and installed in Tehran an Islamist regime adamantly hostile to the United States. The second was the Soviet invasion of Afghanistan, which put the Red Army in a position where it appeared to pose a direct threat to the entire Persian Gulf and hence to the West's oil supply.

Faced with these twin crises, Jimmy Carter concluded that treating the Middle East as a secondary theater, ancillary to the Cold War, no longer made sense. A great contest for control of that region had been joined, one that Iran's Ayatollah Khomeini had made unmistakably clear was not simply an offshoot of the already existing East-West competition. This was something quite different.

Rejecting out of hand any possibility that the United States might come to terms with or accommodate itself to the changes afoot in the Persian Gulf, Carter claimed for the United States a central role in determining exactly what those changes would be. In January 1980, to forestall any further deterioration of the U.S. position in the Gulf, he threw the weight of American military power into the balance.

In his State of the Union Address of that year, the president enunciated what became known as the Carter Doctrine. "An attempt by any outside force to gain control of the Persian Gulf region," he declared, "will be regarded as an assault on the vital interests of the United States of America, and such an assault will be repelled by any means necessary, including military force."[7]

From Carter's time down to the present day, the doctrine bearing his name has remained sacrosanct. As a consequence, each of President Carter's successors has expanded the level of U.S. military involvement and operations in the region. Even today, American political leaders cling to their belief that the skillful application of military power will enable the United

States to decide the fate not simply of the Persian Gulf proper but—to use the more expansive terminology of the present day—of the entire Greater Middle East. This gigantic project is the true World War IV, begun in 1980 and now well into its third decade.

What considerations prompted Jimmy Carter, the least warlike of all recent U.S. presidents, to take this portentous step? The Pentagon's first Persian Gulf commander offered a simple answer: his basic mission, Lieutenant General Robert Kingston said, was "to assure the unimpeded flow of oil from the Arabian Gulf."[8]

In fact, General Kingston was selling his president and his country short. What was true of the three other presidents who had committed the United States to world wars—Wilson, FDR, and Truman—remained true in the case of President Carter and World War IV as well. The overarching motive for action was the preservation of the American way of life.

By the beginning of 1980—facing the prospect of a very tough fight for reelection later that year—a chastened Jimmy Carter had learned a hard lesson: it was not the prospect of making do with less that sustained American-style liberal democracy but the promise of more. By the time that he enunciated the Carter Doctrine, the president had come to realize that the themes of his "Crisis of Confidence" speech six months before—sacrifice, conservation, lowered expectations, personal inconvenience endured on behalf of the common good—were political nonstarters. What Americans wanted for themselves and demanded from their government was freedom, defined as more choice, more opportunity, and above all greater abundance, measured in material terms. That meant that they (along with other developed nations whose own prosperity helped sustain that of the United States) needed assured access to cheap oil and lots of it.

In promulgating the Carter Doctrine, the president was effectively renouncing his vision of a less materialistic, more self-reliant democracy. His about-face did not achieve its intended political purpose of enabling him to preserve his hold on the White House—Ronald Reagan had already tagged Carter as a pessimist whose temperament was at odds with the rest of the country—but it did put in motion a huge shift in U.S. military policy, the implications of which gradually appeared over the course of the next two decades.

Critics might cavil that the resulting militarization of U.S. policy in the Persian Gulf amounted to a devil's bargain, trading blood for oil. Carter saw things differently. The contract had a third element. On the surface the exchange might entail blood-for-oil, but beneath the surface the aim was to guarantee the ever-increasing affluence that underwrites the modern American conception of liberty. Without exception, every one of President Carter's successors has tacitly endorsed this formula. It is in this sense that World War IV and the new American militarism manifest the American will to be free.

From the Carter Doctrine came a new pattern of U.S. military actions, one that emerged through fits and starts. Although not fully apparent until the 1990s, changes in U.S. military posture and priorities gradually converted the Persian Gulf into the epicenter of American grand strategy and World War IV's principal theater of operations.

"Even if there were no Soviet Union," wrote the authors of NSC-68 in the spring of 1950, "we would face the great problem of the free society, accentuated many fold in this industrial age, of reconciling order, security, the need for participation, with the requirement of freedom. We would face the fact that in a shrinking world the absence of order among nations is becoming less and less tolerable."[9]

Drafted during some of the most challenging days of the Cold War, NSC-68 remained the definitive statement of U.S. grand strategy during World War III. Some three decades later, with the Soviet Union headed toward oblivion, the great problem of the free society to which NSC-68 alluded had become if anything more acute. As far as the United States was concerned, the world had continued to shrink, and the absence of order had become less tolerable still, especially if disorder erupted in a region critical to America's own economic well-being.

The combination of interests and disorder that gave rise to World War IV did not soon yield a statement of U.S. grand strategy comparable to NSC-68. Conceiving the principles to guide U.S. policy in World War IV turned out to be a more daunting proposition than it had been during any of the three previous world wars. Throughout the 1980s and 1990s, U.S. policymakers grappled with this challenge, reacting to crises as they occurred and then insisting after the fact that their actions conformed to some larger design. In fact, only after 9/11 did a fully articulated grand strategy emerge, with George W. Bush seeing the antidote to intolerable disorder as the transformation of the Greater Middle East through the sustained use of military power.

Further complicating this challenge of devising a strategy for World War IV was the fundamental incompatibility of two competing U.S. interests in the region. During the last quarter of the twentieth century, the importance that the United States attached to each of these interests grew. At the same time, so too did the difficulty of reconciling one with the other.

On the one hand was a dependence on oil from the Middle East that steadily increased over time. Dependence meant vulnerability, as the crippling oil shocks of the 1970s, administered by the Organization of Oil Exporting Countries (OPEC), amply demonstrated.[10] During the latter half of the twentieth century, that vulnerability inexorably grew as the United States depleted its once fabulous domestic sources of petroleum. As late as World War II, the United States itself had been the world's Saudi Arabia, producing enough oil to meet its own needs and that of its friends and allies.[11] By the end of the twentieth century, with Americans consuming one out of every four barrels of oil produced worldwide, remaining U.S. reserves accounted for less than 2 percent of the world's total. The United Arab Emirates and tiny Kuwait alone each had reserves four times larger than the United States', Iraq almost six times greater, and Saudi Arabia twelve times greater. Projections showed the leverage of Persian Gulf producers mushrooming in the years to come, with oil exports from the region expected to account for between 54 percent and 67 percent of world totals by 2020.[12]

Juxtaposed against Arab oil was Israel. America's commitment to the security and well-being of the Jewish state complicated U.S. efforts to maintain cordial relations with oil-exporting states in the Gulf. Prior to the Six Day War, the United States had tried to manage this problem by maintaining a certain equidistance in matters relating to the Arab-Israeli dispute, supporting Israel's right to exist but resisting Israeli entreaties to forge a strategic partnership. After 1967, that changed dramatically. The United States became Israel's preeminent international supporter and a generous supplier of economic and military assistance.

The Arab-Israeli conflict could not be separated from World War IV, but for U.S. policymakers, figuring out exactly where Israel fit in the larger struggle proved to be a perplexing problem. Was World War IV a war of blood-for-oil-for-freedom in which Israel figured at best as a distraction and at worst as an impediment? Or was it a war of blood-for-oil-for-freedom in which the United States and Israel stood shoulder to shoulder in a common enterprise? For the first twenty years of World War IV, the American response to these questions produced a muddle.

During his final year in office, Carter himself initiated the first action of America's new world war. Through his typically hapless and ineffectual effort to rescue the Americans held hostage in Iran, Carter sprinkled the first few driblets of American military power onto the floor of the desert, where they vanished without a trace.

Although Desert One remained thereafter the gold standard for how not to use force, it by no means curbed America's appetite for further armed intervention in the region. On the contrary, notwithstanding the apparent strictures of the Weinberger Doctrine, Ronald Reagan gave the spigot labeled "military power" a further twist—and in doing so opened the floodgates. To put it another way, while Carter may have declared World War IV, it was on Reagan's watch that the war was fully—if somewhat haphazardly—engaged.

Granted, Reagan himself professed to be oblivious to that war's existence. After all, his immediate preoccupation was with World War III. For public consumption, the president was always careful to justify the U.S. military buildup of the 1980s as a benign and defensive response to Cold War imperatives. "We're not in the business of imperialism, aggression, or conquest," he declared. "We threaten no one."[13] Reconstituting the nation's armed forces had but a single object: to avert conflict. "War will not come again, other young men will not have to die," the president assured his listeners at Memorial Day ceremonies in 1982, "if we will speak honestly of the dangers that confront us and remain strong enough to meet those dangers."[14] All that the United States sought was to be at peace. "Our country has never started a war," Reagan told the annual VFW convention in 1983. "Our sole objective is deterrence, the strength and capability it takes to prevent war."[15] "We Americans don't want war and we don't start fights," he insisted on another occasion. "We don't maintain a strong military force to conquer or coerce others."[16]

This was, of course, at least 50 percent bunkum. During the Reagan era, with the first stirrings of revived American militancy, defense and deterrence seldom figured as the operative principles. Since at least Christmas

1776 when George Washington crossed the Delaware to fall on the unsuspecting Hessians garrisoning Trenton, U.S. military practice had always favored offensive action. The American military tradition has never viewed defense as other than a pause, a period of preparation before seizing the initiative. Nothing in the subsequent two centuries of history that followed—certainly not the experience of Vietnam—had caused American commanders or commanders-in-chief to revise this preference for taking the fight to the enemy.

During the period when the commander-in-chief was Ronald Reagan, partisan critics saw the president's muscle flexing as evidence of a reckless ideologue unnecessarily stoking old Cold War tensions. Viewing events in relation to Vietnam and the Cuban Missile Crisis, they forecast dreadful consequences. On the one hand Reagan risked the recurrence of another quagmire, this time in Central America or in Central Asia. On the other hand opponents charged that Reaganesque provocations—especially in strengthening U.S. strategic offensive capabilities and vowing to field comprehensive strategic defenses—threatened to destabilize Soviet-American relations and court a potentially cataclysmic nuclear showdown.

Reagan's partisan defenders, then and later, told a different story, one that credited the president with being a strategic genius. Having intuitively grasped that the Soviet system had reached an advanced state of decay, Reagan proceeded with skill and dexterity to exploit that system's economic, technological, and moral vulnerabilities; the ensuing collapse of the Soviet empire, in their view, proved conclusively that Reagan had gotten it right all along.

From a post-9/11 vantage point, neither interpretation, Reagan as trigger-happy Cold Warrior or Reagan as master strategist, is especially persuasive. To assess the military record of the Reagan years from a present-day perspective—through the prism of World War IV, as it were—yields a set of altogether different and arguably more relevant insights.

In retrospect, we can see that the entire Reagan era was situated on the seam between one world war that was winding down and a successor war, already begun but not yet fully comprehended. Although preoccupied with waging the Cold War, Reagan and his chief advisers almost as an afterthought launched several forays into the Greater Middle East. The results achieved during this first phase of World War IV were mixed. On the one hand Reagan took a series of steps that greatly enhanced the U.S. ability to project military power into the region. On the other hand his initiatives also emboldened the enemy and contributed to the instability that drew his successors more deeply into the region.

In four different instances, the Reagan administration found occasion to use force in the Islamic world: first, the insertion of U.S. Marine "peace-keepers" into Lebanon, culminating in the Beirut bombing of October 1983; second, clashes with Libya, culminating in April 1986 with punitive U.S. strikes against targets in Tripoli and Benghazi; third, the so-called tanker war of 1984–88, culminating in the commitment of U.S. forces to protect the flow of oil from the Persian Gulf; and finally, American assistance throughout the 1980s to Afghan "freedom fighters," culminating in the Soviet army's ouster from Afghanistan.

The nominal stimulus for action in each case varied. In Lebanon, murkiest of the four, Reagan ordered Marines ashore at the end of September 1982 "to establish an environment which will permit the Lebanese Armed Forces to carry out their responsibilities in the Beirut area."[17] This was a daunting proposition given that Lebanon, divided by a civil war and variously occupied by the Syrian army, the Israel Defense Forces, and (until its recent eviction) the Palestinian Liberation Organization, possessed neither an effective military nor an effective government and had little prospect of acquiring either. Vague expectations that a modest contingent of U.S. peace-keepers camped in Beirut might help restore stability to Lebanon motivated Reagan to undertake this risky intervention, which ended disastrously when a suicide bomber drove into the Marine compound and killed 241 Americans.

In the case of Libya, Muammar Qaddafi's declared intention of denying the U.S. Sixth Fleet access to the Gulf of Sidra, off Libya's coast, had led to preliminary skirmishing in 1981 and again in March 1986.[18] But it was Qaddafi's support for terrorism, and especially alleged Libyan involvement in the bombing of a Berlin disco frequented by GIs, that prompted President Reagan to order retaliation on April 15.[19]

In the tanker war, Reagan was reacting to attacks against neutral shipping in the Persian Gulf, perpetrated by both Iran and Iraq. Since 1980, these two nations had been locked in a bloody and inconclusive war. As that struggle spilled over into the adjacent waters of the Gulf, it reduced the availability of oil for export, drove up insurance rates, and crippled merchant shipping. It was an Iraqi missile attack on the USS *Stark* on May 17,

1987, that brought things to a head. Iraq claimed that the incident, which killed thirty-seven sailors, had been an accident and offered compensation. However, the Reagan administration used the *Stark* episode to blame Iran for the escalating violence. In short order, Kuwaiti supertankers were flying the Stars and Stripes, and U.S. forces were conducting a brisk campaign to sweep Iranian air and naval units out of the Gulf.[20]

Finally, in the case of Afghanistan, Reagan built on a program already in existence but hidden from public eyes. In July 1979, the Carter administration had agreed to provide covert assistance to Afghans resisting the pro-Soviet regime in Kabul. According to Zbigniew Brzezinski, Carter's national security adviser, the aim was to induce a Soviet military response, thereby "drawing the Russians into the Afghan trap."[21] When the Soviets did invade in December 1979, they soon became bogged down in a guerrilla war against the U.S.-backed mujaheddin. Reagan inherited this project, initially sustained it, and then in 1985 greatly stepped up the level of U.S. support for the Afghan resistance.[22]

At first glance, these four episodes seem to be all over the map, both literally and also in terms of purpose, means, and outcome. Contemporaneous assessments tended to treat each in isolation from the others and to focus on near-term outcomes. "After the attack on Tripoli," Reagan bragged, "we didn't hear much more from Qaddafi's terrorists."[23] Nonsense, replied critics, pointing to the suspected Libyan involvement (since confirmed) in the bombing of Pan American flight 103 in December 1988 and in the midair destruction of a French DC-10 nine months later. When a ceasefire in 1988 ended the fighting between Iran and Iraq, Defense Secretary Weinberger assessed U.S. involvement in the tanker war as a major achievement. In his 1990 memoir, Weinberger concluded the chapter recounting this episode (entitled "The Persian Gulf Success Story") with this judgment: "We had now clearly won."[24] With several hundred thousand U.S. troops deploying to the Gulf that very same year to prepare for large-scale war, Weinberger's claims of victory seemed at best premature.

To be sure, Reagan himself labored to weave together a comprehensive rationale for the various military actions he ordered. The result, however, tended to be another exercise in mythmaking.

In his public presentations, Reagan justified his actions in terms of ideals rather than interests. Truth began with understanding that evil forces were constantly subverting American efforts to bring to the region that lasting peace "under which mankind was meant to flourish."[25] Soviet leaders pursuing global revolution, fundamentalists bent on propagating Islamic theocracies, Arab fascists like Libya's Qaddafi and Syria's Havez al Assad, fanatical terrorists like Abu Nidal—to listen to Reagan, all of these disparate threats morphed into a single conspiracy. Since to give way to one element of that conspiracy was to give way to all, the essential thing was to hold firm everywhere for peace.

Here is Reagan recalling his dilemma in considering how to react to the bombing in Beirut:

> In the weeks immediately after the bombing, I believed the last thing we should do was turn tail and leave. If we did that, it would say to the terrorists of the world that all it took to change American foreign policy was to murder some Americans.... We'd be saying that the sacrifice of those marines had been for nothing. We'd be inviting the Russians to supplant the United States as the most influential superpower in the Middle East. After more than a year of fighting and mounting chaos in Beirut, the biggest winner would be Syria, a Soviet client.

Despite all that, of course, the United States did turn tail and leave, Reagan in his memoirs blaming "the irrationality of Middle Eastern politics."[26]

Further muddying the waters were administration initiatives seemingly predicated on an assumption that no such overarching conspiracy against peace actually existed, or at least that selective U.S. collaboration with evildoers was permissible. The administration's notorious "tilt" in the Iran-Iraq War in favor of Saddam Hussein, offering intelligence and commercial credits to the region's foremost troublemaker—perhaps the final U.S. effort to enlist a proxy to secure its Persian Gulf interests—provides one example.[27] Its illegal sale of weapons to Iran's Islamic Republic, leading to the infamous Iran-Contra Affair, provides a second. Such opportunism made a mockery of Reagan's windy pronouncements regarding America's role as peacemaker, feeding suspicions that the president's rhetoric was actually intended to divert attention from his administration's apparent strategic disarray.

Considered from a post-9/11 vantage point, however, Reagan-era uses of force in Lebanon, Libya, the tanker war, and Afghanistan do cohere, at least in a loose sort of way. First, and most notably, all four occurred in the Greater Middle East, hitherto not the site of frequent U.S. military activity. Second, none of the four episodes can be fully understood except in relation to global reserves of fossil fuels and America's growing dependence on imported oil. Although energy considerations did not drive U.S. actions in every instance, they always loomed in the background, sometimes figuring prominently. Even in the case of Lebanon, itself not an oil exporter, assertions that a desire to keep the peace prompted the United States to intervene in 1982 stand up to close examination about as well as do claims that Germany's violation of Belgian neutrality prompted Great Britain in 1914 to intervene in what became World War I. Altruistic concern for the well-being of lesser nations, even the most innocent, does not explain the behavior of great powers, even democratic ones. Lebanon's woes mattered to the United States because instability there threatened to undermine the precarious stability of the region as a whole and that, in turn, could threaten the West's supply of oil.

The episodes comprising Reagan's Islamic quartet were alike in one other way. Although each yielded a near-term outcome that the administration touted as conclusive, the actual results turned out to be anything but that. Rather, as subsequent events made clear, each of the four pointed toward ever-deepening American military engagement. Together the four episodes constituted a campaign that deserved the name "Slippery Slope."

In that regard, the true significance of Reagan's several interventions in the Islamic world lies not in the events themselves but in the response that they evoked from the U.S. national security apparatus. Bit by bit during the 1980s, that apparatus began to reorient itself. Government agencies, nudged along by the analysts, insider journalists, and out-of-office officials comprising the foreign policy *nomenklatura*, evolved the beginnings of a new strategic consensus. The essence of that consensus was that the challenges posed by the politically volatile, energy-rich world of Islam were eclipsing all others in the list of pressing U.S. geopolitical concerns. Here, far more than the size of the Soviet nuclear arsenal or the putative ambitions of the Soviet politburo, was where real danger lay.

Given the imperative of meeting popular expectations for ever greater abundance (which meant importing ever larger quantities of oil)—Jimmy Carter's one-term presidency having demonstrated the political consequences of suggesting a different course—the necessary response to that danger was to put the United States in a position to determine the fate of the Middle East. In this regard as in others, Albert Wohlstetter served as something of a bellwether, pressing the case as early as 1981 for "an improved military capability to protect Persian Gulf oil." This meant forces, bases, and infrastructure.[28] Only by enjoying unquestioned primacy in the region—initially defined as "Southwest Asia" but eventually to encompass all of the Persian Gulf, the Caucasus, and Central Asia—could the government of the United States guarantee American prosperity and therefore American freedom.

From the outset, that is, dominance was the aim. What Winston Churchill had said with regard to European maneuvering in the Persian Gulf at the beginning of the twentieth century remained true as the century drew to a close: "mastery itself was the prize of the venture."[29]

Here lay the driving force behind U.S. actions in what became World War IV: not preventing the spread of weapons of mass destruction; not stemming the spread of terror; certainly not liberating oppressed peoples or advancing the cause of women's rights. The prize was mastery over a region that leading members of the American foreign policy elite, of whatever political persuasion, had concluded to be critically important to the well-being of the United States.

Further, at its very core, the problem was one that demanded a military solution; this, at least, was the initial presumption, never thereafter subjected to serious scrutiny. As such, the response to the challenges presented by this region was to be found in enhancing the Pentagon's ability to move U.S. forces into the region and to sustain them there. In March 1984, Donald Rumsfeld, out of power but serving as a Reagan administration troubleshooter, told Secretary of State George Shultz that Lebanon was a mere "sideshow." The main show was the Persian Gulf; instability there "could make Lebanon look like a taffy pull." Rumsfeld worried that "we are neither organized nor ready to face a crisis there."[30] In fact, the effort to reorganize was already under way. This is where Reagan made his most lasting contribution to the struggle to which Jimmy Carter had committed the United States.

The following specific initiatives figured prominently in the Reagan administration's comprehensive effort to ramp up America's ability to wage World War IV.

- The upgrading in 1983 of the Rapid Deployment Joint Task Force, the Persian Gulf intervention force created by Carter after the Soviet incursion into Afghanistan, to the status of full-fledged regional headquarters. As United States Central Command, that headquarters became the chief instrument for U.S. policy, diplomatic as well as military, throughout the Persian Gulf and Central Asia.[31]

- The accelerated conversion of Diego Garcia, a tiny British-owned island in the Indian Ocean, from a minor U.S. communications facility into a major U.S. forward support base. Diego Garcia was used to preposition military stores and subsequently served as a launching pad for combat operations—to include strikes by long-range bombers— along an arc running from Central Asia to the Horn of Africa.[32]

- The establishment of large stocks of supplies and equipment, pre-loaded on ships and positioned to facilitate the rapid movement of U.S. combat forces to the Persian Gulf. By 1990 this Afloat Prepositioning Force consisted of twenty-five vessels.[33]

- The construction or expansion of airbases, ports, and other fixed locations required to receive and sustain large-scale U.S. expeditionary forces in Egypt, Saudi Arabia, Oman, Kenya, Somalia, and other compliant states.[34]

- The negotiation of overflight rights and agreement to permit U.S. military access to airports and other facilities in Morocco, Egypt, and elsewhere in the region to support the large-scale introduction of U.S. troops.[35]

- The refinement of war plans and the development of exercise programs to acclimate U.S. forces to the unfamiliar and demanding desert environment; most notable among these programs was the "Bright Star" series, conducted throughout the 1980s in Egypt— "America's steppingstone to the Gulf"—and several lesser states in the region.[36]

- The redoubling of efforts to cultivate client states through arms sales and training programs, the latter administered by either the U.S. military or American-controlled private contractors employing large numbers of former U.S. military personnel.[37]

Even before the demise of the Soviet Union was fully visible, that is, the Reagan administration was deeply engaged in the preliminaries of the next world war. All that followed was not foreordained, any more than, say, in the 1940s the Soviet-American rivalry itself had been foreordained, but by the time Ronald Reagan retired from office the skids had been greased: the national security bureaucracy was well on its way to embracing a highly militarized conception of how to deal with the challenges posed by the Middle East. Giving Reagan his due, that is, requires an appreciation of the extent to which he advanced the reordering of U.S. national security priorities that Jimmy Carter had barely begun. Reagan's seemingly slapdash Islamic pudding turned out after all to have a theme.

Those who adjudge the present World War IV to be necessary and winnable will see in Reagan's record much to commend; they may well accord Reagan a share of the credit for Operations Enduring Freedom and Iraqi Freedom. It was, after all, Reagan who restored the sinews of American military might after Vietnam, refashioned American attitudes about military power, and began reorienting the Pentagon on the Islamic world, thereby making possible the far-flung campaigns undertaken to overthrow the Taliban and remove Saddam Hussein. George W. Bush had pulled the trigger, but Ronald Reagan had first cocked the weapon.

Those who view World War IV as either sinister in its motivation or misguided in its conception will include Reagan in their bill of indictment. From their perspective, it was Reagan who seduced his fellow citizens with promises of material abundance without limit. It was Reagan who made the fusion of military strength with American Exceptionalism the centerpiece of his efforts to revive national self-confidence. It was Reagan's enthusiastic support of Afghan "freedom fighters"—eminently defensible in the context of World War III—that produced not freedom but a Central Asian power vacuum, Afghanistan becoming a cesspool of Islamic radicalism and a safe haven for America's chief adversary in World War IV. Finally, it was Reagan's inconclusive forays in and around the Persian Gulf that paved the way for still larger if equally inconclusive interventions to come.[38]

Throughout the first phase of World War IV, from 1980 to 1990, the United States viewed Iran as its main problem and even toyed with the idea that Iraq might be part of a solution; Washington saw Saddam Hussein as someone with whom it might make common cause against the mullahs in Tehran. During the second phase of World War IV, extending through the

1990s, Iraq supplanted Iran as the main U.S. adversary, and policymakers saw the Iraqi dictator himself as their chief nemesis. Throughout the decade, U.S. policymakers experimented with ways of dealing with that opponent while also attempting to prevent the twin concerns for oil and Israel from getting in the way of one another.

Various and sundry exertions ensued, but as the U.S. military profile in the region became ever more prominent, the difficulties with which the United States felt obliged to contend also multiplied. Indeed, rather than eliminating Saddam, the growing reliance on military power served only to rouse greater antagonism directed at the United States. Policies intended to shore up the American position in the Greater Middle East only bred challenges to that position. Actions taken to enhance Persian Gulf stability—more or less synonymous with guaranteeing the safety and survival of the Saudi royal family—instead produced instability. In this regard, the mistakes and miscalculations marring U.S. policy during phase two of World War IV led directly to the war's third and current phase.

Phase two began in August 1990 when Saddam Hussein's army overran Kuwait. From the U.S. perspective, Saddam's aim was clear. He sought to achieve regional hegemony and to control, either directly or indirectly, the preponderant part of the Persian Gulf's oil wealth. Were Saddam to achieve those objectives, there was every likelihood that in due time he would turn on Israel.[39]

So after only the briefest hesitation, the administration of George H. W. Bush mounted a forthright response. At the head of a very large international coalition, the nation marched off to war, U.S. forces handily ejecting the Iraqi occupiers and restoring the Al-Sabah family to its throne. Bowing to American pressure, Israel stayed on the sidelines. Its assigned mission accomplished, the officer corps led by Colin Powell had little interest in pressing its luck. The American army was eager to scoop up its winnings and go home.

The elder President Bush dearly hoped that Operation Desert Storm might become a great historical watershed, laying the basis for a more law-abiding international system. In fact, the war turned about to be both less and more than he anticipated. Out of that demonstration of American military prowess, no new world order emerged, but the war saddled the United States with new obligations from which there came yet more headaches and complications.

Saddam survived in power by brutally suppressing those whom the Bush administration had urged to rise up in opposition to the dictator. After first averting its eyes from the fate of the Iraqi Shiites and Kurds, the administration eventually found itself shamed into action. To protect the Kurds (and to prevent Kurdish refugees from triggering a military response by neighboring Turkey, a key U.S. ally), Bush sent U.S. forces into northern Iraq. To limit Saddam's ability to use his army as an instrument of repression, the Bush administration, with British support, declared the existence of "no-fly zones" across much of northern and southern Iraq. In April 1991, Anglo-American air forces began routine combat patrols of Iraqi airspace, a mission that continued without interruption for the next twelve years. During his final weeks in office, as one means of keeping Saddam "in his box," the elder President Bush initiated the practice of launching punitive air strikes against Iraqi military targets.

Thus, a year after what had seemed to be a decisive victory in Operation Desert Storm, the United States had transitioned willy-nilly to a policy that appeared anything but decisive. The Bush administration called that policy containment. As one result of this new policy, the presence of substantial U.S. forces in Saudi Arabia and elsewhere in the Persian Gulf, initially conceived as temporary, became permanent. A contingent of approximately twenty-five thousand U.S. troops remained after Desert Storm as a Persian Gulf constabulary—or, from the perspective of many Arabs, as an occupying army of infidels. As a second result, the United States fell into the habit of routinely employing force to punish the Iraqi regime. What U.S. policymakers called containment was really an open-ended quasi-war.

From a World War IV perspective, this new policy of containment-with-bombs formed just one part of the legacy that President Bush bequeathed to his successor, Bill Clinton. That legacy had two additional elements. The first was Somalia, the impoverished, chaotic, and now famine-stricken Islamic "failed state" into which Bush sent U.S. forces following his defeat in the November 1992 elections. Bush described the U.S. mission as a humanitarian one and promised to have American troops out of the country by the time that he left office. When Clinton became president, however, there they remained. The second element of the legacy inherited by Clinton was the so-called peace process, Bush's post–Desert Storm initiative aimed at persuading the Arab world once and for all to accept Israel.

Although not for want of trying, President Clinton was unable to extract from this ambiguous legacy much of tangible value. Over the course of his eight years in office, he clung to the Bush policy of containing Iraq while ratcheting up the frequency with which the United States used violence to enforce that policy. Indeed, during the two concluding years of the Clinton presidency, the United States bombed Iraq on almost a daily basis, a campaign largely ignored by the media and thus aptly dubbed by one observer "Operation Desert Yawn."[40]

In the summer of 1993, Clinton had also ratcheted up the U.S. military commitment in Somalia. Here the results proved disastrous. With the famous Mogadishu firefight of October 1993, Clinton quickly threw in the towel, tacitly accepting defeat at the hands of Islamic fighters. Somalia per se mattered little. Somalia as a battlefield of World War IV mattered quite a bit. The speedy U.S. withdrawal after Mogadishu affirmed to many the apparent lesson of Beirut a decade earlier: Americans lacked the stomach for real fighting; if seriously challenged, they would fold. At least, this was the lesson that Osama bin Laden drew. In the August 1996 fatwa against the United States, he cited the failure of the U.S. policy in Lebanon as evidence of America's "false courage" and found in Somalia proof of U.S. "impotence and weaknesses." When "tens of your soldiers were killed in minor battles and one American Pilot was dragged in the streets of Mogadishu," crowed the leader of Al Qaeda, "you left the area carrying disappointment, humiliation, defeat and your dead with you."[41]

From Mogadishu onward, the momentum shifted inexorably in favor of those contesting American efforts to dominate the Gulf. For the balance of the Clinton era, the United States found itself in a reactive posture. Over the next several years, the United States sustained a series of minor but painful and painfully embarrassing setbacks: in November 1995, the bombing of SANG headquarters in Riyadh; in June 1996, an attack on the U.S. military barracks at Khobar Towers in Dhahran; in August 1998, simultaneous attacks on U.S. embassies in Kenya and Tanzania; in August 2000, the near-sinking of an American warship, the USS *Cole*, during a port call at Aden.

To each of these in turn, the Clinton administration promised a prompt, decisive response. Whenever a U.S. response actually materialized, however, it proved innocuous. The low point came in late August 1998 following the African embassy bombings. With the United States now locked in combat with what Bill Clinton openly referred to as "the bin Laden net-work," the president ordered cruise missile strikes against a handful of primitive training camps in Afghanistan, with a Sudanese pharmaceutical factory allegedly involved in the production of chemical weapons thrown in for good measure. Although the president spoke grimly of a "long, ongo-ing struggle between freedom and fanaticism" and vowed that the United States was "prepared to do all that we can for as long as we must," the oper-ation, given the code name Infinite Reach, accomplished next to nothing and was over as soon as it began.[42] The disparity between words and actions—between the operation's grandiose name and its trivial impact—spoke volumes. In truth, no one in the Clinton White House had a clear conception of what it was that the United States needed to do and to whom.

Finally, despite Clinton's own energetic and admirable contributions, the peace process did not yield peace. Instead, the final collapse of that process at Camp David in 2000 gave way to a new cycle of Palestinian ter-rorist attacks and Israeli reprisals. An alienated Arab world convinced itself that the United States and Israel were conspiring to humiliate and oppress Muslims. Just as the Israel Defense Forces occupied Gaza and the West Bank, so too the U.S. military seemingly intended to occupy the Middle East as a whole. In Arab eyes, the presence of U.S. troops amounted to "a new American colonialism," an expression of a larger effort to "seek con-trol over Arab political and economic affairs."[43] Moreover, just as Israel appeared callous in its treatment of the Palestinians, so too the United States appeared callous in its attitude toward Iraqis, persisting in a policy of sanctions in which the burden of punishment fell not on Saddam Hussein but on the Iraqi people.

The end of the 1980s had found the Reagan administration engaged in a far-reaching contest for control of the Middle East, a de facto war whose existence President Reagan himself either could not see or was unwilling to acknowledge. Ten years later, events ought to have removed any doubts about whether or not the circumstance facing the United States qualified as a war, but the Clinton administration's insistence on describing the adver-sary as disembodied "terrorists" robbed those events of any coherent polit-ical context. The various episodes constituting the war's major engagements remained inexplicable, unfathomable, and seemingly unrelated.

In the manner of his immediate predecessors, Clinton refused even to concede that the violence directed against the United States might stem from some plausible (which is not to imply justifiable) motivation—even as Osama bin Laden outlined his intentions with impressive clarity. In his 1996 Declaration of Jihad, for example, bin Laden identified his objectives: to overthrow the corrupt Saudi regime that had become a tool of the "Zionist-Crusader alliance"; to expel the infidels from the land of the Two Holy Places; and to ensure the worldwide triumph of Islam. But megalomania does not necessarily preclude shrewdness. As Michael Klare has observed, bin Laden's immediate aim was more limited, namely "to destroy the 1945 compact forged by President Roosevelt and King Abd al-Aziz Ibn Saud."[44] A perfectly logical first step toward that end was to orchestrate a campaign of terror against the United States.[45]

For Clinton even to acknowledge that agenda was also to acknowledge that opposition to the U.S. presence in and around the Persian Gulf did not simply emerge out of nowhere. It had a history, one fraught like all history with ambiguity. In this case, that history exposed the underside of American Exceptionalism. In the Persian Gulf, even as it proclaimed itself democracy's greatest friend, the United States had behaved just like any other nation. For decades it had single-mindedly pursued its own concrete interests, with only occasional regard for how its actions affected others and with even less attention given to how they might give rise to future difficulties. Expediency had dictated that American policymakers avert their eyes from the fact that throughout much of the Islamic world the United States had aligned itself with regimes that were arbitrary, corrupt, and oppressive.

In the annals of statecraft, U.S. policy in the Persian Gulf from FDR through Clinton did not qualify as having been notably harsh or irresponsible, but neither had it been particularly wise or enlightened. Certainly it had not been the handiwork of innocents. In short, bin Laden's campaign, however contemptible, and opposition to the U.S. ambitions in the Greater Middle East more generally, emerged at least in part as a response to prior U.S. policies and actions, in which lofty ideals and high moral purpose seldom figured. The United States cannot be held culpable for the maladies that today find expression in violent Islamic radicalism. But neither can the United States absolve itself of any and all responsibility for the conditions that have exacerbated those maladies. After several decades of acting as the preeminent power in the Persian Gulf, America did not arrive at the end of the twentieth century with clean hands.

Years before 9/11, bin Laden understood that World War IV had been fully joined, and he seems to have rejoiced in the prospect of a fight to the finish. Even as they engaged in a wide array of military activities intended to deflect threats to U.S. control of the Persian Gulf and its environs, a succession of American presidents persisted in pretending otherwise. For them, World War IV remained a furtive enterprise.

Unlike Franklin Roosevelt, who had deceived the American people but understood long before December 7, 1941, that he was steadily moving the United States toward direct engagement in a monumental struggle, the lesser statesmen who inhabited the Oval Office during the 1980s and 1990s in weaving their deceptions also managed to confuse themselves. Despite endless assertions that the United States sought only peace, Presidents Reagan, Bush, and Clinton were each in fact waging war and building toward a larger one. But a coherent strategy for bringing that war to a successful conclusion remained elusive.

Perhaps for that very reason, whereas bin Laden, playing a weak hand, played it with considerable skill, the United States, even as it flung bombs and missiles about with abandon, seemed throughout the 1990s to dither. During that decade, World War IV became bigger and the costs mounted, but its resolution appeared more distant than ever. The Bush and Clinton administrations used force in the region not so much as an extension of policy but as a way of distracting attention from the contradictions that riddled U.S. policy. Bombing something—at times literally almost anything—became a convenient way of keeping up appearances. Thus, despite (or perhaps due to) the military hyperactivity of these two administrations, the overall U.S. position deteriorated even further during the war's second phase.

George W. Bush inherited this deteriorating situation when he became president in January 2001. Bush may or may not have brought into office a determination to finish off Saddam Hussein at the first available opportunity, but he most assuredly did not bring with him a comprehensive, ready-made conception for how to deal with the incongruities that plagued U.S. policy in the Greater Middle East. For its first eight months in office, the second Bush administration essentially marked time. Apart from some politically inspired grandstanding—shunning an international agreement to slow global warming, talking tough on North Korea, accelerating plans to field ballistic missile defenses—Bush's foreign policy prior to 9/11 hewed closely to the lines laid down by his predecessor.[46] Although Republicans had spent the previous eight years lambasting Clinton for being weak and feckless, their own approach to World War IV, initially at least, amounted to more of the same.

Osama bin Laden chose this moment to initiate the war's third phase. His direct assault on the United States itself left thousands dead, wreaked havoc with the American economy, and exposed the acute vulnerabilities of the world's sole superpower.

President Bush's spontaneous response to the events of 9/11—although they were not perpetrated by soldiers and were directed for the most part at nonmilitary targets—was to see them not as vile crimes but as acts of war. In doing so he acknowledged openly the existence of the conflict in which the United States had been engaged for the previous twenty years. World War IV became the centerpiece of the Bush presidency, although the formulation preferred by members of his administration (and soon widely adopted as authoritative) was "global war on terror."

When committing the United States to large-scale armed conflict, presidents historically have evinced a strong preference for explaining the stakes in terms of ideology, thereby distracting attention from geopolitics. Americans ostensibly fight for universal values rather than sordid self-interest. Thus Franklin Roosevelt cast the war against Japan as a contest that pitted democracy against imperialism. The Pacific War was that, but it was also a war fought to determine the future of East Asia, with both Japan and the United States seeing China as the main prize. Harry Truman and his successors characterized the Cold War as a struggle between a Free World and a totalitarian one. It was that, but it was also a competition to determine which of two superpowers would enjoy preponderant influence in Western Europe, with both the Soviet Union and the United States seeing Germany as the nexus of conflict.

During its preliminary phases—that is, from January 1980 to September 2001—World War IV had departed from this pattern. Throughout this period, regardless of who happened to be occupying the Oval Office, universal values did not figure prominently in the formulation and articulation of U.S. policy in the Persian Gulf. In this war, geopolitics routinely trumped values, although few U.S. officials said as much outright. Everyone knew that the dominant issue was oil, with Saudi Arabia understood to be the crown jewel. Only after 9/11 did values (women's rights now enjoying pride of place among them) emerge as the ostensible driving force behind U.S. efforts in the region, indeed, throughout the entire Greater Middle East. Effective September 11, 2001, World War IV had become—like each of its predecessors—a war for "freedom." This was the theme to which President George W. Bush returned time and again.[47]

In fact, President Bush's epiphany was itself a smoke screen. His conversion to the church of Woodrow Wilson left substantive U.S. objectives in World War IV unaltered. Using armed might to secure American preeminence across the region, especially in the oil-rich Persian Gulf, remained the essence of U.S. policy. What had changed was the scope of the military effort that the United States was now willing to undertake in pursuit of those objectives. After 9/11, the Bush administration pulled out all the stops in its determination to impose America's will on the Greater Middle East.

It is in this regard that the Bush administration's invasion of Iraq in March 2003 can be said to possess a certain bizarre logic. As part of a larger campaign to bring the perpetrators of 9/11 to justice, Operation Iraqi Freedom made no sense at all and was probably counterproductive. Yet as the initial gambit of an effort to transform the entire region through the use of superior military power, it not only made sense but also held out the prospect of finally resolving the incongruities bedeviling U.S. policy. Iraq formed the "tactical pivot"—not an end in itself but a way station.[48] By toppling Saddam Hussein, the United States could establish itself in a position of strength and acquire greater freedom of action. "With Saddam gone," Richard Clarke has written, "the U.S. could reduce its dependence on Saudi Arabia, could pull its forces out of the Kingdom, and could open up an alternative source of oil."[49]

Pulling U.S. forces out of Saudi Arabia did not imply removing them from the region. Advocates of the Iraq War saw that war in part as an exercise in military repositioning. "We will probably need a major concentration of forces in the Middle East over a long period of time," Donald Kagan opined in September 2002. A continuing American troop presence was necessary to guarantee U.S. access to energy reserves. "If we have a force in Iraq," Kagan confidently predicted, "there will be no disruption in oil supplies."[50]

This was only beginning: once having demonstrated its ability and willingness to oust recalcitrants, having established a mighty striking force in the center of the Persian Gulf, and having reduced its susceptibility to the oil weapon, the United States would be well positioned to create a new political order in the region, one incorporating values such as freedom, democracy, and equality for women. A Middle East pacified, brought into compliance with American ideological norms, and policed by American soldiers could be counted on to produce plentiful supplies of oil and to accept the presence of a Jewish state in its midst. "In transforming Iraq," one senior Bush administration official confidently predicted, "we will take a significant step in the direction of the longer-term need to transform the region as a whole."[51]

Bush and members of his inner circle conceived of this as a great crusade. At its unveiling, a clear majority of citizens judged this preposterous enterprise to be justifiable, feasible, and indeed necessary. At least two factors help to explain this apparent gullibility.

The first factor is self-induced historical amnesia. Leaning on a senior Pakistani official to accommodate the upcoming U.S. intervention in Afghanistan, Deputy Secretary of State Richard Armitage growled shortly after 9/11: "History starts today."[52] Armitage's sentiment suffused the Bush administration and was widely shared among the American people. The grievous losses suffered in the attacks on the World Trade Center and the Pentagon had seemingly rendered all that had gone before irrelevant. Nothing that had happened previously counted, hence the notable absence of interest among Americans in how the modern Middle East had come into existence or in the role that the United States since World War II had played in its evolution. In an instant, 9/11 had wiped the slate clean; on this clean slate, the Bush administration, in quintessential American fashion, fancied that it could begin the history of the Greater Middle East all over again.

There is a second explanation for this extraordinary confidence in America's ability to reorder nations according to its own preferences. The progressive militarization of U.S. policy since Vietnam—especially U.S. policy as it related to the Middle East—had acquired a momentum to which the events of September 11 only added. Furthermore, the aura that by 2001 had come to suffuse American attitudes toward war, soldiers, and military institutions had dulled the capacity of the American people to think critically about the actual limits of military power.

Nowhere had those attitudes gained a deeper lodgment than in the upper echelons of the younger Bush's administration. The experiences of the previous thirty years had thoroughly militarized the self-described Vulcans to whom the president turned in shaping his global war on terror—both in formulating grand statements like his *National Security Strategy* and in planning campaigns like the invasions of Afghanistan and Iraq. Theirs was a vision, writes James Mann, of "a United States whose military power was so awesome that it no longer needed to make compromises or accommodations (unless it chose to do so) with any other nation or groups of countries."[53] Their confidence in the competence and bravery of the American soldier and in the effectiveness of American arms was without limit. So too was their confidence in their own ability to make war do their bidding. They had drunk deeply of the waters that sustained the new American militarism.

As the epigraph to his book on Vietnam, Norman Podhoretz chose a quotation from Bismarck. "Woe to the statesman whose reasons for entering a war do not appear so plausible at its end as at its beginning."[54] For the architects of the global war on terror—not only President Bush himself, but also Dick Cheney, Donald Rumsfeld, Condoleezza Rice, and Paul Wolfowitz—it's too late to heed the Iron Chancellor's warning. Their reputations have suffered near irreparable damage. But the outsized conflict that is their principal handiwork continues.

As this is written, the outcome of World War IV hangs very much in the balance. American shortsightedness played a large role in creating this war. American hubris has complicated it unnecessarily, emboldening the enemy, alienating old allies, and bringing U.S. forces close to exhaustion. Yet like it or not, Americans are now stuck with their misbegotten crusade.

God forbid that the United States should fail, allowing the likes of Osama bin Laden and his henchmen to decide the future of the Islamic world.

Still, even if the United States ultimately prevails—thereby reinvigorating the several conceits informing the new American militarism—the prospects for the future will be hardly less discouraging. On the far side of World War IV, a time which we are not presently given to see, there await others who will not readily concede to the United States the prerogatives and the dominion that Americans have come to expect as their due. The ensuing collision between American requirements and a noncompliant world will provide the impetus for more crusades. Each in turn will be justified in terms of ideals rather than interests, but together they may well doom the United States to fight perpetual wars in a vain effort to satisfy our craving for freedom without limit and without end.

Chapter Eight

COMMON DEFENSE

THERE IS, wrote H. L. Mencken, "always a well-known solution to every human problem—neat, plausible, and wrong."[1] Mencken's aphorism applies in spades to the subject of this account.

To imagine that there exists a simple antidote to the "military metaphysic" to which the people and government of the United States have fallen prey is to misconstrue the problem. As the foregoing chapters make plain, the origins of America's present-day infatuation with military power are anything but simple.

American militarism is not the invention of a cabal nursing fantasies of global empire and manipulating an unsuspecting people frightened by the events of 9/11. Further, it is counterproductive to think in these terms— to assign culpability to a particular president or administration and to imagine that throwing the bums out will put things right.

Yet neither does the present-day status of the United States as sole superpower reveal an essential truth, whether positive or negative, about the American project. Enthusiasts (mostly on the right) who interpret America's possession of unrivaled and unprecedented armed might as proof that the United States enjoys the mandate of heaven are deluded. But so too are those (mostly on the left) who see in the far-flung doings of today's U.S. military establishment substantiation of Major General Smedley Butler's old chestnut that "war is just a racket" and the American soldier "a gangster for capitalism" sent abroad to do the bidding of Big Business or Big Oil.[2]

Neither the will of God nor the venality of Wall Street suffices to explain how the United States managed to become stuck in World War IV. Rather, the new American militarism is a little like pollution—the perhaps unintended, but foreseeable by-product of prior choices and decisions made without taking fully into account the full range of costs likely to be incurred.

In making the industrial revolution, the captains of American enterprise did not consciously set out to foul the environment, but as they harnessed the waters, crisscrossed the nation with rails, and built their mills and refineries, negative consequences ensued. Lakes and rivers became choked with refuse, the soil contaminated, and the air in American cities filthy.

By the time that the industrial age approached its zenith in the middle of the twentieth century, most Americans had come to take this for granted; a degraded environment seemed the price you had to pay in exchange for material abundance and by extension for freedom and opportunity. Americans might not like pollution, but there seemed to be no choice except to put up with it.

To appreciate that this was, in fact, not the case, Americans needed a different consciousness. This is where the environmental movement, beginning more or less in the 1960s, made its essential contribution. Environmentalists enabled Americans to see the natural world and their relationship to that world in a different light. They argued that the obvious deterioration in the environment was unacceptable and not at all inevitable. Alternatives did exist. Different policies and practices could stanch and even reverse the damage.

Purists in that movement insisted upon the primacy of environmental needs, everywhere and in all cases. Theirs was (and is) a principled position deserving to be heard. To act on their recommendations, however, would likely mean shutting down the economy, an impractical and politically infeasible course of action.

Pragmatists advanced a different argument. They suggested that it was possible to negotiate a compromise between economic needs and environmental imperatives. This compromise might oblige Americans to curtail certain bad habits, but it did not require changing the fundamentals of how they lived their lives. Americans could keep their cars and continue their love affair with consumption; but at the same time they could also have cleaner air and cleaner water.

Implementing this compromise has produced an outcome that environmental radicals (and on the other side, believers in laissez-faire capitalism) today find unsatisfactory. In practice, it turns out, once begun negotiations never end. Bargaining is continuous, contentious, and deeply politicized. Participants in the process seldom come away with everything they want. Settling for half a loaf when you covet the whole is inevitably frustrating.

But the results are self-evident. Environmental conditions in the United States today are palpably better than they were a half century ago. Pollution has not been vanquished, but it has become more manageable. Furthermore, the nation has achieved those improvements without imposing on citizens undue burdens and without preventing its entrepreneurs from innovating, creating, and turning a profit.

Restoring a semblance of balance and good sense to the way that Americans think about military power will require a similarly pragmatic approach. Undoing all of the negative effects that result from having been seduced by war may lie beyond reach, but Americans can at least make them more manageable and thereby salvage their democracy.

In explaining the origins of the new American militarism, this account has not sought to assign or to impute blame. None of the protagonists in this story sat down after Vietnam and consciously plotted to propagate perverse attitudes toward military power any more than Andrew Carnegie or John D. Rockefeller plotted to despoil the nineteenth-century American landscape. The clamor after Vietnam to rebuild the American arsenal and to restore American self-confidence, the celebration of soldierly values, the search for ways to make force more usable: all of these came about because groups of Americans thought that they glimpsed in the realm of military affairs the solution to vexing problems. The soldiers who sought to rehabilitate their profession, the intellectuals who feared that America might share the fate of Weimar, the strategists wrestling with the implications of nuclear weapons, the conservative Christians appalled by the apparent collapse of traditional morality: none of these acted out of motives that were inherently dishonorable. To the extent that we may find fault with the results of their efforts, that fault is more appropriately attributable to human fallibility than to malicious intent.

And yet in the end it is not motive that matters but outcome.

Several decades after Vietnam, in the aftermath of a century filled to overflowing with evidence pointing to the limited utility of armed force and the dangers inherent in relying excessively on military power, the American people have persuaded themselves that their best prospect for safety and salvation lies with the sword. Told that despite all of their past martial exertions, treasure expended, and lives sacrificed, the world they inhabit is today more dangerous than ever and that they must redouble those exertions, they dutifully assent. Much as dumping raw sewage into American lakes and streams was once deemed unremarkable, so today "global power projection"—a phrase whose sharp edges we have worn down through casual use, but which implies military activism without apparent limit—has become standard practice, a normal condition, one to which no plausible alternatives seem to exist. All of this Americans have come to take for granted: it's who we are and what we do.

Such a definition of normalcy cries out for a close and critical reexamination. Surely, the surprises, disappointments, painful losses, and woeful, even shameful failures of the Iraq War make clear the need to rethink the fundamentals of U.S. military policy. Yet a meaningful reexamination will require first a change of consciousness, seeing war and America's relationship to war in a fundamentally different way.

Of course, dissenting views already exist. A rich tradition of American pacifism abhors the resort to violence as always and in every case wrong. Advocates of disarmament argue that by their very existence weapons are an incitement to violence. In the former camp, there can never be a justification for war. In the latter camp, the shortest road to peace begins with the beating of swords into ploughshares. These are principled views that deserve a hearing, more so today than ever. By discomfiting the majority, advocates of such views serve the common good. But to make full-fledged pacifism or comprehensive disarmament the basis for policy in an intrinsically disordered world would be to open the United States to grave danger.

The critique proposed here—offering not a panacea but the prospect of causing present-day militaristic tendencies to abate—rests on ten fundamental principles.

First, *heed the intentions of the Founders,* thereby restoring the basic precepts that animated the creation of the United States and are specified in the Constitution that the Framers drafted in 1787 and presented for consideration to the several states. Although politicians make a pretense of revering that document, when it comes to military policy they have long since fallen into the habit of treating it like a dead letter. This is unfortunate. Drafted by men who appreciated the need for military power while also maintaining a healthy respect for the dangers that it posed, the Constitution in our own day remains an essential point of reference.

Nothing in that compact, as originally ratified or as subsequently amended, commits or even encourages the United States to employ military power to save the rest of humankind or remake the world in its own image nor even hints at any such purpose or obligation. To the contrary, the Preamble of the Constitution expressly situates military power at the center of the brief litany of purpose enumerating the collective aspirations of "we the people." It was "to form a more perfect union, establish justice, insure domestic tranquility, provide for the common defense, promote the general welfare, and secure the blessings of liberty to ourselves and our posterity" that they acted in promulgating what remains the fundamental law of the land.

Whether considering George H. W. Bush's 1992 incursion into Somalia, Bill Clinton's 1999 war for Kosovo, or George W. Bush's 2003 crusade to overthrow Saddam Hussein, the growing U.S. predilection for military intervention in recent years has so mangled the concept of common defense as to make it all but unrecognizable.

The beginning of wisdom—and a major first step in repealing the new American militarism—lies in making the foundational statement of intent contained in the Preamble once again the basis of actual policy. Only if citizens remind themselves and remind those exercising political authority why this nation exists will it be possible to restore the proper relationship between military power and that purpose, which centers not on global dominance but on enabling Americans to enjoy the blessings of liberty.

Such a restoration is long overdue. For over a century, since the closing of the frontier, but with renewed insistence following the end of the Cold War, American statesmen have labored under the misconception that securing the well-being of the United States requires expanding its reach and influence abroad. From the invasion of Cuba in 1898 to the invasion of Iraq in 2003, policymakers have acted as if having an ever larger perimeter to defend will make us safer or taking on burdens and obligations at ever greater distances from our shores will further enhance our freedoms.[3] In fact, apart from the singular exception of World War II, something like the opposite has been the case.

The remedy to this violation of the spirit of the Constitution lies in the Constitution itself and in the need to *revitalize the concept of separation of powers*. Here is the second principle with the potential to reduce the hazards by the new American militarism.

In all but a very few cases, the impetus for expanding America's security perimeter has come from the executive branch. In practice, presidents in consultation with a small circle of advisers decide on the use of force; the legislative branch then either meekly bows to the wishes of the executive or provides the sort of broad authorization (such as the Tonkin Gulf Resolution of 1964) that amounts in effect to an abrogation of direct responsibility. The result, especially in evidence since the end of World War II, has been to eviscerate Article I, Section 8, Clause 11 of the Constitution, which in the plainest of language confers on the Congress the power "To declare War."

The problem is not that the presidency has become too strong. Rather, the problem is that the Congress has failed—indeed, failed egregiously—to fulfill its constitutional responsibility for deciding when and if the United States should undertake military interventions abroad. Hiding behind an ostensible obligation to "support our commander-in-chief" or to "support the troops," the Congress has time and again shirked its duty.

An essential step toward curbing the new American militarism is to redress this imbalance in war powers and to call upon the Congress to reclaim its constitutionally mandated prerogatives. Indeed, legislators should insist upon a strict constructionist definition of war such that any use of force other than in direct and immediate defense of the United States should require prior congressional approval.

The Cold War is history. The United States no longer stands eyeball-to-eyeball with a hostile superpower. Ensuring our survival today does not require, if it ever did, granting to a single individual the authority to unleash the American military arsenal however the perception of threats, calculations of interest, or flights of whimsy might seem to dictate. Indeed, given all that we have learned about the frailties, foibles, and strange obsessions besetting those who have occupied the Oval Office in recent decades—John Kennedy's chronic drug abuse, Richard Nixon's paranoia, and Ronald Reagan's well-documented conviction that Armageddon was drawing near, to cite three examples—it is simply absurd that elevation to the presidency should include the grant of such authority.[4]

The decision to use armed force is freighted with implications, seen and unseen, that affect the nation's destiny. Our history has shown this time and again. Such decisions should require collective approval in advance by the people's elected representatives, as the Framers intended.

Granted, one may examine the recent past—for instance, the vaguely worded October 2002 joint resolution authorizing the use of force against Iraq—and despair of those representatives actually stirring themselves to meet their responsibilities.[5] But the errors and misapprehensions, if not outright deceptions, that informed the Bush administration's case for that war—and the heavy price that Americans subsequently paid as a result— show why Cold War–era deference to the will of the commander-in-chief is no longer acceptable. If serving members of Congress cannot grasp that point, citizens should replace them by electing people able to do so.

The third principle is to *view force as a last resort*. This requires an explicit renunciation of the Bush Doctrine of preventive war, which in arrogating to the United States prerogatives allowed to no other nation subverts international stability and in the long run can only make Americans less secure. In its place, the United States should return to a declaratory policy more consistent with its own established moral and religious traditions, with international law, and with common sense.

Such a policy should consist of three elements. First, that the United States like every other nation reserves the right to act in its own self-defense and to do so unilaterally if necessary—a proviso that would have permitted the United States well before 9/11 to employ force against Al Qaeda at the time and in a manner of its own choosing. Second, that the United States like every other nation will not tolerate behavior posing a proximate threat to itself or its citizens—a proviso that would have permitted the overthrow of the Taliban in 2001 but not the invasion of Iraq in 2003. Third, that the United States, acting in conjunction with other nations of goodwill, will respond with appropriate military force to wholesale violations of human rights, to instances of widespread suffering, or to looming threats endangering international peace and comity. Such a proviso *might* have permitted U.S. forces to engage in an internationally sanctioned multilateral effort to remove Saddam Hussein from power. It emphatically *would* permit the United States to participate in—indeed, to play a leading role in organizing—multilateral efforts to put a stop to horrific events such as genocide or ethnic cleansing. However, it *would not* permit the United States to claim for itself alone the responsibility of serving as the world's conscience.

The doctrine proposed here does not call for passivity or inaction. From time to time in the years to come, it will doubtless be incumbent upon the United States, in the manner of great powers since time immemorial, to resort to force. Still, American policymakers should employ force only with reluctance and after the most careful deliberation. The United States should dispatch its legions with modest expectations regarding the likely benefits to accrue from victory coupled with a lively appreciation of the surprises and disappointments that almost inevitably flow from any armed conflict. And it should do so with one eye cocked on the home front, wary of claims of military necessity being used to compromise our civil liberties.

The fourth principle emerges as a corollary of the third. That is to *enhance U.S. strategic self-sufficiency*. With globalization a fact of life, autarky is more than ever a chimera. The argument here calls for something more modest: taking prudent steps to limit the extent of U.S. dependence on foreign resources, thereby reducing the pressures to intervene abroad on behalf of ostensibly "vital" material interests.

Ever since the onset of the Cold War, Americans have persuaded themselves that their well-being requires the guarantee of unencumbered access to the world's resources—with real or imagined challenges to that access more often than not eliciting a military response, whether direct or indirect, overt or covert. For decades, this notion has provided an infinitely elastic rationale for sticking America's nose in other people's business. In no case has this been more apparent than with regard to energy and the U.S. "need" for foreign oil, which has sucked the United States ever more deeply into the politically and culturally alien world of Islam. The events of 9/11 effectively breathed new life into this notion that nothing should impede our access to oil. As a result, the Bush administration had concluded that the United States cannot rest easy until every regime in the so-called Greater Middle East conforms to Washington's criteria for liberal democracy. In pursuit of that objective, it has thrust U.S. force into the very heart of the region.

"Dependence on foreign oil is America's Achilles heel," observed a respected analyst in the spring of 2004.[6] The statement is indisputably correct and commands automatic assent, but any number of other commentators have been making precisely this point for over thirty years. In all that time, the United States has yet to take any meaningful action to reduce its energy dependence, which instead continues to increase. Indeed, one question sure to puzzle future historians is how a problem of such self-evident seriousness induced such an unserious response. What passes for U.S. energy policy recalls early nineteenth-century attempts to deal with slavery. Politicians talk big but temporize, resorting to expedients and elaborate compromises that dodge the main issue.

No doubt it is unrealistic to expect that the United States will ever regain true energy independence. It is not unrealistic, however, to expect government to act in various ways to substantially reduce the extent to which the United States relies on foreign oil, especially from countries outside our hemisphere.[7]

When Senator John Kerry, as the Democratic candidate for the presidency in 2004, allowed as how "no young American in uniform should ever be held hostage to America's dependence on oil in the Middle East," he was voicing a popular sentiment.[8] But translating that applause line into a reality requires a level of commitment and determination that no political leader in our time has actually been able to muster. Indeed, the refusal of American political leaders of both major parties to make even the semblance of a meaningful effort—even as they, like Kerry, have testified to the urgency of doing so—must rank as the signal failure of American statecraft over the past half century.[9] Further acquiescence in that failure has become simply intolerable.

The fifth principle derives directly from the preceding four: *organize U.S. forces explicitly for national defense*. Focusing on defense rather than power projection implies jettisoning the concept of "national security," an artifact of the Cold War employed as a device to justify everything from overthrowing foreign governments to armed intervention in places that most Americans could not locate on a map. "National security" also undergirds the concept of a "global war on terror," which since 9/11 has provided the rationale for still more misadventures.

Several concrete implications derive from this principle of organizing for defense.

One is to shed unnecessary obligations. Among other things, this means calling on allies possessing the ability to defend themselves to do just that, rather than contracting out that function to the Pentagon. By extension, it means bringing U.S. troops home from stations abroad where an immediate need for their presence no longer exists, withdrawing from the vast "empire of bases" in which U.S. forces have become entrenched ever since World

War II.[10] The list of those fully able to provide for their own security begins with Europe in its entirety but necessarily extends to Japan (including Okinawa) and South Korea.

Drawing down U.S. overseas garrisons may or may not save money, but in any case that is not the object of the exercise. The aim is threefold: first, to reduce the prospects of the United States getting dragged into a conflict in which its own interests are marginal or altogether nonexistent; second, to allow the United States to choose where it will engage its forces rather than handing that decision to others; third, to treat U.S. allies as partners rather than vassals.

In that regard, Washington should make clear its expectations that partners must henceforth pull their share of the load. This is something that European nations (the United Kingdom partially excepted) have in recent years declined to do, with the United States—always ready to make up for shortcomings in Europe's defenses—acting in effect as an enabler.

Bringing the troops home does not necessarily imply abrogating alliances such as NATO. It does mean that in sharing responsibilities the United States should also share authority. In the case of NATO, for example, that might mean that the alliance's top military position—the Supreme Allied Commander Europe—ought to be a European rather than an American officer as has always been the case. Such an appointment would help make clear that except in extremis maintaining peace and stability anywhere between the English Channel and the Urals is Europe's affair.

"Why quit our own to stand upon foreign ground?" George Washington's question, posed in 1796, and also his answer commend themselves to our consideration today. Washington did not recommend that the United States turn its back on the world. Rather he urged that Americans establish that relationship on terms conducive to the well-being of the republic, steering clear of the ambitions, rivalries, interests, humors, and caprices of other nations. Above all, he counseled the United States to maintain "the command of its own fortunes."[11] Critics will dismiss this as camouflaged isolationism. It is not: it is a call for restoring American freedom of action.

The sixth principle is to *devise an appropriate gauge for determining the level of U.S. defense spending.* For decades U.S. intelligence estimates of Soviet military expenditures provided at least a rough answer to the old question "How much is enough?" But how much is enough in the absence of a great power adversary?

Militarists and those who dream of global empire have proposed their own answer. Their requirement is quite simple: they want more next year than last, and more still the year beyond that, regardless of the situation prevailing beyond U.S. borders. For example, they fancy predesignating a certain fixed percentage of the gross domestic product for military spending—say, 4 or 5 percent—counting on the prospect of an ever-growing economy to assure an ever larger pool of money to purchase new weapons and fund new adventures.[12] In effect, they argue for excess military capacity, thereby providing policymakers with greater flexibility and more options.

A better approach, one more likely to limit adventurism abroad while still meeting essential U.S. security requirements, would be to peg U.S. expenditures in relation to what others are spending. To stipulate, for example, that the United States should match the next ten most lavishly spending powers combined would assure U.S. military capabilities not only far in excess of any potential adversary but also in excess of any remotely plausible combination of adversaries. The budgetary impact of such a stipulation—one that if made by another country Americans would view as evidence of rampant megalomania—would be to reap substantial savings. Indeed, at present the United States could earmark for defense as much as the next ten largest military powers combined and still reduce Pentagon outlays by tens of billion dollars per year.[13]

Promoting self-sufficiency, reducing the U.S. troop presence abroad, and capping defense spending will evoke concerns about the United States turning its back on the world. Such criticism is as mistaken as it is predictable.

If anything, it is the present-day excessive reliance on military power that constitutes an open invitation to neo-isolationism. Once the weight of U.S. military adventures and obligations abroad exceeds the willingness of the American people to foot the bill, the popular urge to turn inward could well become overwhelming and irresistible. Rather than lean ever more heavily on the staff of military power, policymakers interested in keeping the United States sensibly engaged abroad should instead be searching for ways to *enhance alternative instruments of statecraft*. This is the seventh principle for countering the new American militarism.

The natural accompaniment to a doctrine that views hard power as a last resort is to increase the attention given to so-called soft power, the ability to influence rather than merely coerce and to build rather than merely demolish.[14] This is an area (as the mismanaged occupation of Iraq has demonstrated) that the United States has undervalued and in which it continues to be grossly deficient.

Whether or not the rap is an entirely fair one, the State Department is dogged by a reputation of being timid, sluggish, and inept. According to its critics, as measured by return on the dollar, it ranks near the bottom of federal bureaucracies.[15] The charge has stuck, leaving the department with little clout and few advocates in Washington. As a consequence, the agency charged with conducting U.S. diplomacy finds itself perpetually underfunded, understaffed, and, in the age of George W. Bush, marginalized.

Whether or not public diplomacy is quite the panacea that some have made it out to be, careful studies have documented the fact that the United States does an altogether miserable job of communicating its message to peoples around the world.[16] The result is a credibility problem that vastly complicates American statecraft.

Whether or not their view is entirely justified, Americans generally have come to see "foreign aid" as money down a rat hole—giveaway programs that seldom if ever produce tangible results or even gratitude on the part of recipients. As a consequence, the United States trails almost all other developed nations in terms of per capita assistance provided to the developing world.[17] As a further consequence, problems plaguing that world continue to fester, with some eventually making their way to our own shores.

In contrast, on issues related to hard power, the United States spares no expense in its efforts to improve what works and to fix what doesn't. Indeed, in developing new weapons, the Pentagon routinely squanders billions of dollars on programs that either fail outright or are made redundant by changing priorities. When this occurs, policymakers don't so much as bat an eyelash. For their part, citizens—even those otherwise alert to governmental waste, fraud, and abuse—raise nary a murmur of complaint.

When it comes to military matters, Americans accept mismanagement as just part of the cost of doing business. In 2004, the U.S. Army canceled its Comanche helicopter program, having doled out $8 billion over twenty-one years without ever producing a single operational aircraft.[18] Two years earlier, the Pentagon terminated development of the Crusader artillery system after expending $2 billion on a weapon that the end of the Cold War over a decade earlier had rendered obsolete.[19] Over the past two decades, the United States Marine Corps has spent $12 billion in an effort to perfect the V-22 Osprey, tilt-rotor transport aircraft. In that time, four Osprey prototypes have crashed during test flights, killing twenty-three marines. The projected price per aircraft has skyrocketed from $24 million to $105 million. With the Marine Corps still insisting that there are no alternatives to this high-risk design, Congress obligingly continues to funnel hundreds of millions of dollars every year into a program that as of 2004 had yet to yield even a single fully operational squadron.[20]

The V-22 may or may not ultimately prove itself. The point here is simply that the Osprey program provides but one illustration of a general rule: when the issue is a military one, money is no object. Nothing like a comparable willingness to undertake bold initiatives or shrug off delays and cost overruns pertains outside the military realm, where the inclination instead is to write off whole agencies when initial results do not meet expectations. When it comes to developing new weapons, profligacy is the rule; when it comes to funding diplomatic missions or development programs, parsimony reigns.

If the United States is to remain effectively engaged with the rest of the world, it needs a highly competent agency to coordinate and manage U.S. diplomacy. It needs mechanisms to counter the negative image of the United States and its policies prevailing in too many parts of the world. And it needs to solve the riddle of development and, once having done so, to invest in implementing that solution. Each one of these capabilities is of far greater importance to the long-term well-being of the United States than is the fielding of a new armored vehicle or the development of the next-generation fighter jet. And each, if it existed, would reduce the likelihood of policymakers confronting future crises in which they perceived no alternative except to send in the marines or let loose a handful of cruise missiles.

The potential savings in money and lives makes this effort highly desirable. The consequence of inaction—of continuing to present what the world sees as an exclusively military face—makes it indispensable.

An eighth principle is to *revive the moribund concept of the citizen-soldier.* Conceived as a response to the anti-military spirit that flourished some three decades ago, the All-Volunteer Force has long since come to be seen as one of the great success stories of recent American public policy. That success deserves a critical second look.

The reference to volunteering in the title "AVF" makes Americans feel good. It suggests threads of continuity to earlier generations that fought at places like Bunker Hill and Gettysburg. But this is mere nostalgia. The actually existing ethos of today's active force is more akin to that of the French Foreign Legion. Members of the post–Cold War AVF are highly trained, handsomely paid professionals who (assuming that the generals concur with the wishes of the political leadership) will go anywhere without question to do the bidding of the commander-in-chief.

Indeed, to the extent that Americans see their future as one of presiding over an informal empire of global proportions, then the present-day AVF (if perhaps too small) does provide a reasonably appropriate model. Although the heated arguments pro and con about the RMA may not have produced "transformation," the press of events has certainly produced change since the time when defending the Fulda Gap was the order of the day. Ours is now an imperial army. Through hard-won experience it has acquired—in Afghanistan and Iraq, continues to acquire—the wherewithal appropriate to the sort of punitive expeditions and constabulary obligations that the management of an empire entails.

The post–Cold War military encounters that have sent American soldiers hurrying from Panama to the Persian Gulf and points in between have produced not only changes in tactics, organization, and hardware. They have also produced a new mindset. "With a heavy dose of fear and violence, and a lot of money for projects, I think we can convince these people that we are here to help them."[21] Offered by a U.S. Army battalion commander assigned to Iraq in December 2003, this sentiment is one that a British officer in the days of Queen Victoria, dealing with subject peoples in Sudan or South Africa or the Northwest Frontier, would have instantly understood and warmly endorsed.

An imperial America will have need for military officers with just the right touch when it comes to meting out fear, violence, and money to pacify those classified in former days as wogs.[22] But those citizens who prefer an American republic to an American empire ought to view the changes under way in the U.S. armed forces as worrisome.

One way that a republic safeguards itself against militarism is to ensure that the army has deep roots among the people. "Standing armies threaten government by the people," the soldier-historian John McAuley Palmer observed between the world wars, "not because they consciously seek to pervert liberty, but because they relieve the people themselves of the duty of self-defense." A people placing responsibility for national defense in the hands of "a special class" render themselves "unfit for liberty." Therefore, concluded General Palmer, "an enduring government by the people must include an army of the people among its vital institutions."[23] Indeed, the ideal relationship between the armed forces and democratic society is a symbiotic one, in which each draws nourishment from the other. Symbiosis implies intimacy. In a civil-military context, it entails a continuous process of rotation in which the ongoing incorporation of citizens into the ranks renews the army, while the return to civilian life of discharged veterans, understanding at first hand the meaning of service, renews civic life.

Whatever its other merits, the present-day professionalized force is not conducive to this civil-military intimacy. Indeed, to the extent that the members of the AVF see themselves as professionals—members of a warrior caste adhering to their own distinctive code—they have little interest in nurturing a close relationship with civilian society. In an off-the-cuff remark just prior to the 2003 U.S. invasion of Iraq, Secretary of Defense Donald Rumsfeld dismissed the citizen-soldiers of the pre-AVF era as "adding no value, no advantage, really, to the United States armed services." The "churning that took place," he said, "took [an] enormous amount of effort in terms of training, and then they were gone."[24] According to Rumsfeld, rotating large numbers of citizens through the military had been more trouble than it was worth. Present-day military leaders, imbued with a narrowly utilitarian view of recruitment and retention, tend to share that conviction. As a consequence, they are untroubled by the extent to which the armed services have become anything but representative of that society. It is not something on which they place any particular value.

But the rest of us ought to: the issue is an important one. In terms of race, region, religion, and ethnicity, but above all in terms of class, America's armed services should—as they once did, at least in a rough way—mirror society. This does not mean that all must serve, but it does mean that the burdens (and benefits) of service to the commonweal should fall evenly across all sectors of society.

What does this mean in practical terms? It does not mean a return to conscription, for which little or no discernible political support exists.[25] It does mean creating mechanisms that will reawaken in privileged America a willingness to serve as those who are less privileged already do. Other writers have outlined in detail what some of those mechanisms might be. They include shorter enlistments, more generous signing bonuses, greater flexibility in retirement options, the forgiveness of college loans upon completion of a term of service, and passage of a new GI Bill that on principle ties federal education grants to citizen service.[26] Put bluntly, citizens who defend the country should get a free college education; those who choose not to do so ought to pay their own way.

How will having a military that reflects society affect prevailing attitudes regarding war and the use of force? Persuading at least some among the sons and daughters of the elite to serve will elevate the risk of domestic blowback if interventions go awry, inducing presidents to exercise greater caution in making decisions that put Americans at risk in the first place. Moreover, as military veterans who are members of that elite eventually take their places in Congress, as editors of newspapers and journals of opinion, and at the head of major national institutions, their voices will help to counter unrealistic expectations about what wars can accomplish and what they cost.[27]

Reviving the tradition of the citizen-soldier should also entail *reexamining the role of the National Guard and the reserve components.* Here is our ninth principle, for it is in this underappreciated quarter of the larger military establishment that part-time soldiers keep the embers of that tradition alive.

Since the end of the Cold War, and especially since 9/11, federal authorities have increasingly called upon these part-timers to serve as a quasi-full-time backup for the ever-lengthening roster of expeditions that regulars start but prove unable to finish. This practice began in the 1990s when the Pentagon started using reservists to relieve the strain placed on regulars, taking on peacekeeping commitments first in the Sinai and then in the Balkans.[28] More recently, tens of thousands of reservists have been pressed into service to fight the insurgents opposing the U. S-led occupation of Iraq.[29]

As a device for concealing the disparity between the publicly stated aims of U.S. strategy (eliminating evil and universalizing democracy) and the means immediately available to achieve those aims (an active duty force of only 1.4 million), this expedient of incorporating reservists into the imperial army makes sense.[30] But as a basis for long-term policy it makes little sense and is doomed to fail. It will fail because it is not sustainable. Mounting demands imposed on reservists will exhaust their willingness to offer continued service—or will produce a recurrence of incidents such as the Iraq prisoner abuse scandal of 2004.

Far better for the health of the reserve components and for the good of the United States to return reservists, particularly those serving in the land component of the National Guard, to their original purpose—a trained militia kept in readiness as the primary instrument for community self-defense. Of course, community in this context refers not to Kosovo and Iraq but to Kansas and Iowa.

Indeed, given the reemergence after 9/11 of homeland security as a primary concern, the United States should be expanding the National Guard, creating a larger, more robust, and more capable force to protect North America. It should do so even if that means shifting resources away from regulars held in readiness for extracontinental contingencies. To state the matter directly, we need more citizen-soldiers protecting Americans at home even if that means fewer professional soldiers available to assume responsibility for situations abroad.

Will the creation of an army once again pervaded by the spirit of the citizen-soldier impede the future use of force for purposes not related to genuinely vital national interests? In all likelihood, yes—and that is precisely the point.

The final principle, disregarded for far too long, is to *reconcile the American military profession to American society.* If the army of a republic ought to be rooted in society, so too should the officer corps. In the United States, however, this is not the case.

From its earliest days, the officer corps has cultivated *separateness* as a key element of its professional identity. Early America evinced a pronounced ambivalence about the very existence of a standing army and the career soldiers who led that army. Members of the fledgling officer corps were quick to reciprocate, viewing society with a certain wariness.

The defining quality of the U.S. Military Academy, which stands in relation to the American military profession as the Vatican does to the Roman Catholic Church, is remoteness, both physical and psychological. Virtually from its founding in 1802, West Point has sought to train, educate, and above all socialize cadets in isolation from the rest of America—or, if permitting contact between cadets and the "outside world," it has sought to dictate the terms under which that interaction occurs. Implicit in this approach has been the conviction that the soldierly ethic ought to be nurtured within the ramparts, since beyond lies temptation and sin.

Even as the modern military took on the accoutrements of other professions such as medicine and the law, it did so in ways consciously designed to keep civilian society at arm's length. Upon concluding that officership ought to entail postgraduate education, for example, senior military leaders decided that the armed services themselves should provide that education. Up-and-coming officers would undergo advanced schooling in institutions created and administered by the services themselves, with military officers designing the curriculum and comprising the faculty—hence the founding in the late 1800s of a Naval War College at Newport, Rhode Island, and soon thereafter of an Army War College in Washington.[31]

As the U.S. military profession reached full maturity during the course of the twentieth century, the officer corps remained aloof from the rest of America. Officers lived and played in special communities called "forts" that served no military purpose as such—Fort Bliss, Texas, does not defend El Paso, nor does Fort Lewis, Washington, defend Tacoma—apart from clearly delineating a largely self-contained existence.

All of these efforts to carefully distinguish between "us" and "them"—soldiers vs. civilians, warriors vs. politicians—once made a certain amount of sense. But much like the nineteenth-century uniforms in which twenty-first-century West Point cadets continue to parade about, they no longer do.

In the contemporary marketplace, lawyers and doctors have discovered that the traditional model of a self-governing and autonomous profession is no longer viable. The same applies to the officer corps in relation to the contemporary international order.

The idea that war and politics constitute two distinct and separate spheres has always been a fiction. In the present day, with interstate conventional armed conflict becoming increasingly rare even as the use of violence wielded by nonstate actors employing unconventional methods is seemingly on the rise, that fiction has become altogether pernicious.

The dangers facing the United States as it attempts to navigate through that world are formidable. So too are the challenges confronting the American military profession. As Washington's appetite for armed intervention has grown, the burdens imposed on the members of that profession have increased, becoming heavier with each passing year. The military's institutional memory, manifesting itself in an abiding suspicion of civilians and a preoccupation with obsolete prerogatives, makes those burdens heavier still. The danger that they may become unbearable—as in Vietnam they did, leading to both defeat and disgrace—is real.

In short, soldiers must recognize that to save their profession they must change it, either taking the initiative to do so on their own or submitting to change imposed from without.[32] Specifically, soldiers must embrace without reservation two fundamental truths to which the officer corps has heretofore paid the barest lip service. The first truth is that war is the handmaiden of politics, not its co-equal and certainly not its arbiter. The second is that harmonizing war with politics, whether American politics or international politics, requires efforts to bind the military profession to the "outside world" rather than vainly struggling to keep that world at bay. The times call not for isolation but for integration, not for propping up old barriers but for tearing them down or at least making them permeable. Relevant to the purpose of this account, binding the officer corps more closely to society will have the ancillary benefit of reducing the likelihood of the armed services running amok or engaging in politically irresponsible behavior.

These two truths have several practical implications for the governance of the military profession. Above all, they demand a thoroughgoing revision of the way that the values defining the military ethic are formed and inculcated.

A military profession rooted in American society is one in which all officers possess a liberal education acquired in the company of their fellow citizens. This means that as a prerequisite to commissioning, *all* officers should earn a bachelor's degree at a civilian university. Under this arrangement, the function of ROTC on university campuses should be not to train officer candidates selected while in high school, as is presently the case. Instead, ROTC should be the mechanism for recruiting potential officers, identifying undergraduates who possess the necessary attributes and screening them to assess their suitability for actual service. Upon earning an undergraduate degree, all officer candidates—regardless of the service into which they will be commissioned—should undergo a common process of socialization and a common introduction to the precepts of the military profession. Thus *all* candidates (not a select minority, as is presently the case) ought to attend a service academy such as West Point or Annapolis prior to commissioning, albeit for an abbreviated period of only a year or so.[33]

The same concept of education in conjunction with their fellow citizens should apply during the officer's years of active service. A requirement for the military to maintain its own system of schools specializing in technical or operational matters—how to employ a weapon, how to plan an attack—

will always exist, but true education on matters related to politics, strategy, and related disciplines ought to take place in a context that encourages free inquiry, accommodates diverse opinions, and promotes interchange across the civil-military divide. Only civilian institutions of higher learning can fully meet these prerequisites. As an integral part of their professional development, all career military officers deserve an opportunity for postgraduate study; all of them—not just a few, as is the case today—should acquire that education at government expense on the campus of a civilian university.

This assumes that America's universities—renowned for many things but not necessarily for encouraging the study of armed conflict—can provide officers with a course of instruction relevant to their professional needs. To be sure, not all soldier-students will arrive on campus with the intention of studying war per se. For those who do, successful programs in "strategic studies" already exist, albeit on a small scale in several select universities.[34] These provide models that other institutions can adopt or modify. Given the backing of far-sighted congressional appropriators and the leadership of even a handful of university administrators, the academic community could over a period of years build a substantial capacity for research and teaching in matters related to politics, war, and strategy.

Critics will complain that the reputed leftward bias of university faculties will prevent this from happening. The response to that complaint is simple: make the money available—endowing chairs, founding institutes, funding research—and they will come. Indeed, participation of the Left in rejuvenating higher education on matters related to national defense is crucial. Few things are more important to promoting a critical appreciation of the dilemmas facing the United States as a military superpower than to induce the Left to recognize that, like it or not, war remains part of the human condition and central to the human experience and hence eminently worthy of study.

In a valedictory marking his withdrawal from public life, George Washington pointedly advised his fellow citizens to be wary of "those overgrown military establishments which, under any form of government, are inauspicious to liberty, and which are to be regarded as particularly hostile to republican liberty."[35]

Himself a soldier of surpassing greatness, Washington was hardly a naïf in matters related to war and peace. He did not see military power as inherently evil. He considered the maintenance of a respectable army to be essential to a nation's well-being. Those citizens who rallied to their country's defense in its time of need he held in highest esteem.

But of this Washington was certain: to cultivate military power for its own sake and to indulge in the ambitions to which large armies gave rise was alien to the entire conception of the New World. To seek safety in an overgrown military establishment was to replicate the errors of the Old World, home to kings and sepulchres and empires but not to freedom and republican virtue.

In 1796, Washington's warning verged on being superfluous; antipathy toward war and a skepticism of armies were at that juncture hardwired into the American self-identity. Two hundred years later, with Europe and the United States having in so many respects reversed roles, his warning has acquired considerable salience.

The twentieth century was a shipwreck. For the Old World, horrendous slaughter once and for all washed away any lingering misapprehensions about war. Not so for the rising power of the New World, which chose to see "the American Century" as a story of triumph, not tragedy, and which drew from the military record of that century radically different conclusions. Misremembering both bad wars and good, Americans fostered a fresh set of illusions. These illusions—not only or even in particular our outsized martial pretensions—constitute the heart of the problem that is present-day American militarism. For from these illusions come expectations that George Washington for one would find astonishing: that through the determined exercise of its unquestioned military dominance the United States can perpetuate American global primacy and impress its values on the world at large.

If it persists in these expectations, then America will surely share the fate of all those who in ages past have looked to war and military power to fulfill their destiny. We will rob future generations of their rightful inheritance. We will wreak havoc abroad. We will endanger our security at home. We will risk the forfeiture of all that we prize.

The new American militarism materialized as a reaction to profound disorientation and collective distress. In the wake of a humiliating defeat and a closely related cultural upheaval, restoring the sinews of U.S. military might, celebrating soldierly virtue, and contriving ways to restore the utility of force seemed in some quarters to offer an antidote. The ailments were real, but the remedy turned out to be toxic. Over the course of three decades, increasingly frequent recurrence to that remedy has produced an addiction at least as harmful as the condition it was intended to cure.

There can be no recovery without first acknowledging the disease. As with any addiction, denial merely postpones the inevitable day of reckoning.

Afterword: Militarism Entrenched

THE FIRST EDITION OF this book appeared when Americans were experiencing a moment of profound disorientation. In the wake of 9/11, widespread confidence in U. S. military power had invested the George W. Bush administration's "global war on terrorism" with a modicum of plausibility. In pursuit of a righteous cause, nothing would or could stop American warriors in their quest to vanquish evil. So Americans believed and expected, with early returns ever so briefly vindicating such expectations. Yet by 2005, when *The New American Militarism* became available, victory as such appeared increasingly unlikely. Meanwhile, the costs (not to mention the moral complications) entailed by campaigns undertaken in Afghanistan and Iraq were turning out to be vastly larger than anticipated.

President Bush's inability to make good on the promises implicit in his war on terror yielded large-scale political consequences. In 2006, capitalizing on widespread dissatisfaction with administration war policies, Democrats regained control of Congress. Two years later, a charismatic candidate with a thin résumé captured the presidency itself. Barack Obama couldn't match the credentials of more seasoned aspirants to the White House. But he unlike they had voiced principled opposition to the Iraq War since its inception—and that made the difference.

Obama's campaign had been all about "Hope"—hope for change and for a new beginning. Nowhere were those hopes greater than with regard to U. S. military policy. Whether fairly or not, George W. Bush left office tagged as a war-monger, and an incompetent one at that. Obama's supporters expected him to reverse course, weaning the United States away from its penchant for military adventurism. Such hopes were not confined to Americans alone: based entirely on his expressed aspirations rather than any actual achievements, the Nobel Committee awarded Obama its 2009 Peace Prize.

In the event, the choice turned out to be a deeply ironic one. Indeed, more than anything else, the massive gap between what the Nobel Committee (and many millions of others) expected of Obama and what actually ensued with regard to U. S. military policy justifies a second edition of this book. American militarism persists.

To unveil his administration's new national security strategy in early January 2012, President Obama made the short trip across the Potomac from the seat of power of the executive branch to the seat of power of America's armed forces. Presidents visit the Pentagon infrequently. In matters relating to national security, they typically conduct business at the White House, receiving high-ranking military officers and senior defense officials rather than calling on them. Yet Obama's advisors had selected this out-of-the-ordinary venue to make a point. That point was identical in intent (if less theatrical in execution) to the one that had inspired a previous set of advisors to land their president on an aircraft carrier in order to proclaim a war won: to highlight the president's role as commander-in-chief and to endow his words with added weight and authority.

In his prepared remarks, Obama depicted the occasion as a momentous one, announcing that "we're turning the page on a decade of war." "Turning the page" meant it was time to reassess the size, stationing, and configuration of U. S. forces. For top members of his administration, doing so had required "asking tough questions, challenging our own assumptions and making hard choices." The president briefly sketched out what making hard choices entailed. The Pentagon was going to rid itself of "outdated Cold War-era systems so that we can invest in the capabilities that we need for the future." A "leaner" military establishment would be one result. Yet the president took pains to guarantee that U. S. forces would remain capable of handling "the full range of contingencies and threats." He promised improvements across the board: in "intelligence, surveillance and reconnaissance, counterterrorism, countering weapons of mass destruction and [operating] in environments where adversaries try to deny us access."

Unquestioned and unchallengeable military superiority was going to remain a hallmark of American statecraft. "The United States of America is the greatest force for freedom and security that the world has ever known," Obama asserted. "And in no small measure, that's because we've built the best-trained, best-led, best-equipped military in history—and as Commander-in-Chief, I'm going to keep it that way."[1]

Of course, critics wasted no time in disputing the president's characterization of his proposed strategy. In their view, Obama was stripping the nation's defenses and forfeiting its position of global leadership. "This is a lead-from-behind strategy for a left-behind America," charged Representative "Buck" McKeon, Republican of California and chairman of the House Armed Services Committee. He dismissed Obama's plan as "retreat from the world in the guise of a new strategy."[2] According to Max Boot, American journalism's preeminent proponent of militarism, the president was launching the United States on a "suicidal trajectory."[3] Hawkish writers manning the ramparts at the *Weekly Standard* concurred. In his brief Pentagon announcement, Obama had issued "an order to retreat." The administration's new strategy was "a bright green light to our enemies and a flashing red one to our friends and allies." By consciously and intentionally denuding America's defenses, Obama had made "a choice for weakness, a choice that will invite war, [and] a choice for American decline."[4]

In fact, both Obama's claims of big change and the fevered rhetoric of his critics fell equally wide of the mark. The president's reference to "turning the page" was, in fact, a model of artful precision. For the actual purpose of the administration's new strategy (and of the president's Pentagon appearance) was not to close the books on war, but in turning the page, to open a new chapter. The decade-long conflict (or more accurately, *conflicts,* since there were more than one) to which Obama referred would not end in the foreseeable future. Indeed, at the moment the president spoke, the new chapter had already commenced.

Among the few to appreciate the charade was the *Washington Post*'s Walter Pincus. The Obama approach to national security preserved far more than it changed, and much of what it was preserving was deeply problematic. "Has President Obama adopted George W. Bush's 'policeman of the world' approach to the fight against terrorism?" the veteran reporter asked.[5] With qualifications duly noted, Pincus answered that question in the affirmative. Stylistically, Obama's approach might differ from Bush's.

But substantively, the two shared the same DNA. To a far greater extent than either his defenders or his critics were wont to admit, Obama was taking the country further down the path toward permanent war that his predecessor had blazed.

Indeed, in his Pentagon presentation, Obama made a point of endorsing the existing fundamentals of U. S. military posture and policy. He offered an unambiguously upbeat assessment of what the previous decade of war had wrought. A few regrettable missteps aside, it had proven to be a smashing success.

> [A]round the globe we've strengthened alliances, forged new partnerships, and served as a force for universal rights and human dignity.... [W]e've succeeded in defending our nation, taking the fight to our enemies, reducing the number of Americans in harm's way, and we've restored America's global leadership. That makes us safer and it makes us stronger.

It followed from this record of success that any new strategy should entail the tweaking of existing practices rather than their wholesale abandonment. So with regard to resources, the president called for judicious trimming, not retrenchment, promising that "the defense budget will still be larger than it was toward the end of the Bush administration." With regard to forces, he emphasized not downsizing but enhanced capabilities. Touting a military that would be "agile, flexible and ready" and require a "smaller footprint," the president revived language that Secretary of Defense Donald Rumsfeld had once employed to describe his vision for transforming U. S. forces. With regard to its global posture, adjustments might be in the offing, but the United States military was not coming home. It was simply reorienting its attention on prospective new threats, notably the putative Chinese challenge in the Pacific. Above all, the president vowed that there would be no backsliding.

> [W]e have to remember the lessons of history. We can't afford to repeat the mistakes that have been made in the past—after World War II, after Vietnam—when our military was left ill-prepared for the future. As Commander in Chief, I will not let that happen again. Not on my watch.

What had already occurred on Obama's watch was notable. Fulfilling a promise he had made as a candidate, the president ended direct U. S. military involvement in the Iraq War, effectively writing off more than eight years of costly military exertions to determine Iraq's fate. Yet the upheaval touched off by Operation Iraqi Freedom continued and, in the wake of the U. S. military withdrawal, showed signs of worsening. Although the American phase of the Iraq War may have ended, the war itself had not. Even so, the Obama administration—and the majority of the American people—did their level best to ignore the evidence suggesting that Iraq itself remained unfinished business.

Then there was Afghanistan. Shortly after taking office, President Obama had committed an additional 17,000 U. S. troops to the war that he had charged his predecessor with neglecting. Yet this proved only the beginning. Near the end of his first year in office, just a week prior to accepting the Nobel Peace Prize, Obama ordered a further escalation in Afghanistan, one that mirrored Bush's 2007 "surge" in Iraq. For a brief interval, Obama even flirted with the nation-building-with-guns approach (formally known as "counterinsurgency") that Bush had pursued in Iraq. As Bush had done in Iraq, the president sought through the use of violence to determine Afghanistan's fate, with similarly inconclusive results.

Notably, Obama's escalation in Afghanistan also included a spatial dimension. He widened that war considerably, incorporating the frontier regions of neighboring Pakistan into the zone of military action. Almost exactly forty years earlier, without Congressional approval and while keeping the American public in the dark, President Richard Nixon had initiated the bombing of Laos, which thereby became an adjunct theater of the much larger Vietnam War. In comparable fashion, without Congressional authorization and with only the most cursory public notification, Obama initiated a campaign of attacks directed against suspected Taliban and al Qaeda operatives seeking sanctuary in Pakistan, which thereby became an adjunct theater of the much larger Afghanistan War. Whereas Nixon employed a blunt instrument—B52s dropping massive bomb loads—Obama relied on missile-firing drones and commando raids.

Failing to prevent North Vietnamese infiltration into South Vietnam, Nixon's secret bombing of Laos succeeded mostly in creating chaos. Failing to prevent cross-border movement in and out of Afghanistan, Obama's quasi-secret attacks into Pakistan served mostly to stoke anti-American outrage and undermine Pakistani stability. Yet whereas Washington in the 1970s attached minimal strategic importance to Laos, nuclear-armed Pakistan reputedly ranks today in the top-tier of countries in which the United States has a vital interest. Obama's single-mindedness—his confidence in the efficacy of force to address proximate problems while disregarding secondary consequences—rivaled Richard Nixon's.

In Pakistan and elsewhere, drone attacks employed pursuant to a campaign of targeted assassination became the signature of Obama's new way of war. In February 2011, Secretary of Defense Robert Gates categorically ruled out any further experiments with the Bush administration's invade-occupy-and-transform paradigm, declaring that "any future defense secretary who advises the president to again send a big American land army into Asia or into the Middle East or Africa should 'have his head examined.'"[6] Most members of the public had long since reached a similar conclusion. In effect, Gates validated such sentiments and invested them with the force of policy. Apart from a few diehards—writing in the *Weekly Standard*, William Kristol accused Gates of "undercutting the troops' mission [in Afghanistan] as though he's resigned to their failure"—this Gates Doctrine evoked little dissent.[7]

Yet a reluctance to commit large-scale land armies did not signify a reluctance to use force. On that score, Obama and his team left little room for doubt. Meanwhile, the American people, despite having lost their stomach for big wars, proved more than willing to indulge the administration's appetite for smaller ones, albeit more out of indifference or inattention than genuine enthusiasm.[8]

Obama's penchant for targeted assassination found application not only in Pakistan but also in places like Yemen and Somalia. In Libya, with allied support, the United State employed airpower on a more sustained basis to help rebels overthrow the regime of Colonel Muammar Gaddafi. With minimal fanfare, the administration also set out to establish "a constellation of secret drone bases" in and around the Arabian Peninsula and the Horn of Africa—new platforms from which to conduct attacks against Islamic radicals wherever they might be found.[9]

As under Bush so under Obama: the United States claimed the exclusive prerogative of striking wherever it needed whenever it chose to do so. And under Obama it continued to act accordingly. This is what turning the page on a decade of war signified.

Notably absent, at least in the halls of government, has been any serious analysis of what a decade of war has actually wrought, and at what price. In terms of outlays, the facts are indisputable. After 9/11, the U. S. military budget—already far and away the world's largest—grew by leaps and bounds. Growth continued without interruption when Obama succeeded Bush. By 2011, Pentagon spending in constant dollars surpassed what it had reached at any time during the Cold War. Even *excluding* the costs of wars in Iraq and Afghanistan, U. S. military spending grew by nearly 50 percent in the decade following 9/11. Regarding war costs, a comprehensive study conducted at Brown University estimated the bill at between $3.2 and 4 trillion—and counting.[10] As for the human toll, as of 2011, the Brown University researchers estimated that conflicts launched in the wake of 9/11 had displaced some 7,800,000 persons and killed another 236,000, among them over 6,000 American troops.[11]

What has this vast outlay of treasure and this harvest of death and human suffering purchased? Simply put, not victory.

George W. Bush's premature claim of mission accomplishment in Iraq in May 2003—much derided after the fact—had accurately reflected prevailing American expectations of how wars were *supposed* to end: neatly and decisively. Once engaging the enemy, superior U.S. forces would quickly prevail, with the conflict concluding on terms consistent with whatever purposes the commander-in-chief had enunciated at war's outset. Outcomes, in short, were expected to express Washington's will, thereby affirming the supremacy of American power.

The actual experience of war after 9/11 demolished all such expectations. Elaborating on the Obama national security strategy shortly after the president's Pentagon appearance, JCS chairman General Martin Dempsey could describe the United States military as a force "that can win any conflict, anywhere." Yet making that claim required Dempsey to sidestep this disturbing fact: The United States military had emphatically not won the conflicts in which he himself had recently participated.[12]

The truth, however unwelcome, is that since 1945 U.S. forces have not achieved a conclusive success in any contest on a scale larger than policing actions such as the 1983 intervention in Granada or the 1989 invasion of Panama. In terms of tactical proficiency and technological sophistication, the military establishment over which Dempsey presided remains without peer: No one else even comes close. To judge by operations such as the one that killed Osama bin Laden in May 2011, America's elite warriors are arguably the best the world has ever seen. Yet even if U. S. forces possess the ability to win just about any *fight*, their capacity to win a serious *war* is subject to considerable question. When it comes to translating military might into desired political outcomes—the nominal rationale for war—they have floundered.

As expectations of triumphant short wars give way to the reality of indecisive long wars, the troops sent to wage those wars demonstrate an admirable, if not entirely untarnished ability to cope, adapt, and endure.[13] Rotation back and forth between home stations and combat theatres has become routine. For their part, senior leaders struggle to explain this new reality of wars that drag on interminably. Shoring up their own claims of professional mastery requires that they devise an explanation that avoids any admission of their having failed to anticipate or grasp the character of modern war.

In the vanguard of this effort was General George Casey. As senior U. S. commander in Baghdad, Casey struggled unsuccessfully for two years to conclude that war. Upon his return from Iraq in 2007, he ascended to the position of U S. Army chief of staff and shortly thereafter began promoting the idea that the United States had become enmeshed in what he called an "era of persistent conflict." Ever since the outbreak of the Korean War, which had caught it unprepared, the army had sought to hold itself in constant *readiness* for what it expected to be *occasional* wars. The implicit assumption was that armed hostilities represented an abnormal condition. Casey's persistent conflict formulation now junked that assumption. War was no longer a sometime thing. It had become, Casey told the House Armed Services Committee in April 2008, "the new normal." Furthermore, it was now incumbent upon the army to "remake itself with that in mind."[14]

In the Pentagon, an implicit new assumption prevailed: for the United States, war had become inescapable. The result was to invert the Melian Dialogue. The great historian Thucydides believed that with power came the possibility of choice while those *lacking* power were obliged to bend to circumstance. "The strong do what they can," he famously wrote, "and the weak suffer what they must."[15] The U. S. military of the 21st century is ostensibly the world's strongest; yet senior officers such as General Casey believe that that it has become the nation's fate to suffer permanent war. The United States apparently has no choice in the matter.

An inability even to conceive of a plausible alternative to war suggests a profound failure of strategic imagination. Yet this aptly describes the condition besetting Washington in the decade after 9/11. By accepting war as a permanent condition, senior officials in the Pentagon and elsewhere in the national security bureaucracy forfeited whatever modest creative capacity they may once have possessed. As a policy priority, conflict management took precedence over conflict avoidance or termination. In the decade after the 9/11 attacks, *peace* had "become something of a dirty word in Washington foreign-policy circles." So wrote Greg Jaffe, the *Washington Post's* military correspondent, adding with considerable justification that "This is the American era of endless war."[16] Jaffe thereby aptly summarized what vast expenditures of blood and treasure had purchased: victory had become a chimera; the acceptance of endless war was now America's destiny.

This new normal has somewhat disconcerting implications for the relationship between American soldiers and the nation they serve. If it were possible, acceptance of war as an open-ended enterprise elevated further the popular standing of those saddled with the burden of waging war. In the eyes of the American people, "the troops" could do no wrong. To the last man and woman, they were heroes, to whom the nation owes an immense debt of gratitude. Making good on that debt—meeting the needs of veterans and of forces in the field—constitutes a sacred obligation. Even in a Washington where Republicans and Democrats agree on little else, this proposition commands something approximating unanimous support.

In some quarters, however, the suspicion developed that American civil-military relations were not as rosy as they appeared. How authentic were the expressions of gratitude that Americans showered on those who wore the uniform? "Thank you for your service." The functional equivalent of the store clerk's "Have a nice day" after completing a sale, this stock phrase creates the illusion of a relationship where none actually exists. Imposing no obligation, such expressions of appreciation for soldiers serve chiefly to gratify the speaker, lionizing the troops as an exercise in self-congratulations. Soldiers were not slow to figure this out.

The Great Recession that staggered the American economy beginning in 2008 created heightened awareness between the well-to-do and the rest of the country. On the one hand were the members of the "1 percent"—the

very rich who just kept getting richer. On the other hand were the "99 percent"—the vast majority of people struggling to get by. For a brief interval,
this gap seemed to define some essential and troubling truth to American
politics and society. Less noted, but arguably even more acute, is another
gap. This is the division between the 1 percent who serve and sacrifice in an
era of open-ended war and remainder of citizens who carry on as if there
were no war. James Wright, former Marine and former president of
Dartmouth College, put the matter succinctly. "We pay lip service to our
'sons and daughters' at war," he observed, "even if the children of some
99 percent of us are safely at home."[17] The "sons and daughters" sent in
harm's way weren't *ours* in any literal sense. To pretend otherwise was
unseemly.

Discomfort with this civil-military gap began gradually to make its
appearance. In a *Time* magazine cover story in November 2011, correspondent Mark Thompson captured the growing unease. "The U.S. military and
American society are drifting apart," he wrote.

> [T]roops in all the military services sense it, smell it—and talk about it.
> So do their superiors. We have a professional military of volunteers that
> has been stoically at war for more than a decade. But as the wars have
> droned on, the troops waging them are increasingly an Army apart.[18]

To camouflage this divide, Americans have invented rituals and made gestures, with corporate American quick to seize what it saw as a marketing
opportunity. In short order, "Proudly Serving Those Who Serve" joined
Anheuser Busch's array of advertising slogans. "Here's to the heroes," the
ad copy cheerfully burbled. "Great times are on deck." For every home
run hit during the 2011 major league baseball season, the nation's leading
brewer promised to donate $100 "to an organization that helps the families
of fallen soldiers." Here was patriotism served in a frosty mug: "Please
raise your Budweiser and join us in honoring those who keep our nation
safe and free every Thirst Inning."[19] Bud's competitors lagged only slightly
behind. "Give a veteran a piece of the High Life," was the Miller Coors
Brewing Company's riposte. "For every High Life cap or tab you drop off
at participating retailers or mail in, Miller High Life will donate 10¢
toward High Life Experiences for returning vets." Money raised was going
to defray the costs of soldier attending sports events and concerts, where

beer was sure to be available for purchase. "Live the High Life. Give the High Life."[20]

The sympathies of Mark Thompson and other journalists lay with the overworked and much-exploited troops. But some sensed in this civil-military gap more insidious implications. Todd Purdum was among them. "Increasingly," he wrote in *Vanity Fair*, "there exist two societies in America." The first Purdum depicted as "a military class, strongly religious, politically conservative, drawn disproportionately from the South and from smaller towns and areas of limited economic opportunity, including the inner cities." The other he described as "an untouched civilian class consisting of everyone else, who wouldn't know a regiment from a firmament or an M16 from a 7-Eleven." The division of America into two camps had already produced pernicious results. "The civilian class can deploy the warriors at will, knowing that most Americans will remain unaffected. In turn, the military class can demand what it wishes, knowing that the civilians have no standing to resist."

Here was an alternative explanation for General Casey's era of persistent conflict. With the creation of its much-celebrated All-Volunteer Force and with its abandonment of the citizen-soldier tradition, Purdum continued, the United States had acquired "something that the country didn't have in the past—a large and permanent warrior caste."[21] The state could employ that caste as it wished.

Perhaps a permanent warrior caste is just what a nation facing persistent conflict needs. Robert Gates for one wasn't so sure. Visiting West Point shortly after stepping down as secretary of defense, he shared his reservations with the assembled cadets. The gap between the military and society was unhealthy, in his view. Among other things, it was fostering in the ranks a sense of moral superiority, members of the armed forces persuading themselves that they "adhered to a set of standards and values that is better than the civilian sector." Gates worried about the emergence of "a cadre of military leaders that politically, culturally, and geographically have less and less in common with the majority of the people they have sworn to defend." Down that road, even if in the far distance, lay the temptation of praetorianism.[22]

The obvious antidote to the dangers posed by a warrior caste set off from society is to reconstitute the tradition of the citizen-soldier. This, however, neither Gates nor any other figure of prominence in either

American political life or the American military profession has ventured to suggest.

The "standing army" created in the wake of Vietnam at least in part to end the divisions created by Vietnam has now become sacrosanct, cherished by the state as an instrument for projecting power and by the country at large as a convenient device for dodging responsibility. Whether either party to this arrangement actually stands to benefit in the long run remains unclear. This much alone is certain: the attitudes and arrangements giving rise to the new American militarism remain intact and inviolable.

Notes

Preface

1. Walter Karp, *The Politics of War* (New York, 2003), p. 130. This is a reprint of a book first published in 1979.

Introduction

1. Gregg Easterbrook, "Out on the Edge: American Power Moves Beyond the Mere Super," *New York Times*, April 27, 2003.
2. Max Boot, "The New American Way of War," *Foreign Affairs* 82 (July/August 2003), p. 44.
3. Bush remarks at the National Cathedral, September 14, 2001.
4. C. Wright Mills, *The Power Elite* (New York, 1956, rpt. 2000), p. 222.
5. *The Oxford English Dictionary*, vol. 6, p. 438, provides the following four-part definition of militarism: "The spirit and tendencies of the professional soldier; the prevalence of military sentiments or ideals among a people; the political condition characterized by the predominance of the military class in government or administration; the tendency to regard military efficiency as the paramount interest of the state." The new American militarism conforms to the latter three elements of this definition, with the caveat that the present-day "military class" in Washington is comprised chiefly of people who are not themselves serving soldiers. They are instead politicians, civil servants, journalists, and hangers-on who are fully imbued with a militaristic mindset and worldview. The definition offered by *The New Oxford Dictionary of English*, p. 1173, "the belief or desire of a government or people that a country should maintain a strong military capability and be prepared to use it aggressively to defend or promote national interests," also applies, but it fails to consider the importance of military values, which also form an element of the new American militarism.

6. Chalmers Johnson, *The Sorrows of Empire* (New York, 2004), pp. 227–29.

7. Michael Mann, *Incoherent Empire* (New York, 2003), p. 267.

8. Michael Sherry, *In the Shadow of War: The United States Since the 1930s* (New Haven, Conn., 1995), p. x.

9. James Madison, "Political Observations," April 20, 1795, in Philip R. Fendall, ed., *Letters and Other Writings of James Madison*, vol. 4 (Philadelphia, 1865), p. 491.

Chapter 1: Wilsonians Under Arms

1. Henry Kissinger, *Diplomacy* (New York, 1994), p. 30. According to Kissinger, even Richard M. Nixon "considered himself above all a disciple of Wilsonian internationalism" (p. 54).

2. Woodrow Wilson, "Address of the President of the United States to the Senate," January 22, 1917, http://www.lib.byu.edu/~rdh/wwi/1917/senate.html, accessed May 10, 2004.

3. "President Woodrow Wilson's War Message," April 2, 1917, http://www.lib.byu.edu/~rdh/wwi/1917/wilswarm.html, accessed May 10, 2004.

4. Andrew J. Bacevich, *American Empire: The Realities and Consequences of U.S. Diplomacy* (Cambridge, Mass., 2002).

5. Lawrence F. Kaplan, "Regime Change," *New Republic*, March 3, 2003.

6. George W. Bush, "President's Remarks to the Nation," September 11, 2002, http://www.whitehouse.gov/news/releases/2002/09/20020911-3.html, accessed May 28, 2004.

7. Kissinger, *Diplomacy*, p. 54.

8. Robert Kagan, *Of Paradise and Power: America and Europe in the New World Order* (New York, 2003), pp. 85–86.

9. None of this is to suggest that idealism alone provides the actual basis for American behavior. Rather, the architects of U.S. policy advert to familiar Wilsonian precepts as a way to justify to the world, to the American public, and perhaps even to themselves the use of American power in pursuit of specific and concrete American interests. This is not an exercise in hypocrisy; policymakers in Washington genuinely believe that the United States acts in response to a higher calling, much as Republicans have no doubt that their party stands for upholding traditional moral values and Democrats really believe that their party genuinely cares about the poor and dispossessed.

10. Quoted in Nancy C. Unger, *Fighting Bob La Follette* (Chapel Hill, N.C., 2000), pp. 252–53.

11. Quoted in Ronald Radosh, *Prophets on the Right: Profiles of Conservative Critics of American Globalism* (New York, 1975), p. 128.

12. Jim VandeHei, "Kerry Assails Bush on Iraq," *Washington Post*, May 13, 2004.

13. "Senator John Kerry Delivers the Weekly Democratic Radio Response,"

March 6, 2004, www.democrats.org/news/20040306o001.html, accessed March 7, 2004.

14. Russell F. Weigley, *History of the United States Army* (New York, 1967), pp. 567–69.

15. For a comparison of current U.S. and British forces, see *The Military Balance, 2002–2003* (London, 2002), pp. 16–26, 60–63.

16. Michael Mann, *Incoherent Empire* (New York, 2003), p. 18.

17. Bruce Berkowitz, *The New Face of War* (New York, 2003), p. 4. Berkowitz cites CIA data indicating that annual worldwide military spending is approximately $750 billion, with the then-current Pentagon budget at $380 billion. If anything, that comparison understates the level of total U.S. defense spending.

18. Tim Reid, "U.S. Defense Spending to Top $500 Billion by 2010," *The Times* [London], February 1, 2003.

19. Steven M. Kosiak, *Analysis of the FY 2005 Defense Budget Request* (Washington, D.C., 2004), p. 1.

20. According to one critic, there are U.S. troops stationed in 150 foreign countries. See Chalmers Johnson, *The Sorrows of Empire: Militarism, Secrecy, and the End of the Republic* (New York, 2004), p. 154. In open sources, the Pentagon acknowledges having bases in some forty countries. See Department of Defense, "Base Structure Report, FY 2003," http://www.globalsecurity.org/military/library/report/2003/basestructure2003.pdf, accessed May 4, 2004. But this report, an inventory of real estate controlled by DoD, seriously understates the U.S. military presence abroad. It does not, for example, make any mention of the U.S. military presence in Iraq, Kuwait, Afghanistan, Uzbekistan, or the Horn of Africa.

21. Chief of Naval Operations Strategic Studies Group XXII, *Coherent Adaptive Force: Ensuring Sea Supremacy for SEA POWER 21*, January 2004.

22. Undersecretary of the Air Force Peter B. Teets quoted in Scott Elliott, "America Must Reach for Space Dominion," *SpaceDaily*, September 30, 2004, www.spacedaily.com/news/milspace-04z.html, accessed September 22, 2004.

23. Cold War episodes included Korea, Lebanon (twice), Vietnam, the Dominican Republic, and Grenada. By some calculations, the U.S. confrontation with Libya culminating in the bombing of Tripoli in 1986 might also qualify.

24. Panama, the Persian Gulf (twice), Kurdistan, Somalia, Haiti, Bosnia, Kosovo, and Afghanistan.

25. Judy Keen, "Cheney Says It's Too Soon to Tell on Iraqi Arms," *USA Today*, January 19, 2004.

26. George W. Bush, "President Addresses the Nation in Prime Time Press Conference," April 13, 2004, www.whitehouse.gov/news/releases/2004/04/20040413-20.html, accessed April 20, 2004.

27. On this point see Azar Gat, *Fascist and Liberal Visions of War* (New York, 1998).

28. Michael Ignatieff, *Virtual War: Kosovo and Beyond* (New York, 2000), pp. 3, 110, 186, 191.

29. Wesley K. Clark, *Waging Modern War* (New York, 2001), pp. 204, 430.

30. Bill Owens with Ed Offley, *Lifting the Fog of War* (New York, 2000), pp. 14-15; Tommy Franks, *American Soldier* (New York, 2004), p. 175.

31. David Skinner, "The New Face of War," *New Atlantis* 2 (Summer 2003), http://www.thenewatlantis.com/archive/2/skinner.htm, accessed March 29, 2004.

32. David C. King and Zachary Karabell, *The Generation of Trust: How the U.S. Military Has Regained the Public's Confidence Since Vietnam* (Washington, D.C., 2003), pp. 1–6.

33. George Will, "Forrestal Lecture Series," U.S. Naval Academy (January 24, 2001).

34. Tom Morganthau, "The Military's New Image," *Newsweek,* March 11, 1991.

35. David Lipsky, *Absolutely American: Four Years at West Point* (Boston, 2003), pp. xii–xiii.

36. Victor Davis Hanson, *Between War and Peace: Lessons from Afghanistan to Iraq* (New York, 2004), p. 282.

37. Gordon Trowbridge, "Today's Military: Right, Republican, and Principled," *Marine Corps Times,* January 5, 2004.

38. Quoted in Thomas E. Ricks, "The Widening Gap Between the Military and Society," *Atlantic Monthly,* July 1997.

39. Mackubin T. Owens, "The Democratic Party's War on the Military," *Wall Street Journal,* November 22, 2000.

40. Colin L. Powell, *My American Journey* (New York, 1995), p. 576.

41. Michael Ignatieff, "The Challenges of American Imperial Power," *Naval War College Review,* Spring 2003, http://www.nwc.navy.mil/press/Review/2003/Spring/art3-sp3.htm, accessed May 12, 2004.

42. Norman Ornstein, "The Legacy of Campaign 2000," *Washington Quarterly* 24 (Spring 2001), p. 102.

43. Cynthia Tucker, "War Doesn't Cost the Moneyed," *Atlanta Journal-Constitution,* January 25, 2004.

44. For a cogent assessment, see Eliot A. Cohen, "Twilight of the Citizen-Soldier," *Parameters* 31 (Summer 2001), pp. 23–28.

45. Edward Walsh and Amy Goldstein, "Cheney's Style," *Washington Post,* July 26, 2000.

46. For a discussion of the changing relationship of citizenship to service, see James Burk, "The Military Obligation of Citizens Since Vietnam," *Parameters* 31 (Spring 2001), pp. 48–60.

47. Ole R. Holsti, "A Widening Gap Between the U.S. Military and Civilian Society? Some Evidence, 1976–1996," *International Security* 23 (Winter 1998/1999), pp. 5–42.

48. On Cheney's appetite for military history, see Mark Leibovich, "The Strong, Silent Type," *Washington Post,* January 18, 2004.

49. Writing at the time of the U.S. invasion of Iraq in 2003, Dunne noted that only a single member of Congress—Senator Tim Johnson, Democrat of South Dakota—had a son or daughter serving as an enlisted member of the U.S. military. John Gregory Dunne, "The Horror Is Seductive," *New York Review of Books,* May 29, 2003.

50. David M. Halbfinger and Steven A. Holmes, "Military Mirrors a Working-Class America," *New York Times,* March 30, 2003. Of the Army's more than sixty thousand enlisted females then on active duty, 46 percent were African American and 38 percent white.

51. Gil Klein, "Uncle Sam Wants You!" *Tampa Tribune,* February 3, 2003.

52. Thomas L. Friedman, "The Home Team," *New York Times,* February 8, 2004.

53. For an elaboration on this point, see the essays and survey data in Peter D. Feaver and Richard H. Kohn, eds., *Soldiers and Civilians: The Civil-Military Gap and American National Security* (Cambridge, Mass., 2001). A superb journalistic treatment is Thomas E. Ricks, *Making the Corps* (New York, 1997).

54. Richard H. Kohn, "The Erosion of Civilian Control of the Military in the United States Today," *Naval War College Review* 55 (Summer 2002), pp. 9–59.

55. Between March 2001 and September 2003, President George W. Bush made appearances at military installations or presentations to specifically military audiences on forty-five separate occasions. Kevin Baker, "We're in the Army Now," *Harper's,* October 2003.

56. Dana Milbank, "Coming to Reelection Campaigns and Toy Boxes Near You," *Washington Post,* August 12, 2003.

57. Robin Toner, "Still the Question: What Did You Do in the War?" *New York Times,* February 15, 2004. No less inevitably, Republicans pushed back against the Democratic attack on Bush's warrior credentials, first contending that Kerry had undermined his own credentials by becoming an outspoken opponent of the Vietnam War and then directly impugning Kerry's Vietnam service.

58. Harold Bloom, "Cometh the Hour . . . ," *Wall Street Journal,* October 14, 2003.

59. Max Boot, "American Imperialism? No Need to Run from Label," *USA Today,* May 6, 2003.

60. C. Wright Mills, *The Power Elite* (New York, 1956, rpt. 2000), p. 184.

Chapter 2: The Military Profession at Bay

1. Charles A. Beard, *The Devil Theory of War* (New York, 1936), p. 29.

2. Quoted in Robert H. Scales Jr., *Certain Victory: The U.S. Army in the Gulf*

War (Washington, D. C., 1994), p. 35. The hundred hours refers to the duration of the ground campaign.

3. Scales, *Certain Victory*, p. 5.

4. Ibid., p. 10.

5. Robert D. Heinl Jr., "The Collapse of the Armed Forces," rpt. in Marvin E. Gettleman et al., *Vietnam and America*, rev. and enlarged ed. (New York, 1995), p. 327. Colonel Heinl's essay first appeared in *Armed Forces Journal*, June 7, 1971.

6. For a brisk account of post-Vietnam institutional reforms, emphasizing the U.S. Army, see Tom Clancy with General Fred Franks Jr., *Into the Storm: A Study in Command* (New York, 1997), pp. 84–127.

7. An unnamed general quoted in Ward Just, *Military Man* (London, 1972), p. 185.

8. The standard biography is Lewis Sorley, *Thunderbolt: General Creighton Abrams and the Army of His Times* (New York, 1992).

9. Clancy with Franks, *Into the Storm: A Study in Command*, p. 78.

10. H. Norman Schwarzkopf, *It Doesn't Take a Hero* (New York, 1992), pp. 379–80.

11. James Kitfield, *Prodigal Soldiers* (New York, 1995), p. 151.

12. General John Vessey quoted in Sorley, *Thunderbolt*, p. 364.

13. Harry G. Summers Jr., *On Strategy: The Vietnam War in Context* (Carlisle Barracks, Pa., 1981), p. 27.

14. Ibid., p. 27.

15. William C. Westmoreland, *A Soldier Reports* (Garden City, N.Y., 1976), p. 410.

16. Ibid., p. 413.

17. The classic account is Roger Trinquier, *Modern Warfare: A French View of Counterinsurgency* (New York, 1964).

18. Summers, *On Strategy*, p. 112.

19. Michael Geyer, "German Strategy in the Age of Machine Warfare," in Peter Paret, ed., *Makers of Modern Strategy from Machiavelli to the Nuclear Age* (Princeton, N.J., 1986), pp. 527–97.

20. Albert Wohlstetter, "The Cold War Is Over and Over and . . . ," *Wall Street Journal*, October 1, 1996. Even before the Soviet Union collapsed, Wohlstetter was writing that expectations of a conventional attack by the Warsaw Pact through the Fulda Gap "were always far-fetched." Albert Wohlstetter and Fred Hoffman, "Confronting Saddam: A Model Danger," *Wall Street Journal*, August 9, 1990.

21. The key primary document is U.S. Army Field Manual 100-5 *Operations*, published in August 1982. For a history, see John L. Romjue, "The Evolution of the AirLand Battle Concept," May–June 1984, http://www.airpower.maxwell.af.mil/airchronicles/aureview/1984/may-jun/romjue.html, accessed April 24, 2004.

22. Paul F. Gorman, *The Secret of Future Victories* (Fort Leavenworth, Kans., 1992), pp. IV-1 to IV-2. Prior to his retirement Gorman had been a four-star general in the U.S. Army and an important contributor to post-Vietnam reforms.

23. Shultz himself explains the Weinberger Doctrine in similar terms. See George P. Shultz, *Turmoil and Triumph: My Years as Secretary of State* (New York, 1993), pp. 649–51.

24. Richard Halloran, "The U.S. Will Not Drift into a Latin War, Weinberger Says," *New York Times,* November 29, 1984.

25. Colin L. Powell, "Why Generals Get Nervous," *New York Times,* October 8, 1992.

26. Eliot A. Cohen, "Playing Powell Politics: The General's Zest for Power," *Foreign Affairs* 74 (November/December 1995), p. 108.

27. Quoted in Michael Steinberger, "Misoverestimated," *American Prospect* 15 (May 1, 2004).

28. Powell, *My American Journey* (New York, 1995), p. 167.

29. The results appeared in Bob Woodward, *The Commanders* (New York, 1991).

30. "About the National Guard," National Guard Bureau, http://www. ngb.army.mil/about/, accessed May 9, 2004.

31. As that war turned sour, Powell, now secretary of state, once again made a point of distancing himself from the decision to use force, providing Woodward with yet more interviews. See Anne Applebaum, "Having It Both Ways," *Washington Post,* April 21, 2004. Woodward's book was published as *Plan of Attack* (New York, 2004).

32. For the authoritative rendering of the Powell Doctrine, see Powell, "Why Generals Get Nervous."

33. Powell, *My American Journey,* p. 437.

34. John Hillen, "Superpowers Don't Do Windows," *Orbis,* Summer 1997, pp. 241–57; Condoleezza Rice, quoted in Michael R. Gordon, "Bush Would Stop U.S. Peacekeeping in Balkan Fights," *New York Times,* October 21, 2000.

35. Wesley K. Clark, *Waging Modern War* (New York, 2001), p. xxxi.

36. Ibid., p. 128.

37. Clark, pp. 119, 129.

38. For accounts of the conflict, see Ivo H. Daalder and Michael E. O'Hanlon, *Winning Ugly: NATO's War to Save Kosovo* (Washington, D.C., 2000), and Andrew J. Bacevich and Eliot A. Cohen, eds., *War over Kosovo: Politics and Strategy in a Global Age* (New York, 2001).

39. Clark, *Waging Modern War,* pp. 278-279, 303, 310-313.

40. The definitive expression of that critique is Wesley K. Clark, *Winning Modern Wars: Iraq, Terrorism, and the American Empire* (New York, 2003).

41. Beginning with the election of 1992, presidential candidates began to solicit the endorsements of recently retired four-star generals and admirals. That year Admiral William Crowe, who had served as chairman of the Joint

Chiefs of Staff for the elder President Bush, announced with great fanfare that he was supporting the candidacy of Governor Bill Clinton. President Clinton subsequently appointed Crowe to be his ambassador to the United Kingdom.

42. H. Josef Hebert, "Bush in Radio Address Says Prison Scandal Will Not Deter U.S. Forces in Iraq," *Boston Globe,* May 8, 2004.

43. Lawrence F. Kaplan, "Officer Politics," *New Republic,* September 13, 2004.

44. Midge Decter, *Rumsfeld: A Personal Portrait* (New York, 2003), pp. 122–25, 132–36.

45. Thomas E. Ricks, "Rumsfeld on High Wire of Defense Reform," *Washington Post,* May 20, 2001.

46. Donald Rumsfeld, "Rumsfeld's Rules," *Wall Street Journal,* January 29, 2001.

47. Michael Mann, *Incoherent Empire* (New York, 2003), p. 9.

48. Interview with Thomas White, "Frontline: The Invasion of Iraq," January 31, 2004, www.pbs.org/wgbh/pages/frontline/shows/invasion/interviews/white.html, accessed May 14, 2004. White was secretary of the Army at the time of the Iraq invasion.

49. In his memoir *American Soldier* (New York, 2004), Franks disputes this view, claiming for himself full credit for the design of the Afghanistan and Iraq campaigns. For an essay that questions the credibility of that claim, see Andrew J. Bacevich, "A Modern Major General," *New Left Review* 29 (September/October 2004), pp. 123–34.

50. For an account of the kneading that transformed OPLAN 1003 from a reprise of Desert Storm into a test-drive of "shock and awe," see Bob Woodward, *Plan of Attack* (New York, 2004), pp. 1, 8, 37, 54–55, 82–83, 96, 101, 121, 133–34, 146, and 237. On Powell's back-channel contacts with Franks, see p. 80. On the marginalization of the service chiefs, see pp. 117–19.

51. Brigadier General Mark Kimmitt quoted in "General Kimmitt Says Coalition Forces Will Pacify Fallujah," U.S. Department of State International Information Programs, April 1, 2004, http://usembassy.state.gov/posts/in3/wwwhiraq92.html, accessed May 10, 2004.

52. John Kifner and Ian Fisher, "U.S. Weighs Falluja Pullback, Leaving Patrols to Iraq Troops," *New York Times,* April 30, 2004.

53. General Richard Myers, "Hearing of the Defense Subcommittee of the Senate Appropriations Committee," May 12, 2004, Federal News Service.

54. Philip B. Davidson, "The American Military's Assessment of Vietnam," in Dennis E. Showalter and John G. Albert, eds., *An American Dilemma* (Chicago, 1993), p. 54. The essays in the collection were prepared for a symposium held at the U.S. Air Force Academy in 1990.

55. Thomas E. Ricks, "Dissension Grows in Senior Ranks on War Strategy," *Washington Post,* May 9, 2004. Ann Scott Tyson, "A Deepening Rift at the Pentagon," *Christian Science Monitor,* May 14, 2004. Sidney Blumenthal, "America's Military Coup," *Guardian,* May 13, 2004.

56. "The Big Story with John Gibson," Fox News Channel, May 14, 2004, http://www.foxnews.com/story/0,2933,120128,00.html, accessed June 25, 2004.

57. "They've Screwed Up," *60 Minutes,* May 24, 2004, http://www.cbsnews.com/stories/2004/05/21/60minutes/main618896.shtml, accessed June 25, 2004.

58. "Bush Should Admit Iraq Is a 'Mess' and Make Plans for a U.S. Troop Pull-out by Next Year," Council on Foreign Relations Interview, May 6, 2004, http://www.cfr.com, accessed June 25, 2004.

59. For the mournful result, see "Article 15-6 Investigation of the 800th Military Police Brigade," n.d. [February 2004], http://www.globalsecurity.org/intell/library/reports/2004/800-mp-bde.htm, accessed May 5, 2004.

60. General Richard Myers, "DoD News Briefing—Secretary Rumsfeld and Gen. Myers," August 5, 2003, http://www.defenselink.mil/transcripts/2003/tr20030805-secdef0525.html, accessed August 11, 2003.

61. James Mann, *Rise of the Vulcans: The History of Bush's War Cabinet* (New York, 2004), p. 307.

Chapter 3: Left, Right, Left

1. Walter Laqueur, "The West in Retreat," *Commentary* 60 (August 1975).

2. Theodore Draper, "The Specter of Weimar," *Commentary* 52 (December 1971).

3. Irving Kristol, "On Conservatism and Capitalism," *Wall Street Journal,* September 11, 1975, rpt. in Christopher DeMuth and William Kristol, eds., *The Neoconservative Imagination: Essays in Honor of Irving Kristol* (Washington, D.C., 1995), p. 179.

4. There is always something slightly arbitrary about lumping individuals into a group and then assigning to the group a political label. The inevitable result is to blur distinctions. But for purposes of political analysis the lumping together is necessary. In describing people as neoconservatives, I do not mean to imply that all individuals so identified agree fully with one another on every issue. I do mean to imply that they share a common outlook and agree on most critical issues. Senator Edward Kennedy of Massachusetts may differ with Senator Hillary Clinton of New York on certain matters, but both are liberal Democrats as the term has come to be understood in the first decade of the twenty-first century—as any neoconservative worth his salt would be the first to testify. It is in this same sense that I take the liberty of labeling people as neoconservatives.

5. Irving Kristol, "The Neoconservative Persuasion," *Weekly Standard,* August 25, 2003.

6. Peter Steinfels, *The Neoconservatives: The Men Who Are Changing America's Politics* (New York, 1980), p. 74.

7. Disingenuous testimonials by neocons professing to be confused by all the fuss stemming from alleged neoconservative influence only serve to reinforce suspicions that a conspiracy of some sort must be afoot. See, for example, Max Boot, "What the Heck Is a 'Neocon'?" *Wall Street Journal*, December 30, 2002.

8. The major works include Norman Podhoretz, *Making It* (New York, 1967), *Breaking Ranks* (New York, 1979), and *Ex-Friends* (New York, 1999). The quotations are from *Making It*, pp. xvii, 3.

9. Steinfels, *The Neoconservatives*, p. 21. With typical immodesty, Podhoretz credits himself with having given "the Movement" much of its initial impetus. This theme permeates the first half of *Breaking Ranks*.

10. H. W. Brands, *What America Owes the World: The Struggle for the Soul of Foreign Policy* (Cambridge, Eng., 1998), p. 284.

11. An interesting illustration of Podhoretz's preoccupation is his essay "Appeasement By Any Other Name," *Commentary* 76 (July 1983). Written in the midst of the biggest-ever peacetime U.S. military buildup, the essay compares Ronald Reagan to Neville Chamberlain and declares that "appeasement by any other name smells as rank, and the stench of it now pervades the American political atmosphere."

12. Norman Podhoretz, "Making the World Safe for Communism," *Commentary* 61 (April 1976).

13. John Ehrman, *The Rise of Neoconservatism* (New Haven, Conn., 1995), p. 108.

14. Norman Podhoretz, *Why We Were in Vietnam* (New York, 1982), p. 11.

15. Norman Podhoretz, "The Reagan Road to Détente," *Foreign Affairs* 63 (America and the World, 1984), p. 452.

16. Norman Podhoretz, "The Neo-Conservative Anguish over Reagan's Foreign Policy," *New York Times Magazine*, May 2, 1982.

17. On McGovern and on the broader danger of isolationism, see Podhoretz, "Making the World Safe for Communism."

18. Podhoretz, *Why We Were in Vietnam*, p. 210.

19. Podhoretz, "Neo-Conservative Anguish."

20. For a concise but thoughtful reflection on the relationship between Wilson and the neoconservatives, see Ronald Steel's review essay "The Missionary," *New York Review of Books*, November 20, 2003.

21. Midge Decter, "America Now: A Failure of Nerve?" *Commentary* 60 (July 1975).

22. Gary Dorrien, *The Neoconservative Mind: Politics, Culture, and the War of Ideology* (Philadelphia, 1993), p. 377. A year after the fall of Saigon, Podhoretz was advocating a revitalization of U.S. foreign policy that would "use American power to make the world safe for democracy." Podhoretz, "Making the World Safe for Communism."

23. Podhoretz, *Breaking Ranks*, p. 322.

24. Ibid., p. 322. The phrase "totalitarian temptation" was borrowed from Jean-François Revel.

25. Norman Podhoretz, *The Present Danger* (New York, 1980, rpt. 1986), p. 86.

26. Ibid., pp. 55, 85.

27. Podhoretz, "Neo-Conservative Anguish over Reagan's Foreign Policy." The new president repaid their support handsomely, appointing neoconservatives to key billets in the State and Defense Departments. Most prominent was Jeane Kirkpatrick, appointed to be U.S. ambassador to the United Nations. But several others—Elliott Abrams, Richard Perle, and Paul Wolfowitz among them—wielded considerable clout even though assigned to less visible second- or third-tier positions in the national security bureaucracy.

28. Norman Podhoretz, "How Reagan Succeeds as a Carter Clone," *New York Post*, October 7, 1986.

29. Podhoretz, "The Reagan Road to Détente,"

30. Podhoretz, "Neo-Conservative Anguish over Reagan's Foreign Policy."

31. Podhoretz, "The Reagan Road to Détente."

32. Norman Podhoretz, "Looking for the Wrong Reagan," *Times* [London], August 14, 1985.

33. Podhoretz, *The Present Danger.* The quotation is from the "Preface to the New Edition."

34. Norman Podhoretz, "The Danger Is Greater Than Ever," *New York Post*, December 1, 1987; Dorrien, *The Neoconservative Mind*, pp. 197–200.

35. John Updike, *Rabbit at Rest* (New York, 1990), pp. 442–43.

36. Norman Podhoretz, "After the Cold War," *Commentary* 92 (July 1991).

37. Norman Podhoretz, "Neoconservatism: A Eulogy," *Commentary* 101 (March 1996).

38. Podhoretz, *Breaking Ranks*, p. 291.

39. Dorrien, *The Neoconservative Mind*, p. 117, quoting Irving Kristol in *Wall Street Journal* columns published on February 3 and March 3, 1986. Kristol's lament did not imply that he for his part was inclined to launch a great crusade to pursue evildoers. "No one can seriously claim," he wrote in 1986, "that the numerous authoritarian regimes now scattered all over the world constitute any kind of threat to liberal America or the liberal West." Quoted in DeMuth and Kristol, *The Neoconservative Imagination*, p. 200. The original quotation comes from Irving Kristol, "Human Rights: The Hidden Agenda," *National Interest*, Winter 1986–87.

40. Joshua Muravchik, "Losing the Peace," *Commentary* 94 (July 1992).

41. Ehrman, *The Rise of Neoconservatism*, p. 184.

42. Podhoretz, "Neoconservatism: A Eulogy." According to Gary Dorrien, the end of the Cold War left the neoconservatives divided between a realist camp and a Wilsonian camp. See Dorrien, *The Neoconservative Mind*, pp. 324–41.

43. Robert Kagan, "Global Mission," *Commentary* 92 (August 1991). Emphasis in the original.

44. Muravchik, "Losing the Peace."

45. George Weigel, "On the Road to Isolationism?" *Commentary* 93 (January 1992).

46. John B. Judis, "Trotskyism to Anachronism," *Foreign Affairs* 74 (July 1995), p. 123ff.

47. William Kristol and Robert Kagan, "Toward a Neo-Reaganite Foreign Policy," *Foreign Affairs* 75 (July/August 1996), p. 23.

48. Charles Krauthammer, "The Bush Doctrine," *Weekly Standard,* June 4, 2001.

49. Robert Kagan, "If Not U.S. Hegemony, Then What?" *Washington Post,* June 23, 1998.

50. Robert Kagan, "American Power—A Guide for the Perplexed," *Commentary* 101 (April 1996).

51. Muravchik, "Losing the Peace."

52. Charles Krauthammer, "The Unipolar Moment," *Foreign Affairs* 70 (America and the World, 1990), p. 25.

53. Charles Krauthammer, "The Anti-Superpower Fallacy," *Washington Post,* April 10, 1992.

54. Charles Krauthammer, "A World Imagined," *New Republic,* March 15, 1999.

55. Charles Krauthammer, "What 'International Community'?" *Washington Post,* December 26, 1997.

56. Krauthammer, "The Unipolar Moment."

57. Krauthammer, "What 'International Community'?" Not that the United States would, as a practical matter, end up acting alone. Neoconservatives believed that if the United States expressed a determination to act, others would follow. In the Persian Gulf War of 1990–91, wrote Krauthammer, "others joined the U.S. effort precisely because President Bush had demonstrated that he was quite prepared to act unilaterally if necessary. Under those circumstances, lesser powers, convinced of American will, joined up. It was a textbook example of an apparently multilateral effort hinging on the fact of American unilateralism." Charles Krauthammer, "Dreams of a Blue Helmet," *Weekly Standard,* October 30, 1995.

58. Krauthammer, "The Unipolar Moment."

59. William Kristol and Robert Kagan, "Foreign Policy and the Republican Future," *Weekly Standard,* October 12, 1998.

60. Robert Kagan, "Power and Weakness," *Policy Review* 113 (June/July 2002).

61. Kagan, "American Power—A Guide for the Perplexed."

62. Podhoretz, *Breaking Ranks,* pp. 181, 219.

63. Nor was there any doubt about what those organizing principles should be. As Krauthammer wrote, "Political philosophy is over. Finished. Solved. . . . [The] triumph of the Western political idea is complete. Its rivals have been routed. . . . What models are left? Islamic fundamentalism? . . . The jig is up. Political theory . . . is finished. The Western idea of governance has pre-

vailed." Charles Krauthammer, "Democracy Has Won," *Washington Post*, March 24, 1989.

64. Robert Kagan, "The Clinton Legacy Abroad," *Weekly Standard*, January 15, 2001.

65. Joshua Muravchik, "The Bush Manifesto," *Commentary* 114 (December 2002).

66. Quoted in Claudia Rosett, "One Down, Dozens More to Go," *Wall Street Journal*, December 16, 2003.

67. Michael Ledeen, "Faster, Please," *National Review Online*, April 1, 2002, http://www.nationalreview.com/ledeen/ledeen040102.asp.

68. From 1991 onward, Powell remained in the eyes of most neoconservatives an untrustworthy figure. Laurie Mylroie, "General's Story," *Commentary* 95 (January 1993).

69. Donald Kagan and Frederick W. Kagan, "Peace for Our Time?" *Commentary* 110 (September 2000). See also Frederick W. Kagan and David T. Fautua, "Could We Fight a War if We Had To?" *Commentary* 103 (May 1997).

70. Charles Krauthammer, writing in 1990, saw "the coming decades [as] a time of heightened, not diminished, threat of war." Krauthammer, "The Unipolar Moment."

71. Donald Kagan and Frederick W. Kagan, *While America Sleeps* (New York, 2000), p. 295.

72. Frederick W. Kagan, "The Decline of America's Armed Forces," in Robert Kagan and William Kristol, eds., *Present Dangers: Crisis and Opportunity in American Foreign and Defense Policy* (San Francisco, 2000), p. 261.

73. Robert Kagan, "When America Blinked," *New Republic*, December 3, 2001.

74. Robert Kagan, "Inside the Limo," *New Republic*, April 10, 2000.

75. Elliott Abrams et al., "Statement of Principles," Project for the New American Century, June 3, 1997.

76. William Kristol and Robert Kagan, "Bombing Iraq Isn't Enough," *New York Times*, January 30, 1998.

77. Robert Kagan, "Saddam's Impending Victory," *Weekly Standard*, February 2, 1998.

78. Michael Ledeen, "American Power—For What?" *Commentary* 109 (January 2000).

79. Michael Ledeen, "U.S. Military Aid Advances Our Values," *Wall Street Journal*, April 25, 2001.

80. The phrase is taken from the title of Schlesinger's influential postwar polemic *The Vital Center: The Politics of Freedom* (Boston, 1949).

81. The implication is not that these writers limited themselves exclusively to foreign policy. Particularly in the case of Brooks and Krauthammer, they did not.

82. "Letter to President Clinton on Iraq," January 26, 1998, Project for the New American Century, http://www.newamericancentury.org/iraqclinton letter.htm, accessed June 27, 2004.

83. HR 4655, "Iraq Liberation Act of 1998," http://www.iraqwatch.org/government/US/Legislation/ILA.htm, accessed June 27, 2004.

84. Robert Kagan and William Kristol, "America's Role: The Burden of Power . . . Is Having to Wield It," *Washington Post*, March 19, 2000.

85. Krauthammer, "The Bush Doctrine."

86. William Kristol and Gary Schmitt, "Take on North Korea, Too," *Australian*, October 25, 2002.

87. Lawrence Kaplan and William Kristol, *The War over Iraq* (San Francisco, 2003), p. 121.

88. See, for example, Bob Woodward, *Bush at War* (New York, 2002), pp. 49, 60–61.

89. Robert Kagan and William Kristol, "Remember the Bush Doctrine," *Weekly Standard*, April 15, 2002. This did not necessarily mean targeting Saddam Hussein first. Some neoconservatives wanted to save Iraq for last. Thus Charles Krauthammer, writing in late September 2001, advocated a strategy that began with the Taliban, then proceeded to Syria, a vulnerable regime that he characterized as "low-hanging fruit." For Krauthammer, overthrowing the governments in Iraq and Iran was best left to stage three. "The war on terrorism," he predicted, "will conclude in Baghdad." Krauthammer, "The War: A Road Map," *Washington Post*, September 28, 2001. The road to Baghdad was not one that Americans would be obliged to travel alone. Where the United States led, others were sure to follow. "An American invasion of Iraq will not be a unilateral action, not by a long shot," Kristol and Kagan assured their readers. "With or without a UN Security Council resolution, the US will not 'go it alone' in Iraq. When President George W. Bush announces that the US is going to war, and the attack begins, the US will have many allies indeed." William Kristol and Robert Kagan, "US Won't Need to 'Go It Alone,'" *Australian*, January 29, 2003. For more on the same point see Charles Krauthammer, "Unilateralism? Yes, Indeed," *Washington Post*, December 14, 2001, and Robert Kagan and William Kristol, "What To Do About Iraq," *Weekly Standard*, January 21, 2002, p. 23.

90. William Kristol et al. to George W. Bush, April 3, 2002, Project for the New American Century.

91. Robert Kagan and William Kristol, "What to Do About Iraq."

92. Kaplan and Kristol, *The War over Iraq*, p. 99.

93. Ibid. See also William Kristol et al., "Statement on Post-War Iraq," Project for the New American Century, n.d. [winter 2003?], which foresaw a U.S. invasion of Iraq as paving the way for "the democratic development of the wider Middle East."

94. Charles Krauthammer, "Victory Changes Everything . . . ," *Washington Post*, November 30, 2001.

95. Kagan and Kristol, "What to Do About Iraq."

96. "Testimony of William Kristol," Senate Foreign Relations Committee, Feb-

ruary 7, 2002, www.newamericancentury.org/defense-20020207.htm, accessed May 14, 2004.

97.   Andrew J. Bacevich and Elizabeth Prodromou, "God Is Not Neutral: Religion and U.S. Foreign Policy After 9/11," *Orbis* 48 (Winter 2004), pp. 43–54.

98.   Victor Davis Hanson, "Our Enemies, The Saudis," *Commentary* 114 (July/August 2002).

99.   Neoconservatives were not happy with Bush in one respect. Although the aftermath of 9/11 saw a quantum increase in U.S. defense spending, neocons lobbied for still more, describing the budget as "inadequate" for a "military with global responsibilities" and arguing for a permanent increase of $70 to $100 billion. William Kristol et al. to George W. Bush, January 23, 2003, Project for the New American Century.

100.   William Kristol, "Taking the War Beyond Terrorism," *Washington Post,* January 31, 2002.

101.   David Frum and Richard Perle, *An End to Evil: How to Win the War on Terror* (New York, 2004), pp. 275, 279.

102.   Norman Podhoretz, "How to Win World War IV," *Commentary* 113 (February 2002).

103.   Ibid.

104.   Norman Podhoretz, "Where Do We Go from Here?" *Jerusalem Post,* March 3, 2003.

105.   Podhoretz, "How to Win World War IV."

106.   Podhoretz, "In Praise of the Bush Doctrine."

107.   Quoted in Dorrien, *The Neoconservative Mind*, p. 49.

108.   Norman Podhoretz, "Syria Yes, Israel No?" *Weekly Standard,* November 12, 2001.

Chapter 4: California Dreaming

1.   Ronald Reagan, "Message to the Nation on the Observance of Independence Day," July 3, 1983.

2.   Podhoretz recounts the episode only briefly, conveying the impression that as a life experience two years in uniform lagged well behind attending even a single dinner party hosted by Diana and Lionel Trilling. Still, the account is an interesting one. Although the notably hawkish Podhoretz describes his fellow soldiers with good-humored respect, he does not gush over them, and he does not wax nostalgic about the Army as an institution. Norman Podhoretz, *Making It* (New York, 1967) pp. 177–93.

3.   Lou Cannon, *President Reagan: The Role of a Lifetime* (New York, 1991), p. 20.

4.   Quotations are from Jimmy Carter, "The Crisis of Confidence," July 15, 1979.

5.   Carter's speech contains a single military reference, a throwaway line alluding to the nation's "unmatched . . . military might."

6. Andrew Higgins, "Pax Americana," *Wall Street Journal Europe*, January 29, 2004.

7. Keith Richburg, "Carter's Rating Rose Nine Percent After Speech," *Washington Post*, July 17, 1979.

8. Garry Wills, *Reagan's America* (Garden City, N.Y., 1987), p. 2.

9. George C. Wilson and Michael Getler, "Anatomy of a Failed Mission," *Washington Post*, April 27, 1980.

10. Jimmy Carter, "Inaugural Address of President Jimmy Carter," January 20, 1977.

11. Jimmy Carter, "State of the Union Address 1978," January 19, 1978.

12. Reagan recounts his wartime service in Ronald W. Reagan, *An American Life* (New York, 1990), pp. 97–102.

13. Norman Podhoretz, "The Reagan Road to Détente," *Foreign Affairs* 63 (America and the World, 1984), p. 453.

14. On this point see Cannon, *President Reagan*, pp. 40–44, 74–75, 251, 427–28.

15. Ronald Reagan, "Inaugural Address," January 20, 1981.

16. According to Weinberger, the Carter administration had postponed the ceremony because it "had not wanted to do anything that reminded the people of Vietnam." Caspar Weinberger, *Fighting for Peace* (New York, 1990), pp. 51–52, 56.

17. Ronald Reagan, "Remarks on Presenting the Medal of Honor to Master Sergeant Roy P. Benavidez," February 24, 1981.

18. Ronald Reagan, "Remarks at Memorial Day Ceremonies Honoring an Unknown Serviceman of the Vietnam Conflict," May 28, 1984.

19. Ronald Reagan, "Remarks on Board the USS *Constellation* off the Coast of California," August 20, 1981.

20. On this point, see Weinberger, *Fighting for Peace*, p. 51.

21. The Reagan administration's fiscal policies obviated the need for collective sacrifice even in a monetary sense. With his tax cuts and emphasis on deficit spending, Reagan left it to future generations to foot the bill for the U.S. military buildup of the 1980s.

22. Ronald Reagan, "Remarks at a Ceremony Commemorating the 40th Anniversary of the Normandy Invasion, D-day," June 6, 1984.

23. Haynes Johnson, *Sleepwalking Through History: America in the Reagan Years* (New York, 1991), pp. 157–58.

24. By 1981, for example, minorities comprised 41.2 percent of the Army's enlisted strength. In terms of mental aptitude, the percentage of recruits scoring in the top two categories had fallen by one-third between 1964 and 1980. Meanwhile, the percentage of those scoring in the lowest category had more than doubled to 33 percent. Desertion rates were double those of the pre-Vietnam era. And due to an increase in indiscipline, personality disorders, job inaptitude, and the like, one in three recruits did not finish his or her initial term of service. Charles C. Moskos, "Making the All-Volunteer Force Work," *Foreign Affairs* 60 (Fall 1981), pp. 18–22.

25. Weinberger, *Fighting for Peace*, p. 52.

26. Derek Leebaert, *The Fifty-Year Wound: The True Price of America's Cold War Victory* (Boston, 2002), pp. 501–2.

27. M. Thomas Davis, "Operation Dire Straits," *Aviation Week and Space Technology*, January 10, 2000.

28. Ronald Reagan, "Remarks in Columbus to Members of Ohio Veterans Organizations," October 4, 1982.

29. Ronald Reagan, "Remarks and a Question-and-Answer Session with Editors of Gannett Newspapers," December 14, 1983.

30. Ronald Reagan, "Remarks at the Annual Convention of the American Legion in Seattle, Washington," August 23, 1983.

31. Ronald Reagan, "Remarks at a White House Ceremony for Medical Students and United States Military Personnel from Grenada," November 7, 1983.

32. Ronald Reagan, "Remarks at a Memorial Service in Fort Campbell, Kentucky, for the Members of the 101st Airborne Division Who Died in the Airplane Crash in Gander, Newfoundland," December 16, 1985.

33. Ronald Reagan, "Remarks and a Question-and-Answer Session with Editors of Gannett Newspapers," December 14, 1983.

34. Ronald Reagan, "Radio Address to the Nation on the Situation in Lebanon," October 8, 1983.

35. Ronald Reagan, "Address to the Nation on Events in Lebanon and Grenada," October 27, 1983.

36. Ronald Reagan, "Remarks to Military Personnel at Cherry Point, North Carolina," November 4, 1983.

37. Vincent Canby, "'Rambo' Delivers a Revenge Fantasy," *New York Times*, May 26, 1985.

38. This was a recurring theme in 1980s film. Liberating American POWs abandoned by the U.S. government was central to the *Missing in Action* films (1984 and 1985), starring Chuck Norris, and to *Uncommon Valor* (1983), starring Gene Hackman, and figured in episodes of television series such as *Magnum, PI* and *Airwolf*. Dewey Gram, "The Politics of Machismo," *The Times* [London], July 7, 1985.

39. Richard Grenier, "Stallone on Patriotism and 'Rambo,' " *New York Times*, June 6, 1985.

40. Gram, "The Politics of Machismo."

41. Vincent Canby, "Vintage Plotting Propels Mach II Planes in 'Top Gun,'" *New York Times*, June 8, 1986; Rita Kempley, "Cruise in Control," *Washington Post*, May 16, 1986. "Be All You Can Be" was at that time a ubiquitous recruiting slogan employed by the U.S. Army.

42. Pauline Kael, "Top Gun," *New Yorker*, June 16, 1986, rpt. in *For Keeps* (New York, 1994), pp. 1107–8.

43. Robert Lekachman, "Virtuous Men and Perfect Weapons," *New York Times*, July 27, 1986.

44. Lekachman, "Virtuous Men and Perfect Weapons."
45. T. Harvey Holt and Peter Samuel, "Tom Clancy, Patriot," *Policy Review* 38 (Fall 1986), p. 84.
46. Revisionism in the worlds of film and popular fiction had its counterpart in the realms of popular music. Country music, which in the 1980s achieved broad mainstream popularity, remained faithful to the patriotic themes that it had always emphasized. The best single illustration of this point is provided by Lee Greenwood's "God Bless The U.S.A." This sentimental, even banal song, produced in 1983, became something of an unofficial anthem of the U.S. armed forces during the Reagan era and beyond. After 9/11, its popularity revived—Greenwood sang it at the 2002 Super Bowl—and it seems likely to become a permanent part of the repertoire of American popular music.
47. The quotations are from Clinton's letter, dated December 3, 1969, to Colonel Eugene Holmes, head of the ROTC program at the University of Arkansas. "A Letter by Clinton on His Draft Deferment," *New York Times,* February 13, 1992.
48. Governor Bill Clinton, "A New Covenant for American Security," Georgetown University, December 12, 1991.

Chapter 5: Onward

1. In contemporary America, evangelical Christians are distinguished by their belief in biblical inerrancy and in the imperative of a personal conversion experience (being "born again"); by their expectations that the Second Coming of Jesus is near at hand; by their commitment to actively preaching the Gospel; and by their aversion to drugs, alcohol, pornography, promiscuity, abortion, homosexuality, and other "lifestyle" choices viewed as undermining the traditional family. Evangelicalism transcends denominational boundaries. Among the principal American Protestant churches that fall under the evangelical rubric are the Assemblies of God, the Church of God, the Church of the Nazarene, the Southern Baptist Convention, various Pentecostal churches, and evangelical offshoots of the Lutheran, Methodist, and Presbyterian denominations. For a brief history and description, see "Evangelicals," n.d., Beliefnet dictionary, www.beliefnet.com.
2. "How Many Evangelicals Are There?" Institute for the Study of American Evangelicals, Wheaton College, http://www.wheaton.edu/isae/defining_evangelicalism.html, accessed June 29, 2004.
3. Anna Greenberg and Jennifer Berktold, "Evangelicals in America," April 5, 2004, http://www.pbs.org/wnet/religionandethics/week733/results.pdf, accessed June 29, 2004. This document reports on the results of a survey conducted in conjunction with the PBS documentary *The Jesus Factor.* The

survey reports that approximately 69 percent of white evangelicals vote Republican. Eighty-two percent of evangelicals polled reported that they had registered to vote, compared to 77 percent of the overall population. Sixty-five percent report that they regularly go to the polls, compared to 61 percent of the general population. The research also suggests that among evangelicals there is a positive correlation between intensity of religious belief and level of political activism.

4. Already by 1963, in his notable encyclical *Pacem in Terris,* Pope John XXIII had declared that "it no longer makes sense to maintain that war is a fit instrument with which to repair the violation of justice."

5. The most important expression of these trends is probably the "U.S. Catholic Bishops Pastoral Letter on War and Peace" of May 1983, which had influence extending well beyond Catholic circles. Among other things, the statement suggested that any use of nuclear weapons was wrong and specifically condemned even the planned use of strategic retaliation against noncombatants—in essence, arguing that the U.S. strategy of deterrence was immoral. The letter is available at http://www.nuclearfiles.org/redocuments/1983/830503-usrcb-war-peace.html, accessed February 17, 2004.

6. Anne C. Loveland, *American Evangelicals and the U.S. Military, 1942–1993* (Baton Rouge, La., 1996), p. 2.

7. Gary Dorrien, *The Remaking of Evangelical Theology* (Louisville, Ky., 1998), p. 154.

8. "History of the NAE," National Association of Evangelicals, undated, http://www.nae.net/index.cfm?FUSEACTION=nae.history, accessed February 17, 2004.

9. Dorrien, *The Remaking of Evangelical Theology,* pp. 7, 56.

10. See, for example, Dale Herendeen, "Graham Preaches Peace in Viet Nam," *Christianity Today,* January 1, 1967. The title of the article is somewhat misleading. The contents make clear Graham's support for U.S. policy in South Vietnam, citing comments at a press conference in Saigon in which Graham "said that Americans should back their President in his decision to make a stand in Viet Nam."

11. Dorrien, *The Remaking of Evangelical Theology,* p. 56.

12. For a synopsis of Graham's rise, see William Martin, *With God on Our Side* (New York, 1996), pp. 25–46.

13. *Time* assessed reports of God's demise in its cover story of April 8, 1966, published to coincide with Easter.

14. On evangelicals identifying the New Class as their domestic enemy, see James Davison Hunter, *American Evangelicalism: Conservative Religion and the Quandary of Modernity* (New Brunswick, N.J., 1983), pp. 107–19.

15. Garrett Epps, "Born-Again Politics Is Still Waiting to Be," *Washington Post,* March 30, 1980.

16. For a comprehensive statement of that purpose, see Jerry Falwell, *Listen,*

America! (New York, 1980). All specific references are to the paperback edition published in 1981.

17. Quoted by Martin, *With God on Our Side*, p. 201. Contrast this with the establishment's view, in its baldest form characterizing evangelicals as "largely poor, uneducated, and easy to command." Michael Weisskopf, "Energized by Pulpit or Passion, the Public Is Calling," *Washington Post*, February 1, 1993.

18. Kenneth A. Briggs, "Christians on Right and Left Take Up Ballot and Cudgel," *New York Times*, September 21, 1980.

19. At times, Falwell varied this litany to include "pro–strong national defense" as one of his four tenets. Deborah Hart Strober and Gerald S. Strober, *Reagan: The Man and His Presidency* (Boston, 1998), p. 33.

20. Loveland, *American Evangelicals and the U.S. Military*, pp. 122, 154.

21. Ibid., p. 156.

22. Quoted in ibid., p. 161.

23. Falwell, *Listen, America!* pp. 6, 8, 9–10.

24. Ibid., pp. 17, 82, 84, 89.

25. John Price, *America at the Crossroads* (Wheaton, Ill., 1979), pp. 105, 107, 112, 115, 117, 227. Price's book first appeared in 1976. The extracts cited here come from the revised second edition.

26. Rene Noorbergen and Ralph W. Hood, *The Death Cry of an Eagle* (Grand Rapids, Mich., 1980), pp. 134, 180. Interestingly, Noorbergen and Hood worried about American decadence giving rise to American militarism as the government resorted to "force to press for solutions to social problems" (pp. 124–25).

27. G. Russell Evans and C. Gregg Singer, *The Church and the Sword* (Houston, Tex., 1982), pp. vi, 4, 32–33, 35. Throughout their book, Evans and Singer make no effort to conceal their view that the National Council of Churches, the principal umbrella organization of mainstream Protestantism, had been since its inception a Communist front.

28. Ibid., p. 28.

29. Rus Walton, *One Nation Under God* (Nashville, Tenn., rev. ed., 1987), pp. 167–68, 170, 181. Emphasis in the original. According to the cover of the paperback edition, there were 150,000 copies of this book in print.

30. Charles W. Lowry, *Communism and Christ* (New York, 1952), p. 101, quoted in Walton, *One Nation Under God*, p. 181.

31. Michael Lienesch, *Redeeming America: Piety and Politics in the New Christian Right* (Chapel Hill, N.C., 1993), p. 216.

32. For a succinct review of the history, see Donald Wagner, "Evangelicals and Israel: Theological Roots of a Political Alliance," *Christian Century*, November 4, 1998. Also see David Blewett, "Christian Support for Israel," National Christian Leadership Conference for Israel, January 2003, www.nclci.org/Articles/art-blewett-cjrelations.htm, accessed March 8, 2004.

Blewett emphasizes the correlation between conservative Christian activism and the "pro-Arab sentiments [that] increased in the mainline Protestant and Catholic churches."

33. Debra Cohen, "Premier Meets with Evangelicals," *Jewish News of Greater Phoenix*, April 11, 1997, http://www.jewishaz.com/jewishnews/970411/premier.shtml, accessed June 30, 2004.

34. Paul S. Boyer, "When U.S. Foreign Policy Meets Biblical Prophecy," Alternet.org, February 20, 2003, http://www.alternet.org/story.html?StoryID=15221, accessed March 4, 2004.

35. Reliable numbers are difficult to come by, but one estimate from the mid-1980s said that there were eight million dispensationalists. John Herbers, "Religious Leaders Tell of Worry on Armageddon View Ascribed to Reagan," *New York Times*, October 21, 1984.

36. For an assessment of conservative Christian support for Israel, see Howard Fineman and Tamara Lipper, "A Very Mixed Marriage," *Newsweek*, December 19, 2003, http://msnbc.msn.com/id/3761368/, accessed March 4, 2004.

37. For a review of Israeli strategic doctrine, see Eliot A. Cohen, Michael Eisenstadt, and A. J. Bacevich, *Knives, Tanks, and Missiles: Israel's Security Revolution* (Washington, D.C., 1998).

38. For an account that contrasts evangelical support for Israel with mainline Protestant anti-Zionism, see Paul Charles Merkely, *Christian Attitudes Towards the State of Israel* (Montreal, 2001), especially pp. 162–83, 201, 208–11.

39. L. Nelson Bell, "Unfolding Destiny," *Christianity Today*, July 21, 1967; A. Roy Eckhardt and Alice Eckhardt, "Again, Silence in the Churches," *Christian Century*, August 2, 1967, available at http://www.nclci.org/resolut.htm, accessed March 8, 2004.

40. Timothy P. Weber, "How Evangelicals Became Israel's Best Friend," *Christianity Today*, October 5, 1998

41. Joshua Brilliant, "Evangelists Strike a Chord with Israelis," *Washington Times*, November 27, 2003.

42. Grace Haskel, *Prophecy and Politics* (Westport, Conn., 1986), pp. 59–67.

43. Merkely, *Christian Attitudes*, p. 218.

44. Hal Lindsey, *The 1980s: Countdown to Armageddon* (New York, 1980), pp. 141–57, 149, 154. Page citations refer to the Bantam Books paperback edition published in 1981.

45. Ibid., p. 157.

46. Jerry Falwell, "Introduction," Richard A. Viguerie, *The New Right: We're Ready to Lead* (Falls Church, Va., 1981), n. p.

47. Martin, *With God on Our Side*, pp. 173–81, 189–90.

48. Strober and Strober, *Reagan*, p. 31.

49. Allan J. Mayer, "A Tide of Born-Again," *Newsweek*, September 15, 1980. Emphasis in the original.

50.   Martin, *With God on Our Side,* pp. 207–10.

51.   Ibid., pp. 221–37. For a chastened assessment by two of Falwell's key Moral Majority aides, see Cal Thomas and Ed Dobson, *Blinded by Might: Can the Religious Right Save America?* (Grand Rapids, Mich., 1999), pp. 21–26.

52.   Haynes Johnson, "A Preacher for 'Peace Through Strength,' or, Maybe, the Bomb," *Washington Post,* April 3, 1983.

53.   Frances FitzGerald, "Reagan's Band of True Believers," *New York Times Magazine,* May 10, 1987.

54.   Quoted in Loveland, *American Evangelicals and the U.S. Military,* p. 220.

55.   Sara Diamond, *Spiritual Warfare: The Politics of the Christian Right* (Boston, 1989), pp. 157–58.

56.   Quoted in Loveland, *American Evangelicals and the U.S. Military,* p. 223.

57.   For an imaginative discussion of SDI's larger cultural context, see Edward Tabor Linenthal, *Symbolic Defense: The Cultural Significance of the Strategic Defense Initiative* (Urbana, Ill., 1989).

58.   Ibid., pp. 66, 69–70; Loveland, *American Evangelicals and the U.S. Military,* p. 224.

59.   [Unsigned editorial], "Are Churchmen Failing Servicemen in Viet Nam?" *Christianity Today,* August 18, 1967.

60.   Nancy M. Tischler, "Onward, Christian Soldiers?" *Christianity Today,* February 2, 1973. The author is identified as professor of English and humanities at Pennsylvania State University.

61.   Loveland, *American Evangelicals and the U.S. Military,* p. 164.

62.   Association of Graduates, U.S. Military Academy, "1972 Sylvanus Thayer Award—Citation," http://www.aog.usma.edu/AOG/AWARDS/TA/thayer 72.txt, accessed December 5, 2003.

63.   Quoted in Loveland, *American Evangelicals and the U.S. Military,* p. 166, from "Dr. Graham Receives Thayer Award," *Assembly* 31 (Spring 1972), pp. 4–5.

64.   Edward M. Coffman, *The Old Army: A Portrait of the American Army in Peacetime, 1784–1898* (New York, 1986), pp. 78–79, 391–92.

65.   Loveland, *American Evangelicals and the U.S. Military,* pp. 23, 26, 299.

66.   Ibid., p. 98.

67.   Ibid., p. ix.

68.   Colonel Tom Wilhelm, U.S. Army, quoted in Robert D. Kaplan, "The Man Who Would Be Khan," *Atlantic* 293 (March 2004), http://www.theatlantic.com/issues/2004/03/kaplan.htm, accessed April 9, 2004.

69.   The quotations are from James Ridgeway and Kris Jacobs, "Onward, Christian Soldiers," *Village Voice,* March 17, 1987.

70.   Quoted in William A. Arkin, "The Pentagon Unleashes a Holy Warrior," *Los Angeles Times,* October 16, 2003. General Boykin was speaking to a group of evangelical Christians in Sandy, Oregon.

71. Jay Tolson, "The New Old-Time Religion," *U.S. News and World Report*, December 8, 2003; Paul A. Marshall, *Their Blood Cries Out: The Untold Story of the Persecution of Christians in the Modern World* (Dallas, Tex., 1997); Abigail Noll, "Awakening to the Scandal of Sex Trafficking," *Faith and Freedom*, Spring 2000.

72. Jeffrey Goldberg, "Washington Discovers Christian Persecution," *New York Times Magazine*, December 21, 1997.

73. Elisabeth Bumiller, "Evangelicals Sway White House on Human Rights Issues Abroad," *New York Times*, October 26, 2003.

74. Jeffrey L. Sheler, Joannie M. Schrof, and Dorian Friedman, "Holy War Doctrines," *U.S. News and World Report*, February 11, 1991.

75. Charles Colson, "The Silence of the Sheep," *Breakpoint Online*, April 12, 1999.

76. Charles Colson, "Anchors Away?" *Breakpoint Online*, November 11, 1999.

77. Daniel Benjamin and Steven Simon, *The Age of Sacred Terror* (New York, 2003), p. 488. The reference is to the afterword written for the paperback edition.

78. Gustav Niebuhr, "Muslim Group Moves to Meet Billy Graham's Son," *New York Times*, November 20, 2001.

79. Quoted in Max Blumenthal, "Onward Christian Soldiers," Salon.com, April 15, 2003, http://archive.salon.com/news/feature/2003/04/15/in_touch .html, accessed March 6, 2004.

80. Mark Tooley, "Praise the Lord and George W. Bush," *Seattle Post-Intelligencer*, March 21, 2003.

81. "Washington Insight," National Association of Evangelicals, October 2002, quoted in "Excerpted Statements: U.S. Churches on Iraq," *Faith and Freedom*, Winter 2003.

82. See, for example, the full-page ad entitled "Jesus Changed Your Heart. Now Let Him Change Your Mind," that the National Council of Churches placed in the *New York Times* on December 4, 2002. In reference to Iraq, the NCC declared categorically that "this is not a just war" and argued that "it is inconceivable that Jesus Christ . . . would support the proposed attack."

83. Martin Marty, "At the Crossroads," *Christianity Today*, February 2, 2004, www.christianitytoday.com/ct/2004/002/2.38.html, accessed February 16, 2004.

84. A Catholic author cannot leave this question of the relationship between American religiosity and American militarism without making one final point. If in the aftermath of the Cold War a religious counterweight to the evangelical influence on U.S. policy were to have emerged, that counterweight ought to have been the Roman Catholic Church. Great in numbers, political influence, and material resources, with anti-Catholicism largely a thing of the past, the church was eminently well-positioned to put its

stamp on public policy. In America, the Catholic moment seemed at hand—not least of all because of the charismatic leadership of John Paul II, whose long papacy spans most of the period covered by this account. With great eloquence, John Paul II has spoken against war and militarism and on behalf of an international order based on genuine freedom and respect for the human person. That testimony and the pope's enormous prestige, transcending religious boundaries, ought to have enabled American Catholics to comment with some authority on the moral dimension of war and U.S. military policy. But by the end of the twentieth century a corrupt hierarchy had thrown that opportunity away. The bishops discredited themselves and silenced the voice of the church, in effect enhancing other voices. This may not be the greatest effect of the clergy sex scandal, but it should not be overlooked.

Chapter 6. War Club

1.   George W. Bush, "Remarks by the President at 2002 Graduation Exercise of the United States Military Academy," West Point, New York, June 1, 2002.

2.   George W. Bush, "Remarks by President Bush at Boeing, St. Louis, Missouri," April 16, 2003.

3.   George W. Bush, *A Charge to Keep* (New York, 1999), p. 55.

4.   Quoted in Fred Kaplan, *The Wizards of Armageddon* (New York, 1983), p. 9. Although dated, Kaplan's book remains the best introduction to the leading lights of nuclear strategy.

5.   Bernard Brodie et al., *The Absolute Weapon: Atomic Power and World Order* (New York, 1946), p. 76.

6.   Dexter Masters and Katharine Way, eds., *One World or None: A Report to the Public on the Full Meaning of the Atomic Bomb* (New York, 1946).

7.   Brodie, *Absolute Weapon*, pp. 9, 21.

8.   Kaplan, *Wizards*, pp. 34, 43, 45.

9.   For an example of Wohlstetter in full attack mode, see his "Critique of a Brookings Agenda for the Nation on Military Strategy, Military Forces, and Arms Control," October 1968, http://www.rand.org/publications/classics/wohlstetter/DL17910/DL17910.html, accessed February 9, 2004.

10. For an effusive assessment, see James Digby and J. J. Martin, "On Not Confusing Ourselves: Contributions of the Wohlstetters to U.S. Strategy and Strategic Thought," in Andrew W. Marshall, J. J. Martin, and Henry S. Rowen, eds., *On Not Confusing Ourselves: Essays on National Security Strategy in Honor of Albert and Roberta Wohlstetter* (Boulder, Colo., 1991), pp. 3–16.

11. Richard Perle, "Albert Wohlstetter, 1912–1997," eulogy rpt. in *Congres-*

sional Record (105th Congress, 1st Session), vol. 143, no. 14, February 6, 1997. *An End to Evil*, Perle's treatise on the global war on terror, written with David Frum and published in 2004, is dedicated to Wohlstetter.

12.   A. J. Wohlstetter, "Economic and Strategic Considerations in Air Base Location: A Preliminary Review," December 29, 1951, http://www.rand .org/publications/classics/wohlstetter/D1114/D1114.html, accessed February 9, 2004.

13.   Thomas C. Schelling, "What Went Wrong with Arms Control?" *Foreign Affairs* 64 (Winter 1985–86), p. 221. Emphasis in the original.

14.   Kaplan, *Wizards*, p. 110.

15.   Wohlstetter developed this theme most memorably in his essay "The Delicate Balance of Terror," prepared for RAND in 1958 and published the following year in *Foreign Affairs*, http://www.rand.org/publications/classics/ wohlstetter/P1472/P1472.html, accessed February 9, 2004.

16.   Wohlstetter, "Delicate Balance of Terror."

17.   Robert Dallek, *An Unfinished Life: John F. Kennedy, 1917–1963* (Boston, 2003), pp. 289, 337–38.

18.   Albert Wohlstetter and Henry Rowen, "Objectives of the United States Military Posture," May 1, 1959, http://www.rand.org/publications/classics/ wohlstetter/RM2373/RM2373.html, accessed February 13, 2004.

19.   Albert and Roberta Wohlstetter, "Notes on the Cuban Crisis," October 28, 1962, http://www.rand.org/publications/classics/wohlstetter/DL10647/DL 10647.html, accessed February 11, 2004. See also Albert Wohlstetter, "Strength, Interest, and New Technologies," January 24, 1968, paper originally presented at the Ninth Annual Conference of the Institute of Strategic Studies.

20.   An example from a 1959 RAND study coauthored by Wohlstetter: "The ability of our vehicles which survive an attack to penetrate defenses and seriously damage the Soviet Union is doubtful. For example, neither a small surviving force of bombers nor the relatively naked Polaris [submarine-launched ballistic] missile would appear to have an easy prospect of penetrating well-designed Soviet active defenses." To suggest in 1959 that the Soviets possessed an effective ballistic missile defense system was patently absurd. Wohlstetter and Rowen, "Objectives of the United States Military Posture."

21.   Khurram Husain, "Neocons: Men Behind the Curtain," *Bulletin of the Atomic Scientists* 59 (November/December 2003), pp. 62–71.

22.   Herman Kahn, *On Thermonuclear War* (Princeton, N.J., 1960), p. 240.

23.   For a pioneering exposition of these ideas, see William W. Kaufmann, "Limited Warfare," in Kaufmann, ed., *Military Policy and National Security* (Princeton, N.J., 1956), pp. 102–36.

24.   Wohlstetter and Rowen, "Objectives of the United States Military Posture."

25. Albert Wohlstetter, "Scientists, Seers, and Strategy," *Foreign Affairs* 41 (April 1963), pp. 477–78.

26. Lawrence Freedman, *The Evolution of Nuclear Strategy* (London, 1981), p. 231.

27. Deborah Shapley, *Promise and Power: The Life and Times of Robert McNamara* (Boston, 1993), pp. 187–89.

28. Kaplan, *Wizards*, pp. 332–36.

29. Ibid., pp. 336, 341.

30. Albert Wohlstetter, "On Vietnam and Bureaucracy," July 17, 1968, http://www.rand.org/publications/classics/wohlstetter/D17276.1/D17276.1 .html, accessed March 20, 2004.

31. Wohlstetter, "On Vietnam and Bureaucracy."

32. Albert Wohlstetter, "Who Are 'Good' and 'Bad' Guys?" *Los Angeles Times*, August 3, 1969; Albert Wohlstetter, "Safeguard Critics Contradict Selves," *Los Angeles Times*, August 4, 1969.

33. Albert Wohlstetter, "Threats and Promises of Peace: Europe and America in the New Era," *Orbis* 17 (Winter 1974), p. 1135.

34. Albert Wohlstetter, "The Political and Military Aims of Offense and Defense Innovation," in Fred S. Hoffman, Albert Wohlstetter, and David S. Yost, eds., *Swords and Shields: NATO, the USSR, and New Choices for Long-Range Offense and Defense* (Lexington, Mass., 1987), p. 14. For evidence that senior U.S. officials did consider—only to reject—preventive war as an option during the early Cold War, see Marc Trachtenberg, *History and Strategy* (Princeton, N.J., 1991), pp. 100–152.

35. Albert Wohlstetter, "Between an Unfree World and None: Increasing Our Choices," *Foreign Affairs* 63 (Summer 1985), p. 990; Albert Wohlstetter, "The Uses of Irrelevance," *New York Times*, February 25, 1979.

36. "Deputy Secretary Wolfowitz Interview with Sam Tannenhaus, Vanity Fair," May 9, 2003, www.defenselink.mil/transcripts/2003/tr20030509 -depsecdef0223.html, accessed March 29. 2004.

37. Wohlstetter, "Threats and Promises of Peace."

38. Albert Wohlstetter, "Bishops, Statesmen, and Other Strategists on the Bombing of Innocents," *Commentary* 75 (June 1983), p. 19.

39. Wohlstetter, "Between an Unfree World and None."

40. For more on this point, see Neil Swidey, "The Mind of the Administration," *Boston Globe*, May 18, 2003.

41. The other cochair was Fred C. Ikle. Among the members of the commission were Zbigniew Brzezinski, Andrew J. Goodpaster, Samuel P. Huntington, and Henry Kissinger.

42. Report of the Commission on Integrated Long-Term Strategy, *Discriminate Deterrence* (January 1988), pp. 8, 29, 49, 65

43. *Discriminate Deterrence* in no way anticipated the demise of the Soviet Union and generally depicted the United States as lagging behind the Soviets in terms of military power (pp. 1, 9, 19, 24–25, 28, 39, 45, 53).

44. Albert Wohlstetter and Fred Hoffman, "Confronting Saddam: A Model Danger," *Wall Street Journal*, August 9, 1990.

45. Fred Frostic, *Air Campaign Against the Iraqi Army in the Kuwaiti Theater of Operations* (n.p., n.d. [1993]), p. 63.

46. James F. Dunnigan and Austin Bay, *From Shield to Storm* (New York, 1992), pp. 492–93.

47. Norman Friedman, *Desert Victory* (Annapolis, Md., 1991), p. 5.

48. Albert Wohlstetter, "Help Iraqi Dissidents Oust Saddam," *Wall Street Journal*, August 25, 1992, p. A14.

49. In his final years, Wohlstetter became preoccupied with urging on moral and humanitarian grounds American military intervention in the Balkans, a region of little or no strategic relevance to the United States.

50. Wohlstetter had something of a reputation as a gourmand and bon vivant. See Robert L. Bartley, "Foreword," in Marshall et al., *On Not Confusing Ourselves*, pp. vii–x.

51. For a fawning profile, see Jay Winik, "Secret Weapon," *Washingtonian*, April 1999, or John Barry and Evan Thomas, "The Pentagon's Guru," *Newsweek*, May 21, 2001. For a more balanced but still admiring appraisal, see Thomas E. Ricks, "Warning Shot: How Wars Are Fought Will Change Radically," *Wall Street Journal*, July 15, 1994.

52. Marshall likened the U.S. situation in 1990 to that of Great Britain between the world wars: dominant, but its dominance subject to rapid decline if it failed to respond to the changes in warfare then at hand. Peter Schwartz, "Warrior in the Age of Intelligent Machines," *Wired*, April 1995, http://www.wired.com/wired/archive/3.04/pentagon.html, accessed March 28, 2004. The article reprints an interview with Marshall.

53. For an introduction to the literature on military revolutions, see Andrew Krepinevich Jr., "Cavalry to Computer: The Pattern of Military Revolutions," *National Interest* 37 (Fall 1994), pp. 30–42, and Richard O. Hundley, *Past Revolutions, Future Transformations* (Santa Monica, Calif., 1999), pp. 7–20.

54. Andrew W. Marshall, "Strategy as a Profession for Future Generations," in Marshall et al., eds., *On Not Confusing Ourselves*, pp. 310–11.

55. For an early evaluation prepared by Marshall's office in the immediate aftermath of the Persian Gulf War, but not made publicly available until 2002, see Andrew F. Krepinevich Jr., *The Military-Technical Revolution: A Preliminary Assessment* (Washington, 2002), http://www.csbaonline.org/4Publications/Archive/R.20021002.MTR/R.20021002.MTRpdf, accessed April 1, 2004.

56. Andrew W. Marshall, "Foreword," in Zalmay Khalilzad and John P. White, eds., *Strategic Appraisal: The Changing Role of Information in Warfare* (Santa Monica, Calif., 1999), pp. 5–6.

57. On another occasion, Marshall identified the key elements of the RMA as precision weapons married to sensors; the seamless coordination of opera-

tions across the force; increased reliance on robotic devices such as pilotless aircraft; and the exploitation of performance enhancing drugs. Douglas McGray, "The Marshall Plan," *Wired*, February 2003, www.wired.com/wired/archive/11.02/marshall_pr.html, accessed March 4, 2004.

58. On Marshall's concern about China, see Robert G. Kaiser, "2025 Vision: A China Bent on Asian Dominance," *Washington Post*, March 17, 2000.

59. Azar Gat, *Fascist and Liberal Visions of War* (Oxford, 1998), pp. 3, 6.

60. Thomas L. Friedman, "A Manifesto for the Fast World," *New York Times Magazine*, March 28, 1999, pp. 40, 42.

61. Winston S. Churchill, *The World Crisis* (New York, 1923), chap. 6.

62. General John M. Shalikashvili, *Joint Vision 2010* (Washington, 1996). For a discussion and critique, see Andrew J. Bacevich, *American Empire: The Realities and Consequences of U.S. Diplomacy* (Cambridge, Mass., 2002), pp. 130–40.

63. Michael Ignatieff, *Virtual War: Kosovo and Beyond* (New York, 2000).

64. Harlan K. Ulmann and James P. Wade, *Shock and Awe: Achieving Rapid Dominance* (Washington, 1996), chap. 1, http://www.ndu.edu/inss/books/books%20-%201996/Shock%20and%20Awe%20%20Dec%2096/ch1.html, accessed on April 2, 2004. Listed on the title page as contributors to this study are General Frederick M. Franks, General Charles A. Horner, and Admiral Jonathan T. Howe.

65. William Greider, *Fortress America: The American Military and the Consequences of Peace* (New York, 1998).

66. George W. Bush, "A Period of Consequences," The Citadel, Charleston, S.C., February 9, 2000.

67. Thomas E. Ricks, "Pentagon Study May Bring Big Shake-Up," *Washington Post*, February 9, 2001.

68. Thomas E. Ricks, "For Rumsfeld, Many Roadblocks," *Washington Post*, August 7, 2001.

69. For a critical assessment of service foot-dragging prior to 9/11, see Michael Catanzaro, "The 'Revolution in Military Affairs' Has an Enemy: Politics," *American Enterprise*, October 2001, http://www.taemag.com/issues/articleID.15477/article_detail.asp, accessed February 18, 2004.

70. For an assessment of RMA thinking as it stood during the interval between the invasion of Afghanistan and the invasion of Iraq, see Bill Keller, "The Fighting Next Time," *New York Times Magazine*, March 10, 2002. For an incisive critique of Donald Rumsfeld's vision of transformation, see James Kurth, "Iraq: Losing the American Way," *American Conservative*, March 15, 2004.

71. Richard Perle quoted in Neil Swidey, "The Mind of the Administration," *Boston Globe*, May 18, 2003.

Chapter 7: Blood for Oil

1. Norman Podhoretz, "How to Win World War IV," *Commentary* 113 (February 2002), pp. 19–29.

2. "Like the Second World War," President Bush has stated, "our present conflict began with a ruthless, surprise attack on the United States." "Remarks by the President at the United States Air Force Academy Graduation Ceremony," June 2, 2004.

3. Daniel Yergin, *The Prize: The Epic Quest for Oil, Money, and Power* (New York, 1991), pp. 403–5.

4. "The Secret CIA History of the Iran Coup, 1953," National Security Archive Briefing Book no. 28, http://www.gwu.edu/~nsarchiv/NSAEBB/NSAEBB28/, accessed April 21, 2004.

5. Yergin, *The Prize*, pp. 565–66.

6. "Office of the Program Manager, Saudi Arabian National Guard Modernization Program," http://www.globalsecurity.org/military/agency/dod/opm-sang.htm, accessed April 21, 2004. Today Vinnell continues its work with the Saudi National Guard under the terms of a five-year contract worth over $800 million.

7. Jimmy Carter, "State of the Union Address, 1980," January 21, 1980.

8. Quoted in Jay LaMonica, "RDF's Bright Star," *Washington Quarterly* 5 (Spring 1982).

9. NSC-68, "United States Objectives and Programs for National Security," April 14, 1950, sec. VII ("Present Risks"), http://www.fas.org/irp/offdocs/nsc-hst/nsc-68-7.htm, accessed April 26, 2004. The principal author of this document was Paul Nitze, then State Department director of policy planning.

10. Yergin, *The Prize*, pp. 613–2, 674–98.

11. In 1940, for example, 63 percent of world oil production came from wells in the United States, while the entire Persian Gulf region produced less than 5 percent. Yergin, *The Prize*, p. 393.

12. Andrew Higgins, "Power and Peril: America's Supremacy and Its Limits," *Wall Street Journal*, February 4, 2004.

13. Ronald Reagan, "Remarks at the Annual Washington Conference of the American Legion," February 22, 1983.

14. Ronald Reagan, "Remarks at Memorial Day Ceremonies at Arlington National Cemetery," May 31, 1982.

15. Ronald Reagan, "Remarks at the Annual Convention of the Veterans of Foreign Wars in New Orleans, Louisiana," August 15, 1983.

16. Ronald Reagan, "Radio Address to the Nation on the Observance of Armed Forces Day," May 21, 1983.

17. The quotation is from the mission statement provided to the U.S. Commander-in-Chief Europe by the Joint Chiefs of Staff in a JCS Alert Order of September 23, 1983. Quoted in *Report of the DoD Commission on Beirut*

International Airport Terrorist Act, October 23, 1983 (December 20, 1983), p. 35, http://www.ibiblio.org/hyperwar/AMH/XX/MidEast/Lebanon-1982 -1984/DOD-Report/, accessed February 5, 2004.

18. In 1981, that skirmishing had resulted in aircraft from the Sixth Fleet shooting down two Libyan MiGs. In March 1986, Libyan air defenses had engaged patrolling American F-14s. The United States responded by attacking a Libyan air defense site and destroying several Libyan gunboats.

19. For a brief account, see Walter J. Boyne, "El Dorado Canyon," *Air Force Magazine* 82 (March 1999).

20. The origins and conduct of the tanker war are discussed in "Operation Earnest Will," n.d., http://www.fas.org/man/dod-101/ops/earnest_will.htm, accessed February 5, 2004.

21. "How Jimmy Carter and I Started the Mujahideen [*sic*]," interview with Zbigniew Brzezinski, *Le Nouvel Observateur*, January 15–21, 1998, p. 76, http://www.counterpunch.org/brzezinski.html, accessed February 6, 2004. Bill Blum translated the Brzezinski interview from the French. See also John Prados, "Notes on the CIA's Secret War in Afghanistan," *Journal of American History* 89 (September 2002), pp. 466–71 and Robert M. Gates, *From the Shadows: The Ultimate Insider's Story of Five Presidents and How They Won the Cold War* (New York, 1996), pp. 146–49.

22. Steve Coll, "Anatomy of a Victory: CIA's Covert Afghan War," *Washington Post*, July 19, 1992.

23. Ronald W. Reagan, *An American Life* (New York, 1990), p. 520.

24. Caspar Weinberger, *Fighting for Peace* (New York, 1990), p. 426. Weinberger treated as incidental the fact that U.S. involvement in the tanker war had included the accidental shooting down of an Iran civilian airliner by the USS *Vincennes*, killing all 290 civilians aboard.

25. Ronald W. Reagan, "Address to the Nation on National Security," February 26, 1986.

26. Reagan, *An American Life*, p. 462.

27. For details see Joyce Battle, ed., "Shaking Hands with Saddam Hussein: The U.S. Tilts Toward Iraq, 1980–1984," National Security Archive Electronic Briefing Book, February 25, 2003, http://www.gwu.edu/~nsarchiv/ NSAEBB/NSAEBB82/, accessed April 28, 2004.

28. Albert Wohlstetter, "Meeting the Threat in the Persian Gulf," *Survey* 25 (Spring 1981), pp. 128–88.

29. Winston S. Churchill, *The World Crisis* (New York, 1923), p. 136.

30. George P. Shultz, *Turmoil and Triumph* (New York, 1993), p. 235.

31. Dana Priest, "A Four Star Foreign Policy? U.S. Commanders Wield Rising Clout, Autonomy," *Washington Post*, September 28, 2000.

32. Between 1980 and 1983, appropriations for Diego Garcia totaled $435 million. Sheila Ryan, "Countdown for a Decade: The U.S. Build-Up for War in the Gulf," in Phyllis Bennis and Michel Moushabeck, eds., *Beyond the Storm: A Gulf Crisis Reader* (New York, 1991), p. 96.

33. Salvatore R. Mercogliano, "Military Sealift Command: Ships That Wait," n.d., http://www.usmm.org/msts/wait.html, accessed February 9, 2004.

34. "Air Bases Beefed Up for Rapid Deployment," *Engineering News-Record*, June 12, 1984. This article notes that in 1984 alone the United States was spending over $500 million on six air bases in the Middle East and Africa.

35. Richard Halloran, "Poised for the Persian Gulf," *New York Times Magazine*, April 1, 1984, p. 61.

36. "Bright Star," Federation of American Scientists, http://www.fas.org/man/dod-101/ops/bright_star.htm, accessed February 8, 2004; "The Host with the Most," *Economist*, June 6, 1981. U.S. military exercises also occurred in Jordan, Sudan, Somalia, Kenya, and Oman.

37. By 1984, the Department of Defense was providing weapons, training, and other security assistance to fourteen of the nineteen nations falling under the purview of U.S. Central Command. The total value of the contracts was $7.7 billion and rising. Halloran, "Poised for the Persian Gulf." On arms sales to Saudi Arabia, for U.S. weapons manufacturers the most lucrative market after the fall of the Shah, see Ryan, "Countdown for a Decade," pp. 96–100.

38. Reagan himself did not doubt the feasibility of politically transforming the Islamic world. Discussing Saudi Arabia, for example, he remarked, "I think they want to be part of the West. They associate more with our views and our philosophy." Ronald Reagan, "Remarks and a Question-and-Answer Session at a Working Luncheon with Out-of-Town Editors," October 16, 1981.

39. George Bush and Brent Scowcroft, *A World Transformed* (New York, 1998), pp. 319–24.

40. Patrick Clawson, "Stealth Bombing: Our Silent War in Iraq," *New Republic* 221 (September 6, 1999).

41. Osama bin Laden, "Declaration of War Against the Americans Occupying the Land of the Two Holy Places," August 23, 1996, http://www.geocities.com/dcjarviks//Idler/vIIIn165.html, accessed July 2, 2004.

42. Bill Clinton, "Address to the Nation on Terrorist Sites in Afghanistan and Sudan," August 20, 1998.

43. Abdel Mahdi Abdallah, "Causes of Anti-Americanism in the Arab World," *Middle East Review of International Affairs* 7 (December 2003), p. 66.

44. Michael T. Klare, "The Geopolitics of War," *Nation,* November 5, 2001.

45. Osama bin Laden, "Declaration of War Against the Americans Occupying the Land of the Two Holy Places," and "Text of Fatwah Urging Jihad Against Americans," (1998), http://www.mideastweb.org/osamabinladen1.htm, accessed May 5, 2004.

46. Andrew J. Bacevich, *American Empire: The Realities and Consequences of U.S. Diplomacy* (Cambridge, Mass., 2002), pp. 198–215.

47. For a notably impassioned statement, see "Remarks by the President at the United States Air Force Academy Graduation Ceremony," June 2, 2004; but more important still is "President Bush's Address to a Joint Session of Congress and the American People," September 20, 2001.

48.   John Donnelly and Anthony Shadid, "Iraq War Hawks Have Plans to Reshape Entire Middle East," *Boston Globe*, September 10, 2002.

49.   Richard A. Clarke, *Inside America's War on Terror* (New York, 2004), p. 283.

50.   Quoted in Jay Bookman, "Bush's Real Goal in Iraq," *Atlanta Journal-Constitution*, September 29, 2002.

51.   Zalmay Khalilzad, "The Future of Iraq Policy," *Policywatch* Number 667, Washington Institute for Near East Policy, October 8, 2002, http://www.washingtoninstitute.org/watch/Policywatch/policywatch2002/667.htm, accessed May 21, 2004.

52.   Quoted in James Mann, *Rise of the Vulcans* (New York, 2004), p. 299.

53.   Mann, *Rise of the Vulcans*, p. xii.

54.   Norman Podhoretz, *Why We Were in Vietnam* (New York, 1982), p. 6.

Chapter 8: Common Defense

1.   H. L. Mencken, "The Divine Afflatus," *Prejudices: Second Series* (1920), p. 158.

2.   "Smedley Butler on Interventionism," http://www.fas.org/man/smedley.htm, accessed March 23, 2004. When he leveled that charge in 1933, Butler was a recently retired U.S. Marine who had twice been awarded the Medal of Honor.

3.   The historian John Lewis Gaddis dates this phenomenon from the War of 1812. Ever since that war, he writes, the United States has adhered to the principle that "safety comes from enlarging, rather than from contracting, its sphere of responsibilities." John Lewis Gaddis, *Surprise, Security, and the American Experience* (Cambridge, Mass., 2004), p. 13.

4.   Kennedy's most recent biographer reports that as a candidate and as president JFK was routinely injected with drug cocktails that included painkillers, amphetamines, steroids, cortisone, procaine, testosterone, codeine, and Ritalin. Robert Dallek, *An Unfinished Life: John F. Kennedy, 1917-1963* (Boston, 2003), pp. 398–99, 471-473. On Reagan and Armageddon, see Grace Haskell, *Prophecy and Politics* (Westport, Conn., 1986), pp. 40-50.

5.   That resolution authorized the president "to use the Armed Forces of the United States as he determines to be necessary and appropriate in order to (1) defend the national security of the United States against the continuing threat posed by Iraq; and (2) enforce all relevant United Nations Security Council resolutions regarding Iraq." On the operative questions of the day—namely, whether or not to invade Iraq and forcibly remove Saddam Hussein from power—the resolution was silent. "House Joint Resolution Authorizing Use of Force Against Iraq," October 10, 2002, http://usinfo.state.gov/regional/nea/iraq/text/1010res.htm, accessed April 10, 2004. It passed by a 77 to 23 vote in the Senate and 296 to 133 in the House.

6.   Gal Luft, "Terror's Big Prize," *New York Sun*, April 30, 2004.

7.   For a good starting point, see the comprehensive energy strategy outlined in

Timothy E. Wirth, C. Boyden Gray, and John D. Podesta, "The Future of Energy Policy," *Foreign Affairs* 82 (July/August 2003), pp. 132–55.

8. John Kerry, "Remarks at Campaign Event," Providence, R.I., April 13, 2004.

9. Kerry piled on with his own promise, if elected, to "make this country energy independent of Mideast oil within ten years. So our sons and daughters will never have to fight and die for it." John Kerry, "Fighting a Comprehensive War on Terrorism," University of California at Los Angeles, February 27, 2004.

10. The phrase comes from Chalmers Johnson, *The Sorrows of Empire: Militarism, Secrecy, and the End of the Republic* (New York, 2004).

11. "Washington's Farewell Address," 1796, www.yale.edu/lawweb/avalon/washing.htm, accessed April 6, 2004.

12. See, for example, "Time for the Bush Military Build-up," Center for Security Policy, January 7, 2002, http://www.centerforsecuritypolicy.org/index.jsp?section=papers&code=02-F_02, accessed April 15, 2004.

13. For a nation-by-nation comparison, see "Worldwide Military Expenditures" at http://www.globalsecurity.org/military/world/spending.htm, accessed April 8, 2004.

14. The term "soft power" is Joseph F. Nye's. For an introduction, see his *Bound to Lead: The Changing Nature of American Power* (New York, 1990), pp. 173–201.

15. For a scathing example that describes the State Department as "ineffective," "incoherent," and "pathetic" and charges it with engaging in a "deliberate and systematic effort to undermine the President's policies," see Newt Gingrich, "Transforming the State Department," a speech delivered at the American Enterprise Institute on April 22, 2003, http://www.aei.org/news/newsID.16992/news_detail.asp, accessed on April 13, 2004; this presentation subsequently appeared as "The Failure of U.S. Diplomacy," *Foreign Policy* (July/August 2003), pp. 42–48.

16. See, for example, the State Department report *Changing Minds, Winning Peace: A New Strategic Direction for U.S. Public Diplomacy in the Arab and Muslim World,* October 1, 2003, http://www.state.gov/documents/organization/24882.pdf, accessed April 13, 2004.

17. In a comprehensive survey by the Center for Global Development published in 2003, the United States ranked twentieth out of twenty-one countries in terms of its commitment to developing countries. The results of the survey appeared in the May/June 2003 issue of *Foreign Policy* magazine. For an online version of results see "Ranking the Rich," http://www.foreignpolicy.com/story/cms.php?story_id=24, accessed April 13, 2004.

18. "Army Cancels Comanche Helicopter Program," *Govexec.com,* February 23, 2004, http://www.govexec.com/dailyfed/0204/022304cdpm2.htm, accessed April 11, 2004. This report projects that the Pentagon will pay an additional $2 billion in cancellation charges.

19. Linda D. Kozaryn, "Pentagon Terminates Crusader Program," May 8, 2002,

http://www.defenselink.mil/news/May2002/n05082002_200205085.html, accessed April 11, 2004.

20. "FY '05 Request for Selected Weapons Systems," Center for Arms Control and Non-Proliferation, http://64.177.207.201/static/budget/annual/fy05/weapons.htm, accessed April 20, 2004. For fiscal year 2005, the Pentagon requested $1.75 billion for eleven V-22s.

21. Dexter Filkins, "Tough New Tactics by U.S. Tighten Grip on Iraq Towns," *New York Times,* December 7, 2003. "You have to understand the Arab mind," the article quotes another U.S. officer as saying. "The only thing they understand is force—force, pride and saving face."

22. For a profile of an American soldier as agent of empire, see Robert D. Kaplan, "The Man Who Would Be Khan," *Atlantic* 293 (March 2004), http://www.the atlantic.com/issues/2004/03/kaplan.htm, accessed April 9, 2004.

23. John McAuley Palmer, *Statesmanship or War* (New York, 1927), p. 74.

24. "DoD News Briefing—Secretary Rumsfeld and Gen. Myers," January 7, 2003, http://www.defenselink.mil/transcripts/2003/t01072003_t0107sd.html, accessed May 1, 2004.

25. Not everyone agrees on this point; 9/11 did evoke some support for restoring conscription. See, for example, Charles Moskos and Paul Glastris, "Now Do You Believe We Need a Draft?" *Washington Monthly,* November 2001.

26. For a discussion of these proposals, see Charles Moskos, "From College to Kosovo," *Wall Street Journal,* August 25, 2000; Charles Moskos, "Reviving the Citizen-Soldier," *Public Interest* 147 (Spring 2002), pp. 76-85.

27. The point here is not that veterans will be automatically dovish, any more than nonveterans are automatically hawks. Rather it is simply that military service and especially service in combat can offer insights relevant to thinking about current and future policy. As this is written, Senator Chuck Hagel, Republican of Nebraska, and Senator John McCain, Republican of Arizona, both Vietnam veterans, differ about the ongoing Iraq War, with Hagel a critic and McCain a critical supporter, but in both cases their Vietnam service enables them to "see" the war in ways that their nonveteran colleagues do not. Were they not in the Senate, the generally insipid debate about U.S. policy in Iraq would be poorer still. For empirical evidence showing that "the higher the proportion of American policymakers with military experience, the lower the probability that the United States would initiate a militarized dispute," see Peter D. Feaver and Christopher Gelpi, *Choosing Your Battles: American Civil-Military Relations and the Use of Force* (Princeton, N.J., 2004), chap. 3. The quotation is from p. 94.

28. Most Americans are unaware of the fact that for over twenty years U.S. troops have been serving as peacekeepers in the Sinai, forming the backbone of an organization called "the Multilateral Force and Observers," or MFO. See the organization's website at http://www.mfo.org/Homepage/home page.ASP, accessed April 11, 2004.

29.   Thom Shanker, "The Struggle for Iraq: Rotation," *New York Times,* January 9, 2004. The article reported that reservists were expected to comprise 46 percent of the 110,000 troops to be committed to the "second rotation" of occupying Iraq.

30.   It makes sense but is of dubious legality. According to federal statute, the purpose of the reserve components is to supplement the regular forces during national emergencies whenever "more units and persons are needed than are in the regular components." The clear implication of that statute is that activation of the reserves is intended as a temporary bridge, not as a way of dodging the requirement to expand the regular active-duty forces. See Title 10, subtitle E, pt. I, chap. 1003, sec. 10102, United States Code, "Purpose of Reserve Components," www4.law.cornell.edu/uscode/10/10102.html, accessed April 15, 2004. I thank John Richardson for bringing this provision to my attention.

31.   These colleges continued to proliferate. After World War II, the Army War College moved to Carlisle Barracks, Pennsylvania, the real estate that it vacated in Washington becoming the site of a National War College, which has since mushroomed into a National Defense University consisting of several colleges. There are still other colleges of various types on military installations at Norfolk and Quantico, Virginia; Montgomery, Alabama; Leavenworth, Kansas; and Monterey, California—all of these in addition to the military's three separate undergraduate institutions at West Point, Annapolis, and Colorado Springs.

32.   In practice, fundamental military reform has tended to be imposed upon the services from the outside. A recent example is the Goldwater–Nichols legislation of the 1980s—passed despite determined opposition by the Pentagon. An earlier example is the so-called Root reforms of the early 1900s, imposed on the U.S. Army by a reform-minded secretary of war, Elihu Root.

33.   The service academies would thus no longer have the mission of providing an undergraduate education. Since any of the three academies could accommodate the entire annual commissioning class for all of the services, the other two could be shut down at considerable savings to the government.

34.   An eminent example is the Strategic Studies Program of the Johns Hopkins School of Advanced International Studies. For a description of this program, directed by Professor Eliot A. Cohen, see http://www.sais-jhu.edu/programs/ir/strategic/index.html.

35.   "Washington's Farewell Address."

Afterword

1.   "Obama's Remarks on Military Spending," *New York Times* (January 5, 2012), http://www.nytimes.com/2012/01/06/us/text-obamas-remarks-on-military-spending.html?pagewanted=all, accessed January 31, 2012.

2. Robert Burns, "Obama Vows U. S. Will Stay World's Top Military Power," *Providence Journal* (January 5, 2012), http://hosted2.ap.org/RIPRJ/f7ded 15e4d4846268a17b79c1c4b7cb8/Article_2012-01-05-US-Defense-Strategy/ id-78a336f336844447aa6968c4931f7105, accessed February 2, 2012.

3. Max Boot, "Slashing America's Defenses: A Suicidal Trajectory," *Commentary* (January 2012), http://www.cfr.org/defense-policy-and-budget/slashing-americas-defense-suicidal-trajectory/p26989, accessed February 2, 2012.

4. Gary Schmitt and Tom Donnelly, "No Superpower Here," *Weekly Standard* (January 16, 2012), http://www.weeklystandard.com/articles/no-superpower-here_616157.html, accessed February 2, 2012.

5. Walter Pincus, "Has Obama Taken Bush's Preemption Strategy to Another Level?" *Washington Post* (January 9, 2012), http://www.washingtonpost.com/world/national-security/has-obama-taken-bushs-preemption-strategy-to-another-level/2012/01/06/gIQAHDImmP_story.html, accessed February 2, 2012.

6. Thom Shanker, "Warning Against Wars Like Iraq and Afghanistan," *New York Times* (February 25, 2011), http://www.nytimes.com/2011/02/ 26/world/26gates.html, accessed February 3, 2012.

7. William Kristol, "The Gates of Resignation," *Weekly Standard* (March 14, 2011), http://www.weeklystandard.com/articles/gates-resignation_552957 .html, accessed February 3, 2012.

8. Public opinion regarding Afghanistan provides an example. A Gallup Poll in March 2012 showed a remarkable 82% of Americans with an "unfavorable" view of the Afghanistan War. Comparable unhappiness with Korea had dissuaded Harry Truman in 1952 from seeking another term in office. The same thing recurred in 1968: Dissatisfaction with his handling of Vietnam sent Lyndon Johnson packing back to Texas. Yet in the presidential election year of 2012, the political salience of an inconclusive and unpopular war was nearly non-existent. President Obama's Republican challengers made little effort to capitalize on his vulnerability regarding Afghanistan. Few if any commentators suggested that the war was likely to determine Obama's prospects for re-election. Gallup Poll on "Afghanistan," March 24, 2012, http://www.gallup.com/poll/116233/afghanistan.aspx, accessed March 24, 2012.

9. Craig Whitlock and Greg Miller, "U. S. Assembling Secret Drone Bases in Africa, Arabian Peninsula, Officials Say," *Washington Post* (September 20, 2011), http://www.washingtonpost.com/world/national-security/us-building-secret-drone-bases-in-africa-arabian-peninsula-officials-say/2011/09/20/gIQAJ8rOjK_story.html, accessed February 4, 2012.

10. Neta C. Crawford and Katherine Lutz, et al, *Costs of War*, http://costsofwar.org/, accessed February 4, 2012.

11. Carl Conetta, *Going for Broke: The Budgetary Consequences of Current U. S. Defense Strategy*, Project on Defense Alternatives (October 25, 2011).

12. Elisabeth Bumiller and Thom Shanker, "Defense Budget Cuts Would Limit Raises and Close Bases," *New York Times* (January 27, 2012).

13. Episodes of misconduct by U. S troops—in Iraq, the abuses at Abu Ghraib prison and the infamous Haditha massacre; in Afghanistan, the reprehensible actions of the 5th Stryker Brigade's "kill team" and the murderous rampage of Staff Sergeant Robert Bales in March 2012—demonstrate that American soldiers are by no means immune to the perversions to which war gives rise. Yet it would be wrong to see these as emblematic or commonplace.

14. "The War Nobody Wanted," *Postscripts* (April 21, 2008), http://notorc.blogspot.com/2008_04_01_archive.html, accessed February 6, 2012.

15. Thucydides, *The Peloponnesian War,* translated by Richard Crawley, Book 5, Chapter 17, http://www.wellesley.edu/ClassicalStudies/CLCV102/Thucydides-MelianDialogue.html, accessed February 6, 2012.

16. Greg Jaffe, "A Decade after the 9/11 Attacks, Americans Live in an Era of Endless War," *Washington Post* (September 4, 2011), http://www.washingtonpost.com/world/national-security/a-decade-after-the-911-attacks-americans-live-in-an-era-of-endless-war/2011/09/01/gIQARUXD2J_print.html, accessed February 6, 2012.

17. James Wright, *Those Who Have Borne the Battle* (New York, 2012), p. 23.

18. Mark Thompson," An Army Apart: The Widening Military-Civilian Gap," *Time* (November 10, 2011).

19. http://www.budweiser.com/en/world-of-budweiser/mlb/default.aspx#/en/world-of-budweiser/mlb/index, accessed July 11, 2011.

20. http://www.millerhighlife.com/high-life-experiences/, accessed July 11, 2011.

21. Todd S. Purdum, "One Nation, Under Arms," *Vanity Fair* (January 2012), http://www.vanityfair.com/politics/2012/01/Todd-Purdum-on-National-Security, accessed February 7, 2012.

22. Robert Gates, "Thayer Award Remarks," (October 6, 2011), http://www.westpointaog.org/page.aspx?pid=4843, accessed February 7, 2012.

Index